PRAIRIE SON

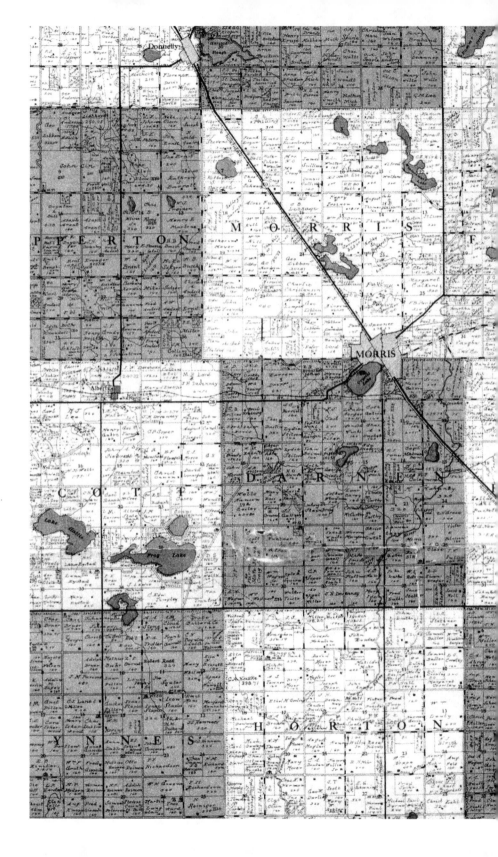

PRAIRIE SON

DENNIS M. CLAUSEN

Library of Congress Cataloging-in-Publication Data
Clausen, Dennis M.
     Prairie son / Dennis M. Clausen
         p.   cm.

     1. Clausen, Lloyd Augustine, 1922-1980. 2. Adoptees—United States—Biography. 3. Birthparents—United States—Identification. I. Title.
     HV874.82.C53C52   1998
     362.82'98'092—dc21   98-46831
     [B]   CIP

Manufactured in the United States of America
First printing: February 1999

To Dad and Delores

CONTENTS

Prologue   1

From the Orphanage to the Farm   7

The Prairie Wind Song   18

Life, Death, and Hay Thieves   30

Death is a Constant Companion   45

A Blind Horse Leads Us Home   58

Windmills and Wells   71

I Lose My Parents   84

Family Secrets   99

Ivar, King of the Hired Men   111

We Almost Starve to Death   123

Dirt, Drought, and Death   135

At the End of the Field   149

Skinning Skunks   162

Searching for the Past   177

Echoes From a Distant War   192

At Last, the Mountaintops   205

The Search Continues   216

New Voices in the Prairie Wind   230

Postscript   241

ACKNOWLEDGMENTS

I want to extend my heartfelt thanks to Marianne Leslie Nora, Lane Stiles, and everyone associated with Mid-List Press for their support, encouragement, and editorial assistance. I am deeply grateful to them for the faith they have demonstrated in this project. Without them, my father's story would never have been told.

The Stevens County Historical Society has been a source of background information and some of the photographs I have used in this book. Larry Hutchings, Tami Plank, and Karen Berget provided valuable research assistance and professional advice.

For over thirty years, I have subscribed to the Morris *Sun & Tribune*. During that time, I have faithfully read and recorded the excerpts from old newspaper articles in the column "Looking Back," edited by Carol M. Day. This information, especially as it pertains to the 1920s and 1930s, provided much background information regarding the period of time when my father grew up south of Alberta. Other Morris *Sun & Tribune* articles on file at the Stevens County Historical Society were also useful sources of information.

The University of San Diego provided me with the necessary reassigned time to write and edit parts of this manuscript, and for that I am grateful.

Many Stevens County residents, too numerous to identify individually, have assisted me in my research. The stories they shared about early Stevens County history, and in some cases their memories of my father, were significant contributions to this book. Some of these people are direct descendants of the farmers south of Alberta who assisted my father in his youth—so my gratitude extends to their parents and grandparents as well.

My wife Alexa provided invaluable feedback, research assistance, and editorial advice throughout the writing of this book. Without her keen insights and support, I would be at a great disadvantage in all of my writing projects.

My three-year-old son, Derl Edward, prefers to watch the balloons float across the screen of my computer. But he has learned to accept the fact that his Dad occasionally has to turn off the screen saver and get back to work. So I thank him for his patience.

My mother, Arlene Benson, who died in April of 1995, and my sisters—Patricia Schmidgall, Beverly Clausen-Kieffer, and Renee Clausen—have supported my efforts in a variety of ways.

My father, Lloyd Augustine Clausen, was a storyteller—and a very good one. He instinctively recorded the details of his life's experiences and shaped them into the stories he told and retold throughout his life. Without his gift for storytelling, I could not have written this book.

Delores Cudrio Hampton provided me with numerous stories and memories about the childhood experiences she shared with my father. Before she died in December of 1995, she gave me many of the photographs I have used in this book. She also encouraged me to write this book so others would understand the forces that had shaped my father's life. As an adopted child herself, she alone understood what he had endured. She was convinced that his story had meanings that transcended the rural area where he grew up.

Delores's voice merges with my father's voice in *Prairie Son*.

PROLOGUE

In 1979 my father was diagnosed with terminal lung cancer. He made one last trip to the Minnesota prairie where he had been born and raised. After that, he settled into a small trailer home in Houston, Texas, for the last year of his life.

During that time, I suggested that he write a memoir of his experiences growing up on the Minnesota prairie earlier in the century. I suppose I had two motives for making such a suggestion. I wanted my father to find some peace in his life by thinking about something other than the cancer. I also thought that someday, when I read what he had written, perhaps I would understand him better. I had no idea if he would take me up on my suggestion, but I hoped that he would.

I called him virtually every night the year before he died, and we talked about his life's experiences. I also flew out to Houston to be with him during the last few months of his life. We often talked while I sat by his bedside.

Shortly after his death in October of 1980, I was sorting through his belongings when I found three yellow legal tablets. I was somewhat surprised, but also pleased that he had taken me up on my suggestion to write down the memories of his early life on the Minnesota prairie.

But when I read what he had written, especially as he described his experiences as an adopted child who struggled to escape from an abusive home and find his way back to his birth mother, I was unable to get through the first few pages. It was almost as painful, I believe, for me to read as it must have been for him to write. So I set the legal tablets aside with a promise to myself that someday I would try once again to read what he had written.

Many years later, as I approached the age my father had been when he died, I returned to his legal tablets and read them through from beginning to end. I noted how his handwriting grew progressively weaker as the cancer stripped him of his energy, and yet he remained determined to write his life's story as I had asked him to do. I believe it was his final gift to me.

What he had written was more of a general summary of some of his experiences than a detailed narrative. Still, it was more than I had expected. I felt I had an obligation to take his notes and complete what he had started by trying to remember our many conversations, and by talking to the few remaining friends and relatives who remembered my father as a boy. I would also have to play detective to check the veracity of his story because the way he described some of the people in his life was quite different from the way I remembered them as a boy. Before I attempted to write and publish anything, I had to be certain that what he had written, and what he had told me in the months before he died, was an honest account of his life—and not some excuse for a life that he admitted was filled with mistakes and regrets.

My father's attempt at autobiography was a heroic effort. But his energy and strength gave out long before he could finish the project. How was I to complete what he had started? It would mean weeks, if not months, of sorting through old boxes of family memorabilia. It would mean countless hours reading ancient copies of small town newspapers and researching county historical archives. And it would mean walking along the dirt roads and through the fields of Minnesota's prairie—as my father once did.

Still, as I envisioned my father trying to write his life's story for me while he was dying of cancer, all other concerns became irrelevant. I decided to plunge ahead, because my father's story deserved to be told. It had purpose. Maybe I could reconnect with him and resolve some of the lingering questions and doubts I had harbored for too many years.

But selfish or personal motivations aside, I believed that something about my father's life transcended the narrow confines of Alberta, Minnesota, and spoke to a whole lost generation of adopted children whose stories will never be told to anyone. These were the adopted children who were taken out of orphanages and brought into homes, not to be raised as sons and daughters, but rather to be exploited as cheap sources of labor.

Few people will attach significance to the name Lloyd Augustine Clausen, but to adopted children who have devoted their lives to a search for their natural parents, his story will probably evoke painful memories of their own experiences. Children who were adopted by parents who exploited their innocence will undoubtedly share many of his emotions. Certainly, they will understand his anguish—and his small victories may appear to be larger triumphs.

My father was an enigma. He was impossibly distant, and yet he was always somehow close at hand. He was a wanderer who, after growing up in Alberta and living for several years in Minneapolis, moved across the country from construction job to construction job, never setting down permanent roots. Yet, during his wanderings, he found the time to write weekly letters back home to me. He was a devoted, albeit absent parent—if there is such a thing.

My father and my mother were married for only a short time before they divorced. He had several other failed marriages and relationships. But for some reason, I remained his anchor in a lifetime of insecurity and uncertainty.

In spite of the difficulty he had establishing lasting relationships, my father's saving grace was that he was always able to laugh at himself. With his marvelous sense of humor, he readily acknowledged—and laughed at—his own weaknesses, his own mistakes. But it was clear that he felt great pain and distress over a broken life that he could not repair.

My father's life is the story of a young boy who somehow remembered the early love of his natural mother, who held him for only a few short months before she gave him up for adoption. And it is the story of his steadfast refusal to accept the destiny his adoptive parents had chosen for him, as well as his determined efforts to find his way back home to his birth mother.

Despite my father's unhappy personal experiences, he often expressed great admiration for parents who adopt babies and take them into their homes to be raised as their own children. He considered those parents to be the finest people who walk the face of God's earth. He was convinced that adoption most often makes children's lives more tolerable. He knew that a home and loving parents are our greatest gifts to one another.

I believe my father would want his story to be dedicated to adopted children everywhere. And he would insist that they have a legal, ethical, and moral right to know their natural parents. He was denied that right. He was deprived of his own past, and, therefore, refused an emotional necessity of life. The pain of his early childhood undoubtedly caused some of his restless uncertainty.

After my father died, I found a box in which he had saved nearly every birthday card, Father's Day card, and Christmas card he had ever received. I was not surprised by this discovery. The smallest gift or memento would bring an immediate flood of tears to his eyes. He remains, to this day, the most unabashedly sentimental man I have ever met.

My father's life was plagued by cruel paradox. He didn't want to be alone. Yet, every decision he made in life seemed to create a set of circumstances that guaranteed he would be even more alone. What he wanted more than anything else was someone who would walk beside him through life. Yet, he could not make relationships work. He lived for the unattainable, the elusive romantic vision lingering somewhere out of reach.

In the months that he lay in his bed in a small trailer house in Houston, Texas, dying of cancer, he must have reviewed his life many times over. He forgave the people who had harmed him. He asked the people he had harmed to forgive him. When my siblings and I came out to see him for the last time, he told each of us that he would have done things differently if he had his life to live over again. To me, he added, "You were the only one who ever understood."

The truth of the matter was: I didn't understand him at all.

So almost fourteen years after he died, I decided to reconstruct my father's early life on the Minnesota prairie, to unravel the paradox of the child who was adopted and renamed Lloyd Augustine Clausen. I entered my father's world and relived the forces that shaped his enigmatic personality and gave form to his massive dreams.

I was in for some big surprises. But perhaps nothing surprised me more than the overwhelming sense that my father's story needed to be told in his own voice. No omniscient author could do justice to it. So I immersed myself in my father's writings, and went on many long walks while I recollected my many conversations with him. I also talked for hours to Delores Cudrio Hampton, the one person who knew him better than anyone else. It did not take long for my father's voice to become a very real presence in my life again.

I heard his voice inside of me as I read old newspaper accounts of life in Stevens County earlier in the century. I saw with his eyes the old photographs of the people and places he had known as a boy. I heard his voice when I walked for many hours over the old abandoned farm sites where he had been raised. I listened to his voice until it became a part of me. And then I sat down to write this account of his life.

Dennis M. Clausen
San Diego, California
1999

From the Orphanage to the Farm

I

Dear Son:

I've been told that most people can't remember anything from the first years of their lives. I disagree. I have one very vivid memory from a time when I was only a few months old. I remember it as well as I remember what I was doing five minutes ago. I am a baby, very small, and I am being held by someone who cares very much for me. I can feel the warmth and the love of this person reach out and envelop me in a way I have never felt at any other time in my life. I know instinctively that this person is my mother, and I feel secure and loved in her arms. I am at peace with myself and my life. I only want to be with her and no one else.

Then two strange arms reach out for me and pull me away from my mother. I know something is very wrong, and I get very upset. I cry, I kick, I cling to my mother's clothing with my tiny hands. I know that she is crying too, for I can hear her. She sounds just like me. Then I am pulled away from her. I feel the world moving on all sides of me, and I fall asleep.

When I wake up, I am in a strange place. It is not the place I remember, and again I start to cry. I reach out for my mother, who had held me and loved me, but she is not there. I want her to hold me again. I want that more than anything else in the world. Then someone else, another stranger, picks me up and tries to comfort me, but I do not stop crying. For many days, nothing can console me. I want my mother. No one else can comfort or console me.

Then many strangers walk by and peer into the area where I lie awake, looking at the ceiling and crying. Eventually, two of the strangers pick me up and carry me away from the small cubicle that has been my home since I was taken away from my mother.

Somehow, as the strangers carry me away, I cling to the memory of my mother. I still remember how she held me, and I want to feel her arms around me again. I want that more than anything else in the whole world.

II

Years later, I learned that I was almost five months old when my mother gave me up for adoption. I will not go into her reasons for putting me up for adoption. Not now. That will come much later in my story. But on the day my mother gave me up for adoption, I somehow knew that she was holding me for the last time. And I fought with every bit of strength I had in my little arms to keep the stranger from taking me away from her.

I know now that the place I was taken to was the orphanage, and the many strange faces passing by my tiny cubicle were the people who were checking out the babies to see which one they wanted to adopt. The two people who took me with them one month later, when I was six months old, became my adoptive parents: Claus and Marie Clausen. I learned to call them Ma and Pa. That is what they taught me.

But I have always carried inside of me the memory of my natural mother. I carry it today. At times, when life just didn't seem to be worth living, I would think back to the way I felt in her arms. And somehow I would find the strength to go on. I knew that someday I would feel those arms around me again.

This all took place, you must remember, at a time when adopted parents were not screened as carefully as they probably should have been. In those days, some people who adopted children did not necessarily want to bring a son or a daughter into their family. They adopted a child to bring another "laborer" into the home or onto the farm. Adoption was a cheap source of labor, and some adults took advantage of orphaned and illegitimate children in this way.

I do not want anyone to think that I am opposed to adoptions. To the contrary, people who adopt babies and take them into their homes to be raised as their sons and daughters must be the finest people who walk the face of God's earth. There must be a special place in heaven for them.

My anger is directed at those adults, especially earlier in the century, who promised to raise their adopted children as their own sons and daughters, but didn't. They stripped these children of all dignity, and treated them like beasts of burden. It is unfathomable that anyone could do this to another person, and yet it did happen.

But more about that later. I am getting ahead of myself.

III

My next vivid memory must have taken place when I was four or five years old. I know that I am very small. I am walking across a newly plowed field, and I am very scared. I do not want to be out there, but Ma has told me that I must find Pa and bring him his lunch.

I see dark clouds forming overhead, and I am afraid they will fall on top of me, or grab me and pull me into the sky. The field seems so big, while I am so small. I feel so alone. I am afraid that I will get lost, and no one will ever find me again. Or that the dark clouds will pick me up and drop me someplace far, far away.

I am moving my legs as fast as I can, but since I am carrying a heavy lunch bucket, I can't run fast enough to get away from the dark clouds that are following me. In the distance, I see a team of horses and I yell, "Pa," but he can't hear me over the sound of the horses and the plow cutting into the dark soil. So I have to chase him.

Eventually, I catch up to him with the lunch bucket and yell, "Pa, this is for you." Pa reins in the team of horses and he looks down at me. He is a tall, raw-boned, powerful man with little sense of humor and a very somber manner. In all the time that I knew him, I only saw him laugh once or twice.

"You get on back home now," he says as he reaches for the lunch bucket. "Tell Ma I'll be going over to a neighbor's after I get done out here."

"Can I stay with you, Pa?" I plead. "I don't want to go back across the fields. I'm afraid of the clouds. I'm afraid they will hurt me."

Pa looks at the sky and then back at me. "There's nuthin' to be afraid of. It might rain a little. But it's too cold for a twister to blow in. You get on back home, now."

Pa secures the lunch bucket to the handle of the plow, and then he whips the team of horses with the reins. They plod steadily away from me until I am again alone.

I glance at the dark clouds and start to run in the direction of the small grove of trees in the distance. When I run into the farmyard, I see a car parked next to the house. Ma has told me never to come inside when there is company, unless she calls for me. But I am scared and so I run up to the back porch and knock on the screen door.

"Can I come inside?" I gasp breathlessly when she comes to the door. "I'm afraid of the clouds."

"No, I have company," Ma replies with little emotion. "You'll have to stay outside. Go play with the dogs."

"But I'm afraid of the clouds," I plead. "Please, can I come inside?"

"There's nothing to be afraid of," she insists, shutting the door in my face. "Go play with the dogs."

I run over to where Buster and Minnie are lying in the open doorway of a small shed that serves as their doghouse. I sit down beside them and try not to think about the clouds. Buster is a beautiful German shepherd mix, "police dogs" we called them in those days. Minnie is a mongrel, half the size of Buster, but afraid of nothing that walks.

As I sit next to Buster and Minnie, the clouds grow darker and thicker overhead. Soon it begins to sprinkle and then pour rain. I look at the back door of the house to see if Ma is coming out to tell me to come inside now. But she stays inside with her company. The rain blows in through the open doorway of the shed and trickles through the roof and onto the dirt floor. Lightning streaks through the dark clouds overhead. I cringe and back away from the doorway. I am afraid of what the clouds might do to me if they know I am alone, and there is no one to protect me.

I see a dry spot in the rear of the shed, and I coax Buster and Minnie to join me. We cuddle up together while the thunder roars and crackles overhead. At some point I fall asleep, for the next thing I know Pa is carrying me across the farmyard while the rain streams down, drenching both of us. I know that Pa is very angry, but he doesn't say anything.

Inside the house, he wipes me down with an old rag. He gives me a glass of milk to drink and sends me upstairs to bed. The upstairs of the farmhouse is unfinished, and the rough lumber is exposed on all four walls. I curl up on my small cot in one corner of the room, while the thunder booms overhead and rain pounds on the roof. Downstairs, Ma and Pa are yelling at one another—something they do all the time. Then something breaks on the floor. There is more yelling and screaming.

I pull the covers over my head, wishing that Buster or Minnie could come sleep with me upstairs. But Pa will not let them in the house. So I do what I always do when I am afraid: I think about the woman who held me when I was a baby. I remember how her arms felt around me, and I am comforted.

The yelling and screaming soon stop. Outside, as darkness covers the prairie, lightning flashes across the window next to my cot. I fall asleep.

IV

I learned very early that I was not adopted to be Claus and Marie Clausen's son. Ma clearly didn't even want me around. She booted me out the door early in the morning and told me to fend for myself. I was not allowed back inside unless she called for me later in the day. If Pa was in town playing cards with his friends, sometimes she wouldn't call me until late at night. And if she had company, or there were cars parked in the yard, I was never allowed to knock on the door or disturb her in any way.

Sometimes Ma handed me a bowl of food through the back door. When she did not come to the door to feed me, I usually found something to eat in the garden or apple orchard—or shared some of the scraps she gave to Buster and Minnie. At other times, she fed me very well. Her moods were very unpredictable.

To Ma, I was a nuisance, nothing more. In time, I learned that she never wanted to adopt me. The trip to the orphanage was Pa's idea. I learned many years later that he bragged to some of his card-playing friends that he had gone looking for a champion hired man. He claimed he checked out the size of my hands, arms, and legs, decided I had the makings of a "good farm hand," and adopted me for one reason: to put me to work. To Pa, I was little more than another farm animal born with the potential to become a prize winner.

I cannot remember a single time in my childhood when either Ma or Pa hugged me, kissed me, or held me close. Buster and Minnie became my mother and father. They were the ones who kept me safe and taught me what was right and good about life. They were the only ones who ever showed me any love or affection. Ma and Pa didn't teach me those things. But, then, I don't think they understood those things themselves. I never saw them hug or kiss one another in all the years that I knew them.

Minnie really liked me, but Buster loved me. He and I became inseparable. Here was this powerful police dog, who could chase off a pack of wild dogs, or face down a hog thief with no fear whatsoever, but who was so gentle that he would let me ride on his back. When I was small, he would even lie down on the ground so I could straddle him. Then he would slowly get to his feet with me on top of him. I would ride Buster into the fields, with Minnie walking alongside of us.

I learned more about family life from Buster and Minnie than I ever did from Ma and Pa. Buster was more of a father than Pa could ever have hoped to be. Minnie had more motherly instincts in her front paws than Ma had in her whole body. And if I have any virtues, I learned them from Buster and Minnie. If I am to be reunited with anyone in the next world, I hope it is with Buster and Minnie—and, of course, my birth mother. Just about everyone else can go to hell as far as I'm concerned.

V

Ma was frustrated with her life on the farm and even more so with her marriage. She probably had good reason to be. Although Pa could be a good worker, he preferred to be with his friends in the small town card rooms and bars, or fishing. As a result, he was a very unsuccessful farmer.

Ma was left alone much too often on the farm. Surrounded by the stark, barren prairie, and suffering the impoverished life of a farm wife, she grew increasingly bitter. She vented her unhappiness in a variety of ways, mostly on me.

Very few people ever saw her dark side or guessed it existed. On the surface, she was a small, petite, almost gracious woman—if occasionally high strung and nervous. Most people didn't know her explosive temper, one that raged dangerously out of control. Pa had a temper when it came to politics and some animals, but he was slower to anger. But once he was pushed beyond the point of no return, everyone got out of his way. He was one of the biggest and strongest men in the county, and everyone knew you just didn't mess with him.

About the only good thing you can say about my early life is that I was fortunate that Pa didn't have Ma's temper. If so, someone would have been killed in our house. Most likely it would have been me. As it was, I had much more to fear from Ma's unhappiness than I did from Pa's size and strength.

To make matters worse, since no one in the community had any idea how out of control Ma could be when she lost her temper, I was afraid to tell anyone. I was afraid they wouldn't believe me. I was terrified that they might report what I had said to Ma. All I would get for trying to protect myself would be another beating, or a day in the cellar.

One day, when I was still very young, I gathered the eggs in the hen house as Pa had taught me to do. I was carrying the eggs up to the house in a small bucket lined with straw, when I tripped over something in the yard and fell down. The eggs spilled out of the bucket and smashed onto the ground, creating a huge mess right in front of me.

Ma was outside, and she saw me fall. For some reason, the sight of the broken eggs sent her into an uncontrollable frenzy. She ran over to where I was lying and pulled me up off the ground by my hair.

"You clumsy little fool!" she screamed.

"It was an accident," I cried. "Please, Ma, I didn't mean to do it."

As Ma held me by my hair, she began to beat me with a closed fist on both sides of my head. First one ear, then the other ear, until my head was ringing. I thought I was going to pass out from the pain.

I'm not too sure Ma would have ever stopped beating me. But suddenly, we both heard a low growling sound nearby. Buster was standing a few feet away, his legs firmly planted as though he were about to take a leap at Ma's throat. Only then did she drop me and run into the house, slamming the door shut behind her.

As I lay on the ground, crying and rubbing my hands over my bruised and battered ears, I felt Buster's wet, warm tongue on my neck. He was trying to comfort me in the only way he knew how. I hugged his neck and thanked him for being there for me when I needed him. Buster kept watch on the back door, almost as though daring Ma to come back outside and try something else with me. But she never did. At least not that day. She knew Buster wouldn't stand for it.

VI

Ma knew Buster loved me. And for that reason, she tried in every way to convince Pa to get rid of Buster. Pa refused. Buster was the best protection we had against hog thieves, chicken thieves, and just about every other kind of thief who wandered through the county. One look at Buster, and thieves knew immediately that he would protect his territory.

I always kind of wished that Ma and Pa would both leave the farm for good, so Buster, Minnie, and I could have it to ourselves. I know we would have been a much happier family.

Sometimes I think that when Ma and Pa took me away from the orphanage, God told Buster right then and there that it was his job to protect me and see that I was taken care of. I don't think I would have survived my early years on the farm if Buster hadn't been there to look after me and, at times, to put the fear of God into Ma.

I was always in trouble of one kind or another. Nothing big. Just the kind of mischief little kids get into. But Ma didn't seem to be able to make a distinction between the big problems a kid might get into and mischief. Everything deserved the same punishment—a severe beating.

But sometimes, when Ma's hands were already sore for one reason or another, she wouldn't beat me. She would lock me up in the cellar instead. Ours was a typical farmhouse cellar. The door was outside. Stone steps led down to a dirt floor. There were no window wells to let in the light. When the door closed, there was total darkness.

The walls of the cellar were stone, mostly large rocks mortared together to create the foundation for the house. The stones had been hauled out of the nearby fields when homesteaders first cleared the land for plowing and planting. Along one wall of the cellar, home-canned preserves were stacked on crude wooden shelves, nailed together from pieces of discarded lumber.

When Ma sent me to the cellar, I always asked her if I could take Buster down there with me. She always refused. When I would start to cry as she slowly closed the cellar door, she would ignore my whimperings. The last sound was Ma slipping the latch into place from the other side of the wooden door, securing it so that I could not push my way out. Then I was alone in silent darkness.

I was terribly afraid of the cellar because Ma once told me that snakes crawled out of the holes and cracks where the mortar had fallen out of the stone walls. Ma had said this was especially true if the snakes knew I was down there. So she told me I had to sit real quiet, or else the snakes would get me.

Once Ma latched the door, any distant sound would send me into a state of panic. I would huddle in the corner in case the snakes were slipping out of the holes in the walls and onto the dirt floor. I expected the snakes to be crawling around my feet at any moment. I didn't even whimper, even though I was terrified.

I was probably five or six years old when Ma first locked me up in the cellar. I don't remember what I had done. It probably wasn't much of anything. But that didn't matter to Ma. More than likely, I hadn't done anything at all. Ma probably just decided the cellar was the best place to put me when her company came over. It seemed like I always ended up in the cellar whenever Pa went to town for the day. That's when Ma's company came to visit. Locked in the cellar, I was out of the way—and quiet.

One time as I huddled alone in all that darkness, I shuddered at the sound of awful scratching above my head. I expected at any minute that snakes would start falling down around me. But then I heard Buster's familiar panting and whining. He had found his own crack in the stone wall, near where the house joined the foundation, and he was clearing away the dirt and old mortar with his paws. He was trying to dig me out of my prison, or at least find a place where he could keep me company.

I moved as close as I could to the small crack in the mortar where Buster had his nose. I started talking to him, and he panted and whimpered back in my direction. With Buster nearby, the darkness didn't seem so dark. I also didn't think about the snakes quite so much.

Later, when Ma let me out of the cellar, I went around to the side of the house where Buster had been. He had dug a pretty big hole in the ground next to the foundation. I believe that dog would have excavated the whole foundation to find me.

I chipped a few more pieces of mortar out of the wall to create a bigger hole, and from then on, whenever I was sent into the cellar, I could look up and see Buster's eyes gazing down on me. He seemed to be reassuring me that everything would be all right. He would stay there until Ma let me out of the darkness.

VII

My early life settled into a repetition: chores, beatings, long hours locked up in the cellar, and occasional walks with Buster and Minnie down the county roads or out into the fields and sloughs. It was very easy to get around in those days. Farmers driving by would always offer me a ride in their horse-drawn wagons or on the back of their tractors.

One day when I was preparing to take a long walk with Buster and Minnie, Ma rushed out to the shed. She grabbed me by the arm, stripping off my dirty clothes as she carried me into the house. She scrubbed my body and washed my hair, grumbling something about an important guest. She also threatened that if I wasn't on my best behavior I would be locked up in the cellar for the rest of the week. So I decided right then and there that I wouldn't do or say anything to get Ma upset with me.

I couldn't imagine who our important guest might be, or why Ma wanted me around. But I knew it must be someone real special because Ma almost scrubbed the skin off my body trying to get me clean.

A few minutes later, Pa rushed into the house, carrying some new clothes. They quickly dressed me in the new clothes, then took turns getting into their Sunday best. We sat down by the kitchen table—all clean and presentable for our important guest.

I don't remember what was going through my head at the time. I hoped that maybe Ma and Pa were going to give me back to my birth mother. I was overjoyed at that possibility.

Within the hour, a car pulled into the yard. A knock sounded on the screen door. Ma greeted our important guest in the warmest, friendliest tone of voice I had ever heard her use. Then a tall, gray-haired woman with a very official manner stepped into the kitchen. Ma and Pa talked to her like she was an old friend. They gestured and smiled in my direction. I had never seen Ma and Pa smile so broadly. I knew they were up to something.

I wanted desperately to ask the woman if she were my birth mother, and if she had come to take me home. But I was terrified of what Ma would do to me if I said anything other than "Yes, ma'am," and "No, ma'am," to the questions the woman asked me.

"Lloyd, do you enjoy your life here on the farm?" she asked.

"Yes, ma'am," I replied.

"Are your mother and father looking after you?"

"Yes, ma'am."

"Do they ever hurt you?"

"No, ma'am."

After a few more questions, the woman smiled gently and patted me on the head. Then she laid some papers out on the kitchen table, and Ma and Pa signed them. The woman quickly tucked the papers into her purse and walked toward the screen door. Ma stood in the doorway and waved at her as she drove out of the yard.

"Get those clothes off of him before he gets them dirty," Ma ordered Pa. She turned and walked briskly back into the kitchen.

Once again I was stripped. Only this time I put on the dirty clothes that Ma had hung on a hook behind a door. Pa told me to go back outside to play with the dogs.

For a long time, I thought that maybe our visitor was my birth mother, and she had come out to the farm to see how I was doing. Later, I realized the more likely explanation was that she was someone from the orphanage or the government, and she was doing some kind of final check on me before signing me over to Ma and Pa for good.

THE PRAIRIE WIND SONG

I

I soon learned that I didn't have to do anything to be sent down into the cellar. When a particular black car pulled into our yard, Ma always found some excuse to send me down there. I never knew what that meant at the time. But as soon as I saw that car heading up our dirt road, I knew it was time to take Buster and Minnie and head out to one of the nearby sloughs. Otherwise, I would end up in the cellar until Ma's company left.

One day, as the car drove into the yard, I called to Buster and Minnie and set out down the road toward one of the sloughs. Perhaps I should mention that the roads in the area at that time weren't roads as we know them today. They were narrow dirt trails that were smoothed over for travel. After heavy rains, they were muddy and impassable. Even in dryer weather, the ruts made traveling slow and tedious.

Not too far from the dirt road, in a field about two miles from our house, there was a tall oak tree that was probably one of the first things to grow on the flat prairie lands. Old-timers said that a bird flying by probably dropped an acorn on that spot over a hundred years earlier, and the oak tree grew out of that acorn. They figured the tree was at least that old, if not older.

The unique thing about this oak tree was that it had been struck by lightning long ago, when the early settlers first moved into the area. I was told that everyone thought the tree would certainly die, because it was almost split in half when the lightning took a jab at it. Half of the tree was scorched black and died. But the other half went along from season to season as though nothing had happened, producing leaves and acorns just as it had always done for over a hundred years.

Next to the tree, there was a large pile of rocks that some farmer had cleared out of the nearby fields decades earlier. On that particular day, there was a young girl sitting on top of the pile of rocks. I recognized the girl as my cousin, Delores Cudrio, who was three years older than me.

Delores's situation was similar to mine in some respects. Pa's sister and her husband, who farmed a few miles northeast of us, had adopted Delores. But from everything I could tell, they treated her as a member of the family. I was told that Delores sometimes fought with her adoptive mother, but the fights didn't seem to create any permanent problems in their relationship.

As far as I know, Delores and I were the only adopted children in the area. At times we were teased pretty mercilessly by some of the other children, who called us "illegitimate" or "bastards." Sometimes they would spit at us or try to chase us away. So over a period of time, Delores and I became very close friends. We two adopted children were kindred spirits, and we stood up for each other in all kinds of ways.

There was always something mysterious about the circumstances surrounding Delores's adoption. I couldn't put my finger on precisely why I felt that way. But certain people seemed to speak about her adoption in hushed terms, as though it wasn't something to be talked about at all. Of course, they were that way about all such things—but even more so, it seemed, about Delores's adoption. Eventually, I began to suspect there was another story behind Delores's adoption. But I will talk more about that later.

Delores was sitting on top of the pile of stones, staring at the oak tree, when I walked up to her. We had been together at family functions, but this was one of the first times I had ever seen her outside of those occasions. Pa and his sister didn't get along real well, but Ma enjoyed visiting the Cudrios. When the Cudrios visited us, Pa seemed to be uncomfortable and uneasy. I also sensed a great deal of tension between

Pa and Delores's father, even though on the surface they did their best to create the impression that they got along.

"What are you doing over here?" I asked, walking over and sitting down next to Delores.

"Ma and Pa are visiting one of your neighbors," she replied somewhat evasively. "They dropped me off here so I could listen to this tree."

"How can you listen to a tree?" I asked.

"One of the old hired men told me, if you sit here and listen long enough, you can hear the wind blowing through the crack in the tree trunk, right where the lightning hit it," she explained. "He said it's the sound of people who once lived and died out here on the prairie. He said you can still hear their voices when the wind blows through this tree."

I listened carefully, but I could hear nothing unusual. Since Delores was a rather free-spirited young lady with a vivid imagination, I pretty much decided she must have made the whole thing up.

"Hear it?" she asked, nodding at the tree.

I listened again. "I only hear the sound of the wind blowing through the leaves," I replied.

"Lean closer to the trunk," she insisted.

Since Ma's beatings had already caused some loss of hearing in my left ear, I leaned closer and turned my right ear toward the tree trunk.

"The wind *is* blowing through the crack in the trunk," I marveled. "It sounds like someone whispering from far, far away."

"Then you *can* hear it," she exclaimed proudly. "That old hired man told me when he was a boy they called it the prairie wind song. He said even the Indians placed some kind of special meaning on the sounds the wind made as it passed through that old oak tree, even before it was hit by lightning."

Delores excused herself so she could rejoin her parents. As I watched her run across the field, I continued to listen to the sound of the wind blowing through the split trunk of the oak tree. I had to agree there was something different about the sound, even though I still wasn't too sure if Delores had made up the story about the prairie wind song. I decided it would be just like her to do something like that.

For some reason, I walked back to the house rather than over to the slough. The black car was parked in our yard, so I knew that Ma still had her company. Buster and Minnie lay down next to the water trough, and I walked around the yard thinking about the story Delores had told me about the prairie wind song. I liked the idea that people who had lived and died on the prairie still spoke in the wind that whispered through the split trunk of the old oak tree.

I was circling the house, lost in my thoughts and kicking rocks, when I glanced up at a half-naked man standing in the window of Ma's bedroom. I recognized the man as the driver of the car that was parked in our yard, but I couldn't figure out what he would be doing in Ma's bedroom with his shirt off.

Our eyes locked for a few seconds. Then he jumped back into the shadows. I kept staring at the window, not quite comprehending what I had just seen. The more I thought about it, the more frightened I became. I thought that maybe Ma was in some kind of trouble. I had to tell Pa what I had seen.

When I ran over to the dirt road, I could see Pa in the distance. He was driving a team of horses pulling a wagon full of hay. I ran down the dirt road and out into the field, calling out his name all the way. As I approached the wagon, the team of horses almost spooked, but Pa stood up and reined them in with his powerful arms.

"Watch it," he yelled at me.

"It's Ma," I blurted out breathlessly. "A man's in her bedroom. I think he's trying to hurt her."

Pa quickly lifted me up onto the wagon, and he slapped the reins against the horses' rumps. The horses started to trot across the field and down the dirt road, while the load of hay swayed perilously back and forth on the wagon behind us. As we approached the house, the black car that had been parked in our yard was disappearing into a small cloud of dust farther south. I don't even know if Pa saw the car as he steered the horses into our driveway.

As soon as Pa reined in the horses, he ran into the house, while I sat on the wagon. For several minutes, I heard a lot of screaming and yelling, and then Pa stomped out the front door and walked over to the barn. A few minutes later, Ma appeared at the screen door and glared menacingly in my direction.

I had seen that look before, and I was terrified.

II

Somehow I knew I had done something terribly wrong. Confused and frightened, I stayed away from the house until late that night, and then I slipped quietly inside and fled upstairs to bed. I could hear Ma and Pa talking in their bedroom.

The next morning I awoke and left before Pa got up to go out into the fields. I didn't want to be alone in the house with Ma after he was gone. I took Buster and Minnie with me. We walked over to a nearby slough, where I sat on a log and watched the ducks and loons swimming out in the water. Hours later, when the sun was high overhead, I knew I had no choice but to go back to the house. If I wasn't there by noon to bring Pa his lunch, there would be no telling what Ma might do to me.

Ma was standing on the porch when I walked up to the house. Without saying a word, she opened the screen door and nodded for me to step inside. As I walked past her, my heart was pounding so hard I was certain she could hear it beating. I expected at any moment that she would grab my hair or my ears and start beating on me. But she didn't do anything until we were in the kitchen. Then she gestured for me to sit down on a chair that she had placed next to the stove.

I didn't know what she had in mind for me, but I knew it would be something unforgettable. I briefly considered running out the door. But I sat down in the chair instead.

"What were you trying to do yesterday?" she demanded to know, hovering over me.

"I thought the man in the window was trying to hurt you," I defended myself meekly. "So I ran to get Pa so he could help you."

"There *was* no man in the window," Ma insisted.

"But—"

"You made the whole thing up. Do you understand me?"

"But I didn't make it—"

Ma cuffed me alongside the head. "You made the whole thing up," she insisted again. "And that's what you're going to tell Pa when you bring him his lunch. Do you understand me?"

I knew she was threatening me with some kind of awful punishment, so I quickly nodded to let her know I would tell Pa what she wanted me to tell him.

Ma handed me the lunch bucket. I bolted for the door and ran across the yard. Buster and Minnie joined me. Together we marched across the field in search of Pa. While Buster and Minnie sniffed at gopher mounds along the way, I tried to decide what I would tell Pa.

In the years since I first started bringing Pa his lunch, I had gotten much stronger. I no longer carried the lunch bucket with both hands. But Ma, even though she was a small woman, was still stronger than me.

I knew I had seen a man in Ma's bedroom window. I knew he didn't have his shirt on. At the time, I was too young to understand the implications of all that. But I knew what was going on must have involved something pretty serious to get Pa so upset.

If I told Pa the truth—that I *had* seen a half-naked man in the bedroom window—would he protect me from Ma? I didn't think so. He had never done so before. Why should it be any different this time? And although Ma merely cuffed me in the kitchen, I could tell that she was more angry than I had ever seen her before.

I was convinced I had stumbled into a part of her life that she would kill to protect. So the only thing to do was to tell Pa what she told me to tell him. I was less afraid of what Pa might do to punish me than I was of what Ma would certainly do to me if I didn't lie for her.

I approached Pa and the team of horses. I handed him the lunch bucket and put my hands in my pockets. "Pa," I said nervously, "there's something I've got to tell you."

Pa looked down at me with his somber, humorless eyes. "What is it?" he asked.

"I didn't see a man in Ma's bedroom window," I said. "I made the whole thing up."

Pa stared at me for a few seconds. Then, without betraying any emotion, he slapped the reins against the horses' rumps and continued across the field. I watched Pa and the team of horses disappear in the distance. I started walking in the other direction with Buster and Minnie. I didn't know what kind of trouble I was in now, but Pa's stony silence made me suspect the worst.

The rest of the afternoon, as I explored the slough with Buster and Minnie, I thought about my birth mother. I wondered if she ever thought about me anymore. I wondered if she knew what life was like for me with Ma and Pa. If she did know, would she come and get me and take me back home with her? Or didn't she care what happened to me?

III

We ate a quiet supper that night. After we were done eating, and the dishes were washed and put away, Ma disappeared into the bedroom. Pa immediately pulled out the leather strap he used to sharpen his razor, and he placed me face down across a chair. Without speaking, he pulled down my trousers and underwear, and then he raised the leather strap high in the air. Each time the leather hit my bare skin, I thought my buttocks were going to explode. The pain shot clear up into my head, and my heart started to beat wildly out of control.

I closed my eyes and tried to think about my birth mother. I tried to think about the kind of home I might have had with her. I clung to that vision as the leather strap continued to rise high in the air and slap again and again on my bare skin.

When Pa was finally done, he collapsed in a chair and his chin sank to his chest. The leather strap was covered with blood. For a moment, I thought that maybe he was going to cry. Then I realized, from the salty taste in my mouth, that I had been clenching my teeth so hard I had bitten into my own tongue.

IV

I lay on my stomach that night and tried not to think about the pain. But it was impossible not to think about it. My buttocks were swollen black and blue, and the blood continued to seep from the cuts the leather strap had made in my skin. I had been in pain before, when Ma beat me on both sides of the head, but nothing compared to the way I felt that night.

I had never seen Pa explode like that before. Somehow I think he knew I was lying for Ma. Maybe that made him even madder. But if he knew that Ma made me lie for her, why did he take it out on me and not her? Could Pa know what was going on but be unable to do anything about it? So he took out his rage on me? It was all much too confusing to figure out.

There had never been any love between Ma and Pa. They seemed only to be sharing the same house. Pa must have seen that car parked in our yard many times before when he was working in the fields. The prairie was flat and barren, and you could almost see forever. So what had he been thinking those other times when the car was parked there? Did I reveal to him something he knew but just didn't want to think about?

At the time I didn't understand what was going on between Ma and Pa, but I did hatch a plan for myself as I lay awake that night. We had some neighbors who rented a farm less than a mile to the south. I don't remember their first names, but their last name was Jensen.

When Mr. and Mrs. Jensen drove by in their wagon and team of horses, they would always smile and wave at me. Sometimes, they would stop and talk to me for a minute or two. I could tell that they liked me because on a few occasions they bought some little toys and gave them to me. So I knew they liked kids, and I decided that maybe they would help me.

In the morning, I put a rag inside my underwear so the blood on my buttocks wouldn't weep through my trousers. Then I limped outside and across the fields to our neighbor's farm. Each step was so painful that I feared I would pass out. But eventually I found Mr. Jensen loading hay onto a wagon parked near his house.

"Mr. Jensen," I asked awkwardly, "can I talk to you?"

"Of course, Lloyd," he replied cheerfully. "What's on your mind?"

I hesitated and then I said, "I was wondering if I could come and live with you and your wife?"

"Why would you want to do that?" he replied, obviously puzzled by my request.

"Because Ma and Pa have been beating me," I said as the tears started to flow down my cheeks. "Last night, Pa took the razor strap to me."

I could see the concern and then the anger leap into Mr. Jensen's eyes. He noticed that I was limping and in great pain. "Come inside," he said sympathetically. "Let's have my wife take a look at you."

Once we were inside the house, Mrs. Jensen had me lower my trousers so she could look at my injuries. I could tell, as they stared at my bruised and bloody buttocks, that they were both trying to control their anger. Mrs. Jensen put some warm salve on my wounds, and she replaced the rag I had used as a bandage with a soft, clean towel.

"Are you hungry?" she asked.

"Yes, I am," I replied.

She set a bowl of canned vegetables and some beef jerky on a counter top so I could stand and eat.

While I ate by the kitchen counter, I could hear them talking quietly in the next room. A few minutes later, Mr. Jensen came into the kitchen and announced, "We're going over to have a talk with your Ma and Pa. This kind of thing is going to end right now."

Mr. Jensen walked with me across the fields and over to our house. He told me to stay outside, and then he knocked on the door. When Pa answered, Mr. Jensen pushed past him, leaving me out in the yard. Although I couldn't make out what Mr. Jensen was saying, I could hear his voice rise with anger. About a half hour later, he came back out to the yard alone.

He leaned down next to me and whispered gently, "I told your Ma and Pa if they ever mistreat you again, I will go to the authorities and insist that they let you come and live with me and my wife. If they ever hit you again, for any reason, you come right over and let me know."

I thanked him for helping me, and then he patted me on the shoulder and started walking toward his house.

"Remember," he said, turning around, "if they ever hit you again, I want to know right away."

As I watched Mr. Jensen walk across the field, I could still feel the place where his hand had touched my shoulder. In all the time I had lived with Ma and Pa, neither one of them had ever touched me with that kind of affection. It felt good. I wanted to go running after Mr. Jensen and ask him if I could move in with him and his wife right away. But I knew he had already done enough for me. I didn't want to put him out any further.

V

I wish I could say that there was a dramatic change after Mr. Jensen lectured Ma and Pa on the way they were treating me. But that wouldn't be completely true. Things did get better. There's no question about that. Pa never took the strap to me again, and for that I am grateful. He also seemed to become even more distant—if that were possible—from both Ma and me. He started to disappear from the farm for longer and longer periods of time, playing cards in town or doing whatever else he did when he was away from home. I have no idea how he got his crop in the ground that year. He seemed to be gone all the time.

Ma left me alone for a time, but eventually she returned to her old ways—although she was much more careful not to punish me in ways that would show bruises. She resorted more to shaming me or making me feel guilty, normally for things I didn't do in the first place. It was almost like she was trying to find something that would hurt me more than a good beating but that wouldn't leave as many scars.

At other times, she threatened to send me back to the orphanage, where she promised that I would have to spend the rest of my life. In fact, that became a pretty constant threat. But it didn't bother me too much. I would have missed Buster and Minnie—but that was about all.

During Pa's frequent absences, the black car became a regular feature around our house. It was parked in our yard almost all the time. Whenever I saw it, I just stayed away from the house. Since Pa was gone, and Ma didn't care where I was anyhow, I started to expand the circumference of my world.

One of the people who helped me do that was our mailman, Clyde Roberts. He was another one of the good people God must have put in this world to remedy the damage done by all the bad ones. He delivered the mail by horse and buggy in summer, and by horse and bobsled in the winter.

In the winter, the horses had heavy blankets on to help protect them against the cold weather. They were big, strong, handsome animals. During some snow storms, when the temperature plunged well below zero and no one else would venture outdoors, we would still see Clyde Roberts's horses trotting toward our mailbox—every day, the same time. Frequently, the horses were so matted with snow, they were all white, and all you could see were their eyes. But somehow he got the mail through. I don't know how he did it.

Clyde Roberts took a liking to me, probably because I would help him water his horses at our trough before he continued on his route. I also got to know him better when he stayed overnight with us during some of the more severe winter storms.

One day he asked, "Would you like to go with me for the rest of the route?"

"I would sure like to do that," I replied enthusiastically.

Eventually, it became a regular thing for me to finish the route with him. He found an extra mailman's cap somewhere in the post office, and he had his wife cut and sew the band smaller so it would fit on my head. When Clyde Roberts gave me that cap, I refused to take it off for months. I even slept in it. Ma tried to throw it in the wash tub once or twice, but I wouldn't let her touch it. Not something that valuable.

I know now that there probably were no such things as mailmen's caps in those days. But Clyde Roberts made me believe the cap was

something very special. He must have sensed that I needed kind attention, and he gave it to me. It was the first time in my life I remember
feeling a sense of pride in anything. It was a new emotion. When I woke
up in the morning with my mailman's cap still on my head, it made it
much easier to accept my life with Ma and Pa on the farm.

Just about every afternoon, Clyde Roberts would pull up to our
watering trough to water his horses, and I would climb on board his
buggy and sit down next to the mail sacks. Eventually, he would let me
put some of the mail in the mailboxes. He told me that my hat "showed
that the federal government trusted Lloyd Clausen and authorized him
to make home deliveries," which made me feel proud and important.

Then one day, late in the summer, when Clyde Roberts and I were
finishing the route, he directed the horses right past Mr. and Mrs.
Jensen's mailbox without stopping. I knew the route by heart by that
time, and so I asked him if he had made a mistake, or if they didn't have
any mail.

"No," he said, "They've moved to another part of the state to be
closer to their children. We'll be forwarding their mail to them."

I glanced over my shoulder at the Jensen farm, and then I felt the
tears well up inside of me. I remembered the day I had gone to them
for help, and how kind they were to me. I had always hoped that someday they would let me live with them. Now I could no longer go to
them for help if Ma and Pa started beating me again. I had just lost the
two people who had volunteered to take me into their home if Ma and
Pa mistreated me, and I was devastated.

VI

Sometime after that—I don't remember precisely when—I heard that
Mr. Jensen had died in some distant city. The news of his death took
away another of my dreams. I had hoped that maybe someday Mr.
Jensen and his wife would return to the farm they had rented. Now I
knew that was never to be.

After I heard that Mr. Jensen had died, I walked over to his farm. The
house looked the same, but the front yard and the adjacent fields were
all infested with weeds. Some rusty pieces of old farm equipment lay in
the tall weeds in the middle of a grove of trees. The wind whispered
through the prairie grass that had seemingly sprung up everywhere.

The front and back doors to the house were locked and I could not get inside, but I pulled an old wooden crate over to one of the windows and climbed up on it. The room was empty except for a rocking chair that someone had abandoned right in the middle of the floor. As the sunlight from the window streaked across the rocking chair, it appeared to be one of the loneliest things I had ever seen in my life.

Why, I wondered, would the Jensens take everything except the rocking chair? Wasn't there enough room for it in whatever they had used to move their belongings? Or was it simply forgotten and left behind?

As I looked at the dust filtering across the sunbeams above the rocking chair, I felt even more lonely and abandoned. I don't know why I felt that way. Maybe it had something to do with my own sense of loss now that the Jensens were no longer our neighbors, and Mr. Jensen was dead.

I hadn't really thought too much about death before. But now that Mr. Jensen had gone to a place so far away that I could not even measure the distance in miles, I was overwhelmed by the idea of death. I was suddenly aware of the huge chasm that separates the living from the dead—and I was frightened and more lonely than I had ever been before.

Nothing about life seemed fair at that moment. Life and death made no sense whatsoever. Without the Jensens living down the road from us, I despaired about my future with Ma and Pa.

Later that day, I caught a ride with one of the farmers over to the pile of rocks next to the old oak tree. I sat there until dusk, listening to the sound of the wind blowing through the split trunk of the tree. I wanted to see if I could hear Mr. Jensen's voice in the prairie wind song.

LIFE, DEATH, AND HAY THIEVES

I

My world, which had been largely confined to our farm, became much bigger during my travels with Clyde Roberts. I began to see how our farm compared to some of the other farms south of Alberta. I learned that Pa was not only one of the smallest and least successful of the farmers in the area, but he didn't even own his own land. He rented it from an insurance company that had assumed ownership of the property through foreclosure on some out-of-luck farmer.

Pa's farm, which was located on a couple of hundred acres, consisted of a small two-story house, a granary, a chicken house, a couple of sheds, and a barn that housed a handful of cattle and several work horses. The house itself had three rooms downstairs—a kitchen, small living room, and one bedroom—and an unfinished upstairs, where I slept in the spring, summer, and fall. In the winter months, we closed off the upstairs because it was impossible to heat the whole house. There was no running water, electricity, or indoor toilets. There was a wood burning stove for cooking and heating the house. The house was, in short, four walls and a roof dropped on top of a stone foundation.

Pa didn't own a car, nor did most of the other poorer farmers. If you had a car of any kind in those days, you were considered pretty rich and successful. Most people traveled by horse and buggy, or horse and wagon. I can only assume that Ma's company, the man I had seen in her bedroom window, must have come from a higher social class than we did. But then just about everyone in the county came from a higher social class than we did.

Pa was not a good farmer, and everyone knew it. He stuck with horses when everyone else was switching over to tractors. He seldom got around to planting crops on all of his acreage. He never timed the harvest the way he should have. He was a good worker, but he would rather play cards than work. It was inevitable that he would fail as a farmer—but only after years of futile struggle.

During the time that I traveled with Clyde Roberts on his mail route, he taught me the four points of the compass and how they lined up with the various landmarks in Stevens County. He also taught me how to read a map to identify the various roads. I don't think I ever saw a paved road during the first nine years of my life. Even the roads in Alberta, a small town ten miles north and three miles east of Pa's farm, were dirt roads. Morris, the largest town in Stevens County, might have had paved roads in the 1920s, but I don't know for sure. We never went there until I was older. Whenever we went to town, which wasn't very often, we went to Alberta. But usually Pa went alone, leaving Ma and me on the farm. So I knew almost nothing about town life.

During my travels with Clyde Roberts, I never passed by the Jensen farm without feeling sad and lonely. The farm remained abandoned. Weeds covered the yard and adjacent fields. The house and barn weathered into a kind of gray apparition within a grove of trees.

The contrast between the tilled farm land I had known and the prairie grasses that were reclaiming the land left a lasting impression on me. I learned that homes, which provided protection against wind, rain, and snow storms, eventually fall to the ground and decay back into the prairie soil. Perhaps someday, hundreds of years from now, someone digging in the soil will uncover a decaying shingle or a piece of wood. Maybe he will have no idea what it once was—that it was part of a home. Over the years, as I watched the prairie reclaim the Jensen farm, I was in lonely awe of the forces that govern this universe and control the cycles of life and death.

Pa's farm is the one the prairie should have reclaimed. His farm was an eyesore. It wouldn't have upset the larger scheme of things one bit for it to sink back into the weeds and brush. But not the Jensen farm. It deserved to remain upright, as a memorial to all that is right and good about life and people.

But then, what do I know about those things? I eventually came to the conclusion that human beings are like the autumn leaves when the winds send them scurrying across the fields in directionless patterns. The only thing you can be sure of in life is that things will never come out the way you expect or want them to come out. Some things might be predictable, but I don't know. I haven't had much luck predicting anything.

II

Shortly after Mr. Jensen died, Ma started to hemorrhage internally. Pa, who had been playing cards in Alberta on a regular basis, stayed home to heat water and boil rags for her. For several days and nights, he hauled clean rags into the bedroom and bloody rags out. It became clear that Pa's efforts were not stopping the bleeding. He told Ma he was going to send for the doctor.

Although Ma insisted that she was dying, she still did not want to see a doctor. Weary and worried, Pa told me to ask Clyde Roberts, when he came through on his mail route, to send out Dr. Cumming. I knew then that Ma's condition was serious. Pa had never consulted a doctor before. There was no money for such things.

Dr. Cumming, a small black-haired man with a thin mustache, came out to the farm later that day. He walked into the bedroom, briefly examined Ma, and came back out with the announcement: "If we can't stop the bleeding, she will be gone by morning."

He ordered Pa to boil more water and sterilize more rags. Then he said he didn't want anyone in the bedroom except himself and Ma. He went to work on her with whatever he had in his black bag. Doctors, like everyone else in those days, had to work mostly with home remedies, since there wasn't much in the way of medicines.

Hours later, Dr. Cumming came out of the bedroom for a cup of coffee. He wouldn't say a word, not even when Pa asked him, "How is she doing?" Dr. Cumming seemed to be pondering some deep and terrible secret about Ma's health that he did not want to reveal.

We didn't see Dr. Cumming again for the rest of the night. At six the next morning, shortly after sunrise, he walked out of the bedroom, smiled at both Pa and me, and said, "She's very weak, but she's going to live."

I don't know what my feelings were at that point, but I knew Pa was relieved. He walked into the bedroom to talk to Ma, and Dr. Cumming sat down at the table and drank another cup of coffee.

I watched as Dr. Cumming surveyed the meager contents of our small kitchen. I am convinced to this day that he recognized our poverty during that quick glance around the room, because when Pa came out and asked what we owed for his services, Dr. Cumming replied, "Oh, just a jar or two of home preserves. That would be much appreciated."

Pa was so grateful that he quickly walked outside to the cellar, and came back a few minutes later with two jars of Ma's best jellies.

"Looks like I'm gonna have myself some mighty fine toast and jelly for a spell," Dr. Cumming said as he tucked the two pint jars into his black bag. "I'll be back to check on her tomorrow."

I knew, as I watched Dr. Cumming walk out the door with his tiny black bag, that I had just met another of the truly decent human beings who are put in this world to solve the problems caused by all the selfish ones. Dr. Cumming was a great man at any time, or in any generation. And yet he charged so little for his services.

My view of human nature had been elevated another notch or two.

III

After Ma's close brush with death, there were some changes in our lives—at least for a time. Pa stopped playing cards in Alberta quite so often, and he became a more responsible farmer. Ma stopped seeing her company. Or at least the black car was no longer parked in our driveway when Pa was working in the fields.

Ma was also too weak to do much more than lie in bed, so my life improved considerably. Delores's mother sent her over to help Ma with the housework during the time that she was recuperating. So I got to see a lot more of Delores, and we became very close friends.

I learned a lot when Ma almost died. I learned that people are probably at their best when they finally figure out that they are not going to be on this planet forever. I don't think some people ever figure out what life is all about, or how they should treat other people, until they're at death's door. Of course some people don't figure it out, even then. But Ma's brush with death calmed her down somewhat, and she stopped beating me. Or maybe she just didn't have the physical strength to beat me. In either case, I finally had some peace in my life. For a time, I felt better about my life on the farm.

Two events that occurred in close proximity to one another demonstrated how Pa must have done some soul-searching in the months after he had whipped me with the leather strap. Or maybe Ma's close brush with death had taught him to look at things a little differently, too.

Pa had always taught me, when I brought his lunch out to the fields where he was plowing or disking, that I should walk slowly and wait for the horses to complete their turn so they could see me coming and wouldn't be spooked. If I approached them from behind and surprised them unexpectedly, he said they might think I was an animal and start to run.

Well, one day Buster, Minnie, and I were walking out to the field with Pa's lunch. I was kind of lost in my thoughts, not paying any attention to what I was doing. I walked right up behind Pa and the horses, and sure enough, just as Pa had predicted, they thought some animal was coming at them from behind. They spooked and ran. The plow was down, so dirt flew fifteen feet into the air. Pa pulled back on the reins, but the horses didn't stop running for about a quarter-of-a-mile. Pa managed to bring them to a halt a few yards short of a neighbor's field.

When I realized what I had done, I was so frightened of what Pa would do to me that I set his lunch bucket down on the field and ran over to the slough with Buster and Minnie. I stayed away from the house until nightfall, and when I finally walked inside, I felt like a doomed man about to face the gallows.

Pa was smoking his pipe by the table when I walked into the kitchen. At any moment I expected him to stand up and reach for his leather strap. I decided to go right upstairs rather than risk another beating. But as I walked toward the steps, Pa said, without looking at me, "You'd better eat before you go to bed. Ma has some soup on the stove."

I ate the bowl of soup in silence, while Pa continued to smoke his pipe. He gave no indication at any time that he was going for his leather strap.

A few days later, I made another colossal blunder. Pa had just driven a team of horses and a plow into the yard. When I asked him if I could unhitch one of the horses, he told me to go to work on Tug, the oldest and tamest of the four horses. Pa unhitched the other horses.

When he finished, Pa said, "Giddy up," and started to lead the team back to the barn.

Only I hadn't completely unhitched Tug from the plow. Since the four horses were still hitched together, they spooked. The horses ran across the yard, dragging the plow behind them. They reached the fence and tried to jump it, but couldn't. Their panic created a terrible pile of horses, broken plow parts, and shattered wooden fence posts scattered across the yard.

Once again, I expected the leather strap to come out that night, but Pa didn't say a word. He ate and went to bed as though nothing had happened. So even though the Jensens were gone, I guess Pa still remembered the lecture Mr. Jensen gave him after Pa had beaten me with the leather strap.

IV

A few days later, Buster and I caught a ride with a farmer who dropped us off near Reque Cemetery. I had been in the cemetery with Ma and Pa a few times before, after church services. This was the first time I visited it by myself. I wanted to see if walking through the cemetery would help me understand what death really meant. I hoped, maybe then I would feel a little closer to Mr. Jensen.

I thought I would be afraid to be alone in the cemetery—but I wasn't. Surrounded on all sides by corn and wheat fields, the small country cemetery was quiet, serene. The blue sky and gentle breezes that whispered through the grass made the idea of death seem peaceful, almost pleasant.

As I walked through the cemetery, I noticed that the wind and rain had partially eroded some of the inscriptions on the limestone gravestones. I realized that someday they would be blank blocks of stone—and no one would even know who was buried beneath them. Nature was doing to the gravestones what it was doing to Mr. Jensen's farm. It was reclaiming them.

One of the oldest stones was set off by itself, on the edge of the cemetery. The name on the stone, and the dates of birth and death, had been completely erased by the wind and rain. As the sunlight filtered through the branches of a nearby tree and fell on the old gravestone, it seemed so alone, so isolated, like the rocking chair illuminated by the beams of sunlight in Mr. Jensen's living room.

Mr. Jensen had been buried in some other cemetery—I don't know where. But I decided the nameless gravestone was a fitting memorial to him. I picked some wildflowers and placed them on the ground near the stone. While Buster curled up next to me, I sat on the ground and talked to Mr. Jensen. I thanked him for helping a boy who had no one else to turn to for help. I also asked God to take care of Mr. Jensen for being so kind to me.

V

During the time that Ma was recuperating, Delores came over almost every day to help with the washing, cooking, and cleaning. Delores and Ma hit it off pretty good. I have to confess that I was a little put out by the fact that Ma had so readily rejected me as a son, and yet she so quickly accepted Delores into our home, almost as a daughter.

Delores and I had both been adopted into different branches of the same family tree, and we had to carry the stigma of illegitimacy that was associated with adopted children at that time. We also had to bear the additional stigma of knowing that others considered us part of the lowest social class. Since it was generally understood that adopted children were the product of illegitimate or adulterous relationships, people tended to look down on them. Many people even considered adopted children to be morally inferior to other children.

For some reason, Ma ignored Delores's adoptive status, while she constantly shamed and embarrassed me by threatening to send me back to the orphanage. It was difficult for me to accept that double standard. Still, I was delighted to spend more time with Delores. I liked her very much.

As I said earlier, Delores was three years older than me, so she knew much more about the family history than I did. She had also been treated much better by her adoptive parents. So Delores was less sensitive about some things than I was. For example, she was not the least bit interested in knowing who her birth parents might have been, whereas my dream was to someday find my birth mother. I suppose the way we were treated as adopted children created those differences in us.

Delores also didn't seem to care too much what people thought of her. She was stronger than I was in that way. My self-confidence and self-esteem were always so low that it was important to me to know that people liked me. If they didn't like me, I felt insignificant. If they did like me, it filled me with confidence and a sense of importance. Delores didn't care if people liked her. She was somewhat of a free spirit that way. She just did things her own way and didn't worry too much about the consequences.

She also refused to accept many of the traditional patterns of behavior women were supposed to accept at that time. It was not uncommon for Delores to accompany her father and her brother into the fields with the threshing crew. Most women would have considered that quite improper. They were expected to cook and clean, while the men went out to work in the fields. That didn't bother Delores in the least. She seemed to enjoy intermingling with the men on the threshing crews.

When I think of Delores today, I still see a young girl with a perpetual look of mischief on her face. She appeared as though she had just come from some gay, exciting adventure. She seemed to grab reality, toss in a strong dose of her own imagination, and reshape the world each day into her own image of what she wanted it to be. You had to take everything she said with a few grains of salt. And yet I found everything she told me to be true—in a strange and fascinating way.

Since Ma slept a lot during the time that she was recuperating, Delores would come outside and sit with me and talk. I still wasn't allowed inside the house very much during the day, so I appreciated the fact that she would come outside to be with me. I could also tell that she liked me.

Delores, who was almost eleven years old at the time, filled me in on a lot that had happened in the family before I came along. Her Ma and Pa were much more open about those things. I had lived in a world where I had no meaningful connections to the rest of the human race. Delores, on the other hand, had simply connected her own personal history to the history of her adoptive family, and as a result she was much better adjusted than I was.

She told me that Pa had worked for her father for a time, but there had been a falling out between the two men. Apparently, Pa felt that he had been taken advantage of, and he never quite forgave either his sister or her husband for what they had done to him—whatever that was. Delores also told me she had heard that Pa had married Ma primarily because he wanted someone to cook, clean, and take care of the house for him. For some reason, they could not have children together.

Delores had to explain this to me in a variety of ways, because I didn't know anything about the facts of life at that time. I was completely ignorant of the way babies came into the world. She, however, was quite sophisticated about those things, especially for a girl who was only eleven years old. Delores also said that she had been adopted during the time that Pa worked for her father. Ma became like another mother to her when she was a young girl.

When I asked Delores if she had ever heard any talk in her home about my birth parents, she said that no, she hadn't. But she promised to keep her ears open. She would let me know if she ever found out anything. She knew where some of the family's personal papers and records were stored, and volunteered to see if there was anything there about my adoption or my birth mother.

She explained that many parents rename their adopted children at the time of the adoption. That was news to me. I assumed that my name had always been Lloyd. But Delores told me in all likelihood my birth mother had named me something else. She speculated that I probably went by that name before I was adopted and became Lloyd Augustine Clausen. Of course, that got me to wondering what my name might have been before I was adopted.

VI

Through Ma and Pa, I had already learned that human beings can be selfish and cruel. As I explored more of the world, I began to see evidence that people can also be unexpectedly generous and kind. Every time I would expect something from people, it seemed I would experience the opposite.

I was playing down by a rock pile on our property one day when I saw a wagon in the distance. I recognized the driver as Raymond Kolden, a tough, muscular farm boy who had the reputation of being a bully and a roughneck. There were rumors that Raymond's pa beat him and that Raymond took out his anger and frustration by picking fights with just about anyone who crossed his path. Because of his reputation, Raymond Kolden struck fear in the hearts of every little boy in our part of the county. I didn't know if the rumors were true, but I did know that he was much bigger and stronger than I was, and I sure didn't want to test him. So I ducked behind the rock pile until his wagon had disappeared down the dirt road.

About an hour later, a rough-looking man, with a long dark beard and clothes that looked like he had been sleeping in them for several days, came down the dirt road. He was riding a beautiful black horse with a long mane. At first I thought that surely he must have stolen the horse. No one dressed like he was could possibly own such a beautiful animal. He looked like just about the most down-and-out drifter who had ever passed through the area—and we had many of them who came by looking for work or a free meal.

The stranger stopped near the area where I was playing, and I made nervous small talk with him for a while. He must have seen the glow in my eyes as I ran my hands through his horse's mane, because he asked me, "Would you like to ride Max? He's real tame. He won't throw you."

I was a little hesitant because I had been told about strangers who kidnap children and never let them come back home. But I was overcome with excitement at the prospect of being able to ride a horse. I had sat on Tug a few times as he walked across the yard. But Tug was a plow horse. I had never been on a real riding horse. It was something I had dreamed about, but never thought I would be able to do.

"I'd really like that," I said enthusiastically. "But I don't know very much about riding a horse."

"It's real easy," the stranger explained as he dismounted. "I'll show you how to do it."

He lifted me up onto the back of the horse, who was so big and tall I felt like I was sitting on the gable end of a roof. The stranger had been riding the horse bareback. I held on tightly to the horse's mane so I wouldn't slide off. The stranger showed me how to sit comfortably on the back of the horse, and then he held the reins while he walked Max up and down the dirt road with me on his back.

For what must have been at least an hour, I was in hog's heaven. I was so proud I stuck out my chest and pretended that I was a cowboy, sitting high in the saddle, riding around my ranch. The stranger didn't say much. He just smiled at me every now and then. He seemed to enjoy my innocent delight in my first real horseback ride. Then he said he had to be going, helped me down, mounted his horse, and rode away.

To this day, I don't know what it was about me that made him stop and offer to fulfill what had been one of my life's dreams—to ride a *real* riding horse. Had some higher power whispered in the stranger's ear that this boy needed to feel like a cowboy? Or, perhaps, someone had told the drifter, "A horseback ride would do wonders for this boy's self-esteem."

I never saw the stranger again. I suspect he was just passing through the county that day, looking for work. But I never again expected the worst from a bum or an out-of-work drifter. No matter how tough a guy might look, or how poorly dressed a person might be, a human heart beats inside each of us. I never prejudged anyone again.

VII

Not too long after that, I saw the dark side of human nature play itself out in an equally unusual situation. We had a hay thief who Pa would see out in our fields loading hay into the back of a pick-up truck. But when Pa would try to ride out to catch him, the thief would quickly jump into the pick-up truck and speed away. Pa's horse wasn't fast enough to keep up with the truck. The thief was able to keep stealing our hay without much fear of getting caught.

Then one day, when Pa was chasing the truck off the field, one of the wheels ran over some rocks and the axle broke. When Pa rode up to the truck, he saw that the hay thief was a neighbor from up north. He was a farmer who was too lazy to haul in his own hay during the summer. Instead, he stole from his neighbors' hay stacks during the fall and winter months.

What was most annoying to Pa was that he and others in the area had helped out this same farmer when he had broken his leg a couple of years earlier. Everyone had pitched in to do his chores and feed his cattle and horses. That farmer turned around and stole hay from the same people who had helped him.

VIII

A few months after Ma got sick and almost died, Buster came down with some mysterious illness. Pa and I were both convinced that someone had tried to poison him. Ma thought that he had rabies or some other disease that he had picked up from a wild animal.

We tied Minnie up in the barn so she wouldn't be exposed to whatever it was that Buster had come down with. Buster just lay on his side in the shed all day, panting quietly while the saliva trickled slowly out of his mouth. I stayed with him constantly, except at night when Ma and Pa made me come inside.

Buster didn't have the energy or the desire to eat or drink, so I lifted his head over a bowl several times a day, while he lapped gently at the water. I also soaked pieces of bread in the water and pushed them into his mouth. He tried to swallow, but couldn't. Without any nourishment, Buster lost much of his body weight. The outline of his rib cage showed clearly through his fur.

Every morning I would get up with the sunrise and rush out to the shed to see if Buster had made it through another night. Every morning he would still be lying there, breathing slowly while the saliva dribbled out of his mouth. I didn't see how much longer he could go on like that. He was wasting away right in front of my eyes.

Pa came out to the shed one day, glanced through the open doorway at Buster and me, and just shook his head. "He's not gonna make it," he said. "We're gonna have to put him out of his misery."

"Can we get the veterinarian to look at him first?" I pleaded.

"Nothing will help him," Pa insisted. "He's too far gone."

"Pa, please, can't we at least try?"

"We can't afford to pay someone to tell us what we already know," Pa replied somberly. "There's nothing anyone can do for him."

A knot formed in my throat, and tears filled my eyes. I knelt down by Buster and stroked his huge forehead.

"We'll give him until tomorrow morning," Pa said. "If he isn't any better by then, I'll put him down."

"But maybe a veterinarian can still do something for him," I pleaded.

"We can't spend money we don't have," Pa replied, shaking his head.

Pa was probably right. We were too poor to have all of our livestock vaccinated. How could we afford a special trip for a veterinarian to look at a dog who would probably die with or without medication? Still, the thought of Pa putting Buster out of his misery was more than I could handle.

I don't think I have ever been quite so worried about another living creature in my entire life. I couldn't imagine life on the farm without Buster. He was everything to me—my best friend, comforter, father.

That night I was lying in bed half-awake, thinking about Buster and wondering if maybe there was some way I could get a veterinarian out to the farm to look at him. Suddenly, I heard a terrible, hellish commotion outside. I raced to the window and stared into the darkness. The sounds of dogs snarling, barking, and fighting pierced the night air.

Fearing that Buster in his weakened condition had been attacked by wild dogs, I rushed downstairs. I quickly lit a kerosene lantern and ran out into the darkness. Behind me, I could hear Pa getting dressed in the bedroom. When I ran over to the shed and thrust the lantern into the open doorway, I saw what appeared to be streaks of blood on the wooden walls. Buster was nowhere in sight.

I started to panic. I was convinced that wild dogs had attacked Buster and most likely dragged him out into the surrounding fields. I circled the yard, shining the lantern in all directions. By the edge of our grove of trees, I heard Buster's familiar low, rumbling growl.

I ran toward the sound. Buster was standing with a mouth full of fur, snarling into some thick weeds and underbrush. I held the lantern out in that direction. The light reflected off four eyes staring at me from the darkness.

The underbrush suddenly exploded. Two wild dogs raced out into the prairie and disappeared. I grabbed Buster around the neck so he wouldn't go after them. I talked quietly to him for a few seconds, trying to calm him down.

"What happened?" Pa asked breathlessly as he rushed up to us with his shotgun in hand.

"Buster was attacked by some wild dogs," I explained. "He chased them off."

"Chased them off?" Pa asked skeptically, scratching his head. "He was almost dead the last time I looked in on him."

"You can see the fur in his mouth," I said.

Pa leaned down and examined Buster's mouth. "Well, I'll be damned," he muttered softly as he looked out into the dark field where the dogs had just disappeared.

I locked Buster up in the shed, with the door closed, in case the wild dogs returned. In the morning, when I walked outside to check on him, I expected he would be lying on his side once again, laboring to breathe.

Much to my surprise, when I opened the shed door, Buster bounded out like a young puppy who was eager to play. I couldn't believe my eyes. He was jumping up and down and licking my face like he'd just been released from prison.

It was almost as though Buster had been brought back to life during his fight with the wild dogs. I could only conclude that he was prepared to leave this world, but the thought of two dogs contesting his territorial claim to our farm was more than he could handle. The surge of adrenaline and the flow of blood pumping through that courageous heart of his must have reawakened his desire to live—and to fight once again for his territory.

IX

Delores and I took many walks during the time that she was helping Ma recuperate. I especially enjoyed it when we caught rides with farmers over to Reque Cemetery. Surrounded by the corn and wheat fields, the cemetery had become, for me, a sanctuary from the pain and disappointments in my life. Except for the wind whispering through the grass and the leaves, and an occasional bird chirping contentedly in the trees, the cemetery was silent, peaceful—far removed from human voices and human problems.

One day, as we walked through the cemetery, Delores was especially talkative about the people who were buried there. It seemed that she knew the personal histories of almost everyone whose names were inscribed on the gravestones. And they were interesting and exciting stories, some involving people who had lived and died on the prairie almost a hundred years earlier.

"The farmer buried over there lost his grip on the rope he used to find his way back to the house from the barn during the winter blizzards," she explained, pointing at a moss-blackened cemetery stone protruding out of the grass. "He wandered out into the prairie where he froze to death." She immediately pointed at a smaller gravestone and said, "The woman buried over there became so sad and lonely with her life on the prairie that she swam out into the middle of Frog Lake and drowned herself."

"How do you know all those stories?" I asked. I thought that maybe she was making them up. It would be just like her.

"That old hired man who told me about the prairie wind song used to take me over here after church," she replied. "He knew many of the people who are buried in this cemetery. He said their voices are the ones we still hear in the wind that whispers through that old oak tree."

I tried to say something, but Delores went right on describing the lives and deaths of the people buried in Reque Cemetery.

"That man over there died of a heart attack a few hours after he had completed his harvest. And that woman buried here had a miscarriage," she said, pointing at a gravestone set level with the ground. "They couldn't stop the bleeding. So she died."

"What does it mean to have a miscarriage?" I asked.

"It's when a woman is pregnant," she explained, "but she loses the baby before it's born. A miscarriage can be very dangerous if they can't stop the bleeding."

Later that day, when I was back home with Buster and Minnie, my imagination started to work overtime. Based on what Delores had told me about the farm woman who had bled to death from a miscarriage, I began to question what might have really been going on in Ma's bedroom when she, too, almost bled to death.

Why had Dr. Cumming insisted that no one else should be in the bedroom except him and Ma? Why wasn't Pa allowed to bring the sterilized rags into the bedroom? What had Ma told Dr. Cumming during the time they were in the bedroom together? Had Dr. Cumming charged Pa so little for his services because he recognized our poverty, or had he felt sorry for us for other reasons? What had really happened the day Ma almost died?

I didn't have any answers for those questions. I was just glad that the black car was no longer parked in our yard, and that Ma's company was out of our lives—at least for a time.

DEATH IS A CONSTANT COMPANION

I

I don't know how Pa did it, but somehow he found the money to employ a hired man on the farm. His name was Ivar. I never knew his last name. Ivar spoke very little English. He never volunteered any information about his past, so we knew absolutely nothing about him. He was just one of those people who seem to spring up from nowhere, wander through life from job to job, and then disappear for good.

Ivar let his hands do his talking for him. He could take almost anything apart and put it back together again. I'm convinced that Ivar could have disassembled the Creation—if God would have let him— and I'm pretty sure he could have put it back together again, too.

Ivar was born to work. He was just about the best hired man who ever wandered through our county. He could not sit still. He had to be working to be happy. And since Pa was about the least ambitious farmer in the area, Ivar was the perfect hired man for our farm. Ivar, who slept in the house or the barn, depending upon the weather and Ma's mood swings, did Pa's work, while Pa snuck off to play cards with his friends in Alberta.

With Ivar on our farm, my apprenticeship as one of Pa's future hired men began in earnest. Up until then I had been more or less raised as some kind of farm animal who had the run of the property so long as I did certain basic chores like bringing in the eggs and taking Pa's lunch bucket out to him in the fields. But under Ivar's expert tutelage, Pa clearly expected me to become the champion hired man he bragged that he had chosen in the orphanage. I was taking my first steps toward fulfilling my destiny.

Ivar taught me everything I know about farming and farm equipment. Pa never really took the time to teach me about anything. I proved to be quite mechanically inclined, which was especially surprising since I had failed to unhitch a horse properly and had caused a pile-up of horse flesh, plow parts, and fence posts on our front yard. In time, under Ivar's careful eye, I learned to fix or run just about every piece of equipment on the farm.

II

One of the most ingenious pieces of farm equipment was the cream separator. All cows were milked by hand, and then the milk was poured into a ten-gallon metal drum on top of the separator so the cream could be separated from the milk. There was a cylinder, full of metal discs, on the lower side of the drum. The cylinder was turned by a hand crank on the front of the separator. As the crank was turned, the cylinder would begin to spin. The milk would flow out of one spout, and the cream out of the other spout. To me, as a young boy, there was magic in the separator, and I never tired of watching Ivar run it or repair it when it broke down.

Ivar and I were working on the separator one day when some men rode into the yard on horseback. They were carrying rifles, and they didn't look any too friendly. One of the men pointed his rifle at Buster and yelled, "That's the one! That's him right over there!"

I quickly ran over and stood between Buster and the man with the rifle.

"Get outta the way, boy!" the man demanded as he continued to wave the rifle in our direction.

Pa suddenly rushed out of the barn and over to where we were standing. "What's the problem?" he demanded to know.

"That dog of yours is a sheep killer," the man hollered. "He got two of my sheep last night. They were torn all to pieces."

"This dog's no sheep killer," Pa insisted.

One of the other men quickly intervened. "Mind if we look at his mouth?" he asked.

"Suit yourself," Pa said.

The man dismounted and approached Buster cautiously. The man who had pointed the rifle in our direction also dismounted and joined us. I had to calm Buster down so he would allow the first man to inspect his mouth for traces of blood and wool. A low rumble vibrated in Buster's throat as the man examined all sides of his mouth.

"Can you pull up his lips for me, son?" the man examining Buster's mouth said softly. "I need to take a look inside."

I looked into Buster's big brown eyes. Then and there I decided that if the man looked in Buster's mouth and announced that he had found traces of blood and wool, Buster and I were going to make a run for it together. I didn't care how many horses and men with rifles would be chasing us.

"It's okay, Buster," I assured him softly. "We're just going to look in your mouth."

The man knelt down next to me and closely examined Buster's teeth. Then he stood up and announced, "This dog's clean. He ain't no sheep killer."

The man with the rifle started to protest. But Pa picked him up off the ground by his belt and threw him on top of his horse. Then Pa slapped his huge hand against the horse's rump. The horse bolted across the yard with the man clinging to its neck.

"You're welcome to come on my property if you're looking for a sheep killer," Pa said sternly to the other men. Then he pointed a huge index finger in my direction. "But don't any of you ever point a rifle at this boy. You get outta here now."

The men quickly apologized before riding away, galloping after the other man. I learned later that they found two dogs in the area with wool and blood in their mouths. Both of those dogs were owned by the man who had pointed his rifle at Buster and threatened to kill him.

The dogs with wool and blood in their mouths were immediately shot. Everyone knew that once a dog had tasted sheep's blood, it was sure to kill again. So no one questioned the need to kill dogs who attacked and killed sheep.

But Buster was not a sheep killer. And Pa had just done the most decent thing I remember him doing for me.

III

We had two ways to get the cream to Alberta to sell it. A horse-drawn wagon, carrying a huge tank packed with ice, stopped by the farm once a week to collect our cream and take it back to town. But sometimes it was necessary to make another run to town with the cream, especially if the cows were producing a lot of milk. When another trip to town was necessary, Pa usually went by himself, so he could play cards with his friends. But after Ma got sick, Pa had Ivar drive the cream cans to town. Sometimes I got to go along.

I had been in Alberta a few times before. But Pa always made me sit in the wagon. Ivar allowed me more freedom. After he dropped off the cream cans and parked the wagon, we would go our separate ways. He would shop for supplies. I would walk up and down Main Street, looking into the store windows, but seldom having the courage to go inside.

Alberta wasn't much of a town really. There couldn't have been more than a couple of hundred people living there. The town consisted of a creamery and two cream stations, a bank, two grocery stores, a couple of grain elevators, some hardware stores and other shops, a lumberyard, some restaurants, and a handful of other businesses. There were also clusters of homes located near Main Street. Other people passing through Alberta probably considered it little more than a watering hole in the middle of the prairie. Still, to me, having been confined to the farm for most of my life, it seemed like a huge city. I was enchanted by the new world I had entered.

I must have looked like the strangest thing walking up and down Main Street. I wore second-hand bib overhauls that were several sizes too big, my mailman's cap, and shoes so worn my toes leaked out the end. I was usually covered with dirt. Plus, my hair stuck out in all directions from underneath my cap.

One day, while Ivar was buying supplies, I discovered a building that had some posters tacked on the outer wall. The posters advertised two Charlie Chaplin movies that were showing in Morris. I had never seen a movie, so I was greatly intrigued by the pictures of Charlie Chaplin as the Tramp. He looked just like some of the out-of-work drifters who occasionally stopped by our farm looking for work or a free meal. I couldn't figure out how someone like that had made it into the movies.

I was so preoccupied with the posters that I didn't notice the group of town kids who were gradually surrounding me. When I turned around, I was encircled by grinning, leering faces.

"So, who is this here?" one of them taunted me.

"It looks like one of the farm boys who lives south of town," another jeered.

"You mean the little bastard boy, don't you?" another laughed.

One of them took a grab for my mailman's cap, which set me into a frenzy. I kicked and hit and screamed. But the boys passed my cap to each other, just out of my reach. Finally, I socked one of the bigger boys. He easily wrestled me to the ground and put me into a choke hold. I could not break it. He was much bigger and stronger than I was. Another boy started to tear the bill off my cap.

"Let me go!" I cried. "Please don't tear my cap!"

The boy who was holding my cap leaned down and sneered in my face, "I'll tell you what. You tell us you're a little bastard boy, and I'll give you back your cap."

I continued to struggle on the ground. "No, I won't say that," I cried through clenched teeth as the boy holding me pushed my face into the dirt and gravel. "I won't say it."

"Say it," he demanded.

"No, I won't say it," I insisted.

As I struggled on the ground, it seemed that the boys who had encircled me were flying through the air in every direction. I felt the boy release the choke hold on my neck. He went flying out into the street. In all the commotion, I crawled over to where my cap was lying on the ground. I tried to put the two pieces together, but the brim had been torn away.

As I was sitting on the ground in stunned silence, I heard the sound of departing footsteps. The boys made a hasty retreat down Main Street. Then, as someone knelt down next to me, I heard a husky voice ask, "Are you okay?"

My eyes filled with tears as I stared at the torn pieces of my cap. Except for Buster and Minnie, that cap was the most important thing in my life.

"Maybe you can get someone to sew it back together," the voice said gently.

I looked into the face of my rescuer: Raymond Kolden, the farm boy who had the reputation of being a bully and a roughneck. Only a few months earlier, I had hidden behind the pile of rocks when his wagon passed by our property.

"I was on my way to the creamery," Raymond explained. "I saw them jump you. I figured you could use a little help."

"Thanks," I muttered as I brushed the tears from my eyes.

"Who brought you to town?" he asked.

"Our hired man," I replied, gesturing at our wagon.

"Where is he?"

"Buying supplies."

Raymond looked up and down the street. "I'll wait with you until your hired man returns," he said, "in case any of those boys decide to come back."

He helped me to my feet and escorted me to Pa's wagon. He leaned against the wagon and stared silently at the ground. I noticed that his work boots were laced with twine.

"Town kids are sometimes like that," he said, looking up. "They think they're better than farm kids."

"They were calling me names."

"I know," he replied. "I heard them."

Ivar suddenly stepped out of one of the stores across the street.

"That's our hired man," I said.

Raymond quickly excused himself, walked across the street to his horse-drawn wagon, and drove away.

Later, I learned that Raymond somehow knew that Ma and Pa were mistreating me. He felt sympathy because he, too, had been mistreated. So when the town bullies started to beat up on me, he wasn't about to just drive through town without helping me out.

Raymond and I became good friends. At school, and when we worked on the same threshing crews, he would sometimes share his lunches with me. Ma never did put much of a lunch together for me, just a couple scraps of bread and a little jelly. Raymond also taught me how to wrestle and protect myself. In time, I did right by Raymond. But I remember thinking, as I sat on Alberta's Main Street holding the two pieces of my cap together while he offered me words of encouragement, that he must have been another guardian angel God had sent to look after me. All this kindness from a muscular farm boy everyone considered to be a roughneck and a bully!

So there you have it again. How can you figure people out? They always seem to do the opposite of what you expect from them.

IV

Pa's luck ran alternately good or bad. There just didn't seem to be any in between. We had a good crop that year. The threshing crews arrived in late August, as they always did, moving from farm to farm, harvesting the crops.

Threshing season was a festive time. Farmers, their wives, and the migrant threshing crews worked together until all of the crops in the area were harvested and sold, or safely stored away for the winter. They would finish one farmer's crops and move the steam engine and thresher to another farmer's fields. When everyone's crops were harvested, there would be a party to celebrate. Threshing season was the most enjoyable time of the year for me. I liked watching everyone work together.

But when you're farming, you're always wary of some disaster, or series of disasters, lurking behind every small success you might experience. That particular year the bumper crops caused grain prices to collapse. Grain became practically worthless. Pa said it would have been easier and less expensive to plow it all back into the ground.

As we watched what we thought was going to be a profitable year turn into a devastating loss, we had no idea how many other calamities were waiting for us.

V

Shortly after the harvest, I developed a terrible cough that kept me up all night for several days. It was difficult to eat. When I did, I threw up.

We tried the only remedy we had, which was a red liniment Pa had bought from a Rawleigh peddler, a man who came periodically through the area selling herbs, spices, and various medicines. The red liquid was supposed to be rubbed on the skin for muscle aches and soreness. Hardier souls like Ma and Pa also drank it whenever they got sick. One teaspoonful in a cup filled with cream and sugar, and they would start sweating almost as soon as they swallowed it. Many a fever was broken by the combination of that red potion and a night of sweating under heavy covers. "It'll kill ya, or it'll cure ya," Pa said many times.

The potion didn't do a thing for my cough.

When Dr. Cumming came out to check on Ma, he took one look at me and said, "This boy's got whooping cough." He pulled some herbs and powders out of his black bag and mixed them in a pan of boiling water.

While Dr. Cumming worked over by the stove, I heard him say quietly to Pa, "There's an epidemic of whooping cough all over the county. Some children have died from it."

"How long does it last?" Pa asked.

"Normally five or six weeks," Dr. Cumming explained. "If we can knock it out before then, he'll be okay. If it goes any longer, he probably won't make it. It'll just wear him into the ground—or turn into pneumonia."

I knew Dr. Cumming didn't mean for me to overhear what he was telling Pa, but I did. It was the first time I had ever come face to face with my own mortality, and I was terrified.

Dr. Cumming gave strict directions regarding how much of his medicine I was supposed to take, and then he promised to return in a few days to see how I was doing. I coughed night and day, often until I was blue in the face. I was so tired and weak that I started to hallucinate. At times I thought for sure I was dying. But I kept taking Dr. Cumming's medicine, and almost six weeks to the day that I first started coughing, the fever broke, and I was over the whooping cough. I had survived.

Dr. Cumming pronounced me cured. Pa handed him two jars of preserves as payment for his services. And then Dr. Cumming was out the door and down the road to attend to the other children in the county who were sick or dying from whooping cough.

I was one of the lucky ones. Several new graves were added to the local cemeteries. One of the boys who had jumped me that day in Alberta was among those who died during the whooping cough epidemic.

VI

No sooner had I been cured of the whooping cough, than the creamery in Alberta informed Pa that our cream was contaminated. The problem was in the processing, which could mean only one thing: something was seriously wrong with the separator. Pa did not have the money to buy another one. In order to find the source of the problem, Ivar took the whole apparatus apart, cleaned it, sterilized it, and then put it back together again. That took time.

Meanwhile, most of the milk the cows were producing had to be fed to the hogs. So not only weren't we making any money on our grain crop, but we also weren't making any money on our cream. About all we had left to sell were our eggs. There was very little money, even for essentials. Our very survival depended on whether or not Ivar could repair the separator.

Ivar completed his task. Pa quickly sent a batch of milk through the separator. He brought the cream to Alberta and waited nervously while the cream was being tested. When the cream was given a clean bill of health, Pa gave a sigh of relief. Then he walked across the street to celebrate by playing a few hands of cards with some of his friends.

Later that day, when Pa drove the team of horses into the yard, there was more bad news waiting for him. Ivar had gone out to feed the hogs and had seen two dead sows lying in the hog pen. By the end of the day, three more of the sows were dead. Pa had tried to save a few dollars by not vaccinating the hogs. But it had not been a wise decision because they had all come down with hog cholera. Within a couple of days, we had to dig a pit and bury all of our hogs.

VII

Our troubles, which had begun in autumn and worsened through the winter, continued that spring and into summer. People in our county started dying from some mysterious illness. Rumors were that it was a form of plague—the Black Plague—but I do not know if that was true or not. More likely, it was a form of influenza. I do know that entire families were wiped out by the epidemic.

Everyone retreated indoors. Families did not interact with other families. The only time people went outdoors was to feed the livestock.

Then the farmers hurried back inside, locking the doors behind them—as though that would keep the disease out of their homes.

Nobody knew where the disease came from. Some people believed it must have been dormant in the ground for many years and was released when the fields were plowed. Rather than risk contracting the mysterious illness, many farmers refused to tend their crops. Prairie grasses returned and weeds infested the fields as we hid in our homes and prayed for the epidemic to end.

Ma was looking out the window one morning when she suddenly exclaimed, "Something's happening out there!"

Pa quickly joined her by the window. "What is it?" he asked.

"Looks like someone died," Ma speculated softly.

I walked over to an adjacent window. In the distance, two adults were carrying what appeared to be a blanket-wrapped body into a field. They laid the body on the ground and walked slowly back to the farm-house. Moments later they reappeared, carrying a smaller blanket-wrapped body. They laid that body on the ground next to the first one.

"There are two of them," Pa said solemnly.

Our closest neighbors were new to the area, and we did not know them very well. Still, we felt their grief fill our living room.

We stood silently by the windows, watching the grim funeral service. During the epidemic, many families handled their own dead. We knew that. But this was the first time we had ever witnessed a home burial.

The figures in the field dug two holes in the prairie soil. The bodies were lowered into the ground, then covered with dirt. The surviving members of the family gathered around the new graves and bowed their heads. They stood like that for several minutes.

When I glanced at Ma and Pa, their eyes were closed—and their heads were also lowered.

VIII

While we all waited for some miracle, Ivar was allowed to move out of the barn and into the house. The four of us—Ma, Pa, Ivar, and me—played cards together, or prayed together, until late into the night. When we finally went to bed, we did so wondering how many of us would still be alive the next morning to greet the rising sun. Would we die in our sleep? Or, worse yet, would we find everyone else dead in their beds?

At breakfast, Ma led us in prayer. She would sit by the kitchen table with an open Bible in front of her. We would all join hands and say the Lord's Prayer together. Then Ma would pray, asking God to help us make it through another day. I would recite some of the Psalms I had learned in church. Even Pa seemed to get real serious about religion for a time. He, too, would sometimes offer a short prayer.

Although Ivar would hold hands with us and bow his head, he seemed strangely unmoved by our morning ritual. He wasn't disrespectful or anything like that. But it appeared to me that he had placed his destiny in the hands of the Almighty many years earlier. Ivar was ready to accept whatever might happen to him. I never met a man so unconcerned about death and dying. Because Ivar accepted death as part of his life's experiences, he enjoyed whatever little pleasures came his way. Other than that, he just worked all the time.

The summer of the epidemic was terrifying. And yet it was oddly comforting, because it was one of the few times Ma, Pa, and I truly pulled together as a family. As we stood together at death's door, we seemed to value each other. Ma and Pa were more considerate of one another, and of me. There were no beatings, no black cars parked in the driveway, no threats to send me back to the orphanage, no family fights, and no card playing in smoke-filled rooms in Alberta.

We didn't go so far as to hug and hold each other, but at least we treated each other a little better. In a strange and fascinating way, the mysterious illness brought us together as a family. Maybe it was the same thing that brought the first group of human beings together around the first campfire thousands and thousands of years ago. Maybe we just needed to feel a little bit less alone in the world.

A few weeks later, the mysterious illness passed. We all went back to our old ways. Pa celebrated by getting half drunk on some homebrew he had stored in the cellar. Ma started to beat me on the head again. Ivar was sent back to the barn. And I turned to Buster and Minnie for moral support, and some lessons on how to sustain a sense of family life.

IX

After the epidemic, Delores returned to our farm to help Ma with the cooking and cleaning. I was delighted to see her. I had been terribly worried that she might have been one of the victims of the epidemic. But she was as happy and cheerful as ever. She explained that some people over in her area had become very sick and died, but her family was spared. I think she was as happy to see that we were okay as I was to see that she was okay.

The very first day that Delores came back to the farm, Ma and Pa decided to visit some friends in Alberta to get a firsthand report on who had, or hadn't, survived the mysterious disease. With Ma and Pa gone for the day, Delores and I had the run of the farm. We finished our chores early and took a long walk together. It was the first time I had ever spent an entire day with Delores. I enjoyed myself immensely.

It was one of those beautiful summer days that lingers in your memory for a long time. Not because anything special happened. To the contrary, it was a rather uneventful day, except for the fact that I had Delores to myself.

The thing I remember most about that day was the thought that the prairie had only recently become a dark, foreboding place where mysterious diseases lay just beneath the soil. Yet, as Delores and I walked across the open fields that were teeming with thick green vegetation, everything seemed marvelously and wonderfully alive. The prairie seemed once again to be a place where people could hope—and dream.

We caught a ride with a farmer to the old Jensen farm, where I pulled a wooden crate up to a window and showed Delores the rocking chair sitting all alone in the middle of the living room floor. Later, we caught another ride over to Lake Hattie. While we were sitting on a log, watching the gentle waves rippling against the shore, Delores started to talk about some of the things she wanted to do with her life.

"What do you know about California?" she asked me.

"Nothing," I replied.

"I've been reading about it," she said dreamily. "Someday I want to go there. They don't have winter in California, you know. It's always summer."

"How can it always be summer?" I asked.

"It has something to do with the ocean," she explained, "and the fact that it's closer to the equator than Minnesota."

As she spoke, Delores reached out and held my hand. I immediately felt something deep inside of me that I had never felt before. I think that was perhaps the first time in my life that I felt emotions that would someday change into feelings of love for my adoptive cousin.

"Maybe you can go with me to California," Delores speculated, half teasing.

"I think I would like to live somewhere where it's always summer," I replied as I watched the clouds drift serenely across the blue sky.

X

Later that day, Delores and I walked through Reque Cemetery. So many new graves had been dug. The whooping cough and the mysterious epidemic had taken a terrible toll on county residents. People who had been alive only a few months earlier, and who had celebrated the bountiful harvest with the rest of us the previous autumn, had now joined the growing choir that whispered the prairie wind song from the elusive, immeasurable distance of another world.

A Blind Horse Leads Us Home

I

I awoke the day before Christmas to one of the most magnificent scenes of my childhood. Outside the window, I saw several beautiful horses and three fox hounds running across a field that was completely covered with snow. The entire group, almost as one, leaped gracefully over some object in the field, and then continued chasing a red fox that was fleeing toward a distant grove of snow-covered trees. The horses, riders, fox hounds, and red fox gradually disappeared into the horizon, swallowed up by the whiteness of winter.

I learned later that Pa had decided to earn extra money by renting out our property to some men from Minneapolis who hunted foxes as a hobby. The county was overrun with red foxes. On some farms, the foxes had decimated chicken populations, creating additional financial hardships for area farmers who already had more than their share. Although none of the farmers liked the idea of allowing men from a distant city to ride across his property on horseback, it was a way to earn extra money. At the same time, the sport kept the fox population under control.

The thing I remember most, however, was the beautiful sight of the horses, fox hounds, and red fox bounding toward the horizon. I can still see that image today, as though it were a painting hanging on a wall in my memory.

II

It was a Christmas Eve tradition for Ma, Pa, and me to travel by horse and sleigh over to the Hagen farm, about five miles away. I don't know when or how the tradition started. It seemed kind of strange to me that Pa wouldn't join his sister and her family on Christmas Eve. But like I said earlier, there had been some kind of falling out during the time that Pa worked for his sister's husband as a hired man.

The resentment must have gone pretty deep, because Pa never seemed to be comfortable around his sister and her husband. Ma, on the other hand, didn't hold the same grudges. In fact, she remained close to Pa's sister and would visit her regularly. And, of course, Delores spent quite a bit of time on our farm.

I never did know what to make of all that. But tangled family relationships were common in those days. They still are, I guess, but back then everyone seemed to have a grudge against someone else. So maybe the fact that Pa didn't particularly care for his own sister, while Ma considered her a friend, wasn't all that unusual.

The Hagen home, where we spent Christmas Eve, seemed to be a happy place. Toleph and Bertha Hagen were both very short, no more than five-feet tall, and yet many of their children towered above them. It was somewhat comical to watch those two short parents try to control and discipline their much taller children.

Toleph was a nice, generally even-tempered man. But when he got real angry at someone, everyone got out of his way. I remember Toleph poking his index finger into the chests of men a foot taller than him and reading them the riot act. Still, he was a good father to his children. Many times I wanted to ask if he would let me live with his family. But the Hagens didn't have room for their own growing family. In fact, when they ran out of room, they asked Ma and Pa to take in Alice, one of their children. She stayed with us from time to time, although, for some reason, we never became close.

With all those children around, Christmas was a happy and cheerful event. I was always glad to be a part of it—and to experience the joyful affection that filled the Hagen home. At the same time, I always came away from those Christmas Eve gatherings with a deeper sense of loneliness and emptiness. Life with Ma and Pa was nothing like life on the Hagen farm.

We would arrive at the Hagen home around eight o'clock at night. The kids were immediately sent upstairs, because, we were told, "Santa is coming."

Gunda Hagen, one of the older children, would join us upstairs. She would insist that we stay away from the windows. "Santa Claus is shy, and he will leave if there are people looking at him out the window," she said.

We could hear the bells on the sleigh as it pulled up to the house, and Gunda warned us, "Be very quiet."

Then we would hear a voice that sounded very much like Toleph Hagen's voice, although everyone knew it was Santa Claus talking. The voice would say very clearly, although with a slight Norwegian accent, "Voo Dancer, Voo Prancer, Voo Blitzen—Voo."

The front door downstairs would open, and we could hear Santa's footsteps in the house. Upstairs, we remained quiet as little mice.

We would hear the adults talking to Santa Claus. A few minutes later, Santa would say, "Good-bye, I'll see you next year."

The door would close, the sleigh bells out in the yard would jingle, and Santa would shout, "Go Dancer, Go Prancer, Go Blitzen—Go."

We knew, then, that it was safe to walk downstairs, and we did so very quietly—being the best little boys and girls we could possibly be.

There would be toys on the floor by the Christmas tree, many of them secondhand or homemade, because the Hagens didn't have any more money than we had. But, back then, we were happy to find any toy under the Christmas tree with our name on it. During the rest of the year, there was never any money for extravagances like toys.

Toleph Hagen and his wife would tell all the children that Santa Claus had painted some of the toys just for us. It was their way of making homemade and secondhand toys seem special.

When this Christmas tradition first started, we were so small that we would sit upstairs, somewhat fearful, shivering with anticipation. Later, as we grew older, we knew the adults were playing a trick on us, and yet we went along with it because it was always good fun for everyone.

III

That year—after the whooping cough epidemic, the mysterious illness that killed many area residents, the outbreak of hog cholera, and the other calamities in our lives—every happy occasion seemed to have a disaster lurking somewhere just behind it. When we left the Hagen house late at night, the winds were gently blowing the snow across the frozen fields. But less than a mile into our trip back home, we were suddenly surrounded by a raging blizzard. The two horses, Tug and Reilly, and the sleigh were caught in a howling, screaming whirlwind of white snow.

Pa tried to steer the sleigh into that driving wind. But he gave up. He let go of the reins and joined Ma and me at the bottom of the sleigh.

"I can't see a thing," he muttered as we huddled together. "We'll have to trust the horses, and hope they can find their way back home."

We all knew the many stories—real stories—about people lost in blizzards, and later found frozen in fields. Some weren't discovered until the spring thaw. Cemeteries were filled with the bodies of these poor unfortunate souls. So Ma, Pa, and I huddled together, shivering as much from fear as from the cold.

The blizzard was fierce—gale-force. Pa tried to sit up to stare ahead into the driving snow, but the winds knocked him down. "We'll have to trust the horses," he repeated, huddling closer to Ma and me. "I can't see a thing out there."

Over the howling winds, we could barely hear the horses panting as they struggled to pull the sleigh through the deepening snowdrifts. If the sleigh slipped off the road, or became stuck in some snowbank, we would have frozen to death.

Ma seemed to be especially moved by our predicament. For the only time in my life that I can remember, she pulled Pa and me close to her. Once again, as we confronted the very real possibility that we were going to die, we became a family. For a brief time, we had what the Hagens seemed to have every day of their lives: a family that cared for one another.

We could feel our skin prickling and burning—the early stages of frostbite. Suddenly, the sleigh stopped.

"What happened?" I cried, fearing we were stranded.

Pa sat up and peered into the blinding wind and snow. Then he slowly sat down. "We're home," he said, his face too numb to show any emotion.

We clung together as we fought the wind, stumbling through the snowdrifts and into the house. Pa pushed Ma and me across the threshold. I saw him grab a rope and tie it to a post. Ma and I watched him disappear into the storm, fighting his way back to the horses.

From somewhere in all the blank whiteness, Pa yelled, "Giddy up."

I heard nothing more, except the wind. A few minutes later, I watched the rope stiffen—and knew that Pa had tied the other end to the post just outside the barn door.

Ma and I shivered inside the doorway, waiting for Pa to reappear before us. I had never seen Ma so concerned about him. She gasped, believing she had seen Pa in the middle of all that whiteness. When it turned out to be a mirage created by the swirling snow, she sighed with despair.

Then I saw the rope vibrate. Pa became visible. He clung to the rope with both hands. The winds drove into his body.

As he tumbled through the open doorway, he fought to regain his breath. He rose slowly to one knee. His eyebrows, hair, and face were encrusted with white snow and frost. "Buster, Minnie, and the horses are safe in the barn," he said, panting "But Tug's eyes are covered with frost. I think he's blind."

IV

The morning sky was clear and blue. Snow had drifted and was banked against every building on the farm. Since Ivar had left us for the winter to work in one of the southern states, Pa had to dig us out—with a little help from me.

Pa shoveled a trench all the way from the house to the barn. Then he dug out the water tank and put wood in the tank heater so we could start a fire and get water to the livestock. He milked the cows and watered all the animals, before scooping a path from the house to the chicken coop and the other farm buildings.

I helped Pa whenever I could, but I spent most of my time putting salve on Tug's frostbitten snout. His eyes were swollen shut. Reilly, the other horse that had pulled us through the blizzard, stood nearby, munching on hay. Reilly looked none the worse for wear. But Tug was a pathetic sight to behold. He was so weak he wobbled and swayed on his frostbitten legs.

"How's Tug doing?" Pa asked as he walked into the barn.

"I don't know," I said, shaking my head.

"Reilly kept his head down and his eyes out of the storm," Pa explained, gently stroking Tug's neck. "Tug's the one that got us home. He was leading Reilly."

"Will he be okay?" I asked.

"I don't know," Pa said. "His eyesight was going anyway. We'll just have to see."

Pa continued to excavate around the farm for the rest of the day. I helped with the other chores. Before heading in for supper, Pa and I took another look at Tug. He was still standing in the same place, his head lifted, his swollen eyes seeing nothing.

Pa examined Tug's eyes, and then he shook his head.

"What can we do for him?" I asked.

"Nothing. In the spring, we'll sell him to the slaughter house. They'll give us a couple of dollars for him."

"Pa, he saved our lives," I pleaded. "You can't just send him off to the slaughter house."

Pa shook his head and said, "I got no choice. We'll keep him through the winter. We owe him that much. But in the spring, we'll have to get rid of him. That's just the way things are out here. If something can't pull its own weight, you gotta get rid of it."

"Even if he saved our lives?" I asked.

"Even if he saved our lives!" Pa insisted.

V

Pa and I had just sat down for supper when the winds started to kick up again. In less than an hour, every trench we had dug was obliterated. Exhausted from our labors, we knew we would have to do the same thing again tomorrow, and maybe the next day—or else the horses and livestock would perish.

Of course we did not know it at the time, but Stevens County was in the grip of what everyone would remember as "The Big Snow Storm." Years later, as soon as someone said those words, everyone for a couple of hundred miles in all directions would know immediately which snow storm it was. There was nothing to compare it to. Not before. Not since.

All night the winds pounded against the house and snow gushed from the sky. We watched as it drifted up the side of the house until it covered the windows completely. We were entombed.

"I think we have enough wood," Pa said. "If not, we'll start burning the furniture."

Although Ma cherished her few pieces of furniture, she did not object. She knew we would have to keep a fire burning or freeze to death.

In the morning, Pa opened the front door. But the storm door wouldn't budge. Pa walked upstairs and crawled out a window and onto the roof. The first story of our two-story house was buried under eight-foot drifts. The west side of the house was encased in a huge fifteen-foot drift. Pa stepped off the roof and onto the snowbank.

The yard was deeply blanketed with snow. The chicken house had disappeared. The buried fences twisted across the prairie like huge snakes.

Pa worked his way around to the front of the house, where he tunneled from the top of the snowdrift to the storm door. It took him almost two hours, but finally I heard his muffled voice. I pushed against the storm door with all of my weight. It creaked a bit and popped open. I looked up through a tunnel of snow at the blue sky overhead. It was one of the strangest sights I have ever seen. I thought about how the sky must look to a fish as it swims up into a hole in the ice.

"Come outside," Pa said. The steam was pouring out of his mouth and nose. "We need to dig the trenches again."

Side by side, Pa and I shoveled snow for nearly three days. Once again we had to unearth each structure that housed the animals. The snow had acted as insulation, and they were plenty warm. But they needed food and water—and the cows needed to be milked.

So that was "The Big Snow Storm." There was nothing like it before. There hasn't been anything like it since.

VI

Ma got sick again. Dr. Cumming came through on his rounds to visit the snowbound patients, and he told her she had to have a gallbladder operation immediately. Ma was scared to death because the nearest hospital where such an operation could be performed was in Graceville, almost forty miles away. There was also only one doctor in the area who could perform such surgery. Ma insisted she didn't want to go through with the operation.

"Either those gallstones come out now," Dr. Cumming told Ma, "or else you'll be in so much pain, you'll be begging me to take them out in another week or two."

Well, that pretty much cinched it for Ma. An elderly grandmother was brought over to look after me. A neighbor, who had a stronger team of horses and a huge bobsled, volunteered to take Ma and Pa to Graceville.

The morning Ma and Pa were to leave for the hospital, two magnificent horses pulling a bobsled trotted into our yard. Hay was spread a foot deep on the floor of the wagon box, and blankets were piled up everywhere. Ma laid down on the hay, and Pa covered her with blankets. He sat down next to the driver, and the horses trotted down the road. I heard their labored panting for some time. Then I heard only the sound of the wind blowing gently across the yard.

As I stood alone, I tried to sort through my feelings. Ma had treated me better since she had almost died from the internal hemorrhaging. But I always felt like I was an inch away from another beating. I didn't hate her the way I once did, but I hadn't forgiven her either. I could have forgiven her for almost anything except the beatings and the times I was locked up in the cellar. That was too much to forgive.

The day Ma went to Graceville was the first time I ever had the run of the place. There was only Grandma, and she seemed content to crochet all day by the stove. She would fall asleep periodically, only to wake up a while later, seemingly without missing a stitch. I knew this was an opportunity that would not soon present itself again.

As soon as Grandma nodded off in front of the stove, I snuck quietly past her and into Ma and Pa's bedroom. I searched through all the dresser drawers to see if I could find my adoption papers, or anything else that might yield some information about my birth mother. I found a number of old photographs, including one of Ma and Pa on the day they were married. Neither looked any too happy. I also found a number of souvenir postcards and other items from places like Montana, South Dakota, and Iowa.

After three days of periodic searches, I found nothing in the bedroom regarding my adoption or my birth mother. If those documents existed anywhere in the bedroom, they were well hidden. The more logical explanation was that they were hidden somewhere else in the house. But where?

VII

I gave up my search for the adoption records. Instead, I visited Tug. He and I had become very attached since the night he led us safely through the blizzard. Some of his eyesight had returned, but not much. His overall health had steadily deteriorated, and Pa was still determined to sell him to the slaughter house in the spring.

As I ran my hands through Tug's mane, I thought about how people referred to horses as dumb animals. This "dumb," animal was smart enough to lead three human beings through a raging blizzard and deposit them safely on their doorstep. We couldn't save ourselves. It took a dumb animal to save us. How dumb is that? How many people would be smart enough, or courageous enough, to do what Tug had done? Not very many, I'm afraid.

When Ma and Pa returned from the hospital, Ma had her gallstones with her. They were ugly pieces of grayish-green slime sealed in a glass jar, which she prominently displayed on a kitchen shelf. Many times, when I was eating by the kitchen table, I would look up at Ma's gallstones floating around in that glass jar and almost get sick. I wanted to go outside and feed those hideous things to the chickens. But Ma would've killed me if she woke up some morning to find her prized possessions missing. She'd haul that jar out whenever we had company over, and she would insist that her guests pass it around so everyone could admire her treasure.

Now, tell me something. Is there any other animal dumb enough to do something like that? Is there any animal anywhere dumb enough to cut off some part of its body and put it in a jar, and then pass it around for all the other animals to admire? No, only human beings are that stupid.

I rest my case.

VIII

In late winter of that same year, a young calf got out of the barn by squeezing through some rotting boards. Pa speculated that the mother must have followed her calf, because he found traces of blood and cowhide on the broken lumber. The cow had apparently widened the hole in an effort to go after her calf.

It was late in the day when Pa discovered the two animals were missing. He saw the tracks disappear into the snow-covered fields. He rushed inside to put on some heavier clothes and thicker boots.

"A calf got out of the barn," he explained quickly. "Looks like the mother went after it. I've got to get them back before nightfall. They'll freeze to death out there."

I watched through the window as Pa followed the tracks until he, too, disappeared. Within minutes, the skies darkened and strong winds whipped out of the north. Once again we were in the middle of a raging blizzard.

Ma and I knew that Pa was in serious trouble. She lit three kerosene lanterns and placed them next to the windows to guide Pa home.

"He'll never find his way back," she lamented. "I can't see three feet into that—"

Before the words were out of her mouth, the door burst open and Pa plunged inside. The steam from his breath had coated the hair in his nostrils and his eyebrows white. He was gasping for breath as he sat down next to the kitchen table. "I couldn't find them," he said. "They're gonna have to save themselves."

The storm continued for almost two full days. When it finally subsided, Pa went back out into the fields to look for the cow and her calf. There was no sign of them. The blizzard had erased all of their tracks.

"They're somewhere out there," Pa said after he returned from his search. "Most likely buried under two mounds of snow."

"Shouldn't you tell the other farmers to keep an eye out for them?" Ma asked.

"Yes, I'll do that," Pa agreed with little conviction. He knew the cow and the calf had not found refuge on another farm.

For the rest of that winter, I would search the fields from my window, studying the sizes and shapes of the various mounds of snow, wondering whether the cow and her calf were buried under any of them. The neighboring farmers reported no trace of the two animals. They had simply vanished, swallowed up by the immense prairie that surrounded our farm.

When spring finally came, I set out on my own to look for the cow and her calf. Even though Pa was reconciled to the fact that they were gone and would never return, I needed to know what had happened to them. I think what intrigued me more than anything else was Pa's statement that the cow had probably broken out of the barn to go after her calf. Only a cow with a strong motherly instinct would have done something like that. Most cows would have been content to stay in the warmth and comfort of the barn.

Each day, during my searches, the retreating snow yielded up more of the prairie landscape. But the cow and her calf were nowhere to be found.

Then one day I was walking out in the fields with Buster and Minnie, when I glanced down into a shallow, rock-covered ravine. At the bottom, I saw a small hoof sticking out of the melting snow. A much larger hoof was just beginning to emerge from the snow and ice nearby.

I had found the cow and her calf.

Within a few more days, the sun and warm winds exposed more of their frozen bodies. They were lying right next to each other, looking more peaceful than any two animals I had ever seen before.

As I surveyed the area around the ravine, I speculated about what had happened the day the cow and her calf perished in the snowstorm. That cow was much too savvy to stumble into the ravine on her own. Instinctively, she would have known that once she was at the bottom, she would never have been able to walk back up the icy slopes. So it could not have been stupidity that motivated her.

The more likely explanation was that the calf had slipped down the icy slopes into the ravine and become trapped. The cow had probably paced frantically above the ravine for a few minutes, watching her calf's futile struggle to escape, before she decided to join her offspring. That cow would have known that her decision to descend into the ravine guaranteed that she, too, would perish. But the cow's motherly instincts must have been stronger than her fear of death.

Helpless to reach shelter as the blizzard bore down on them, the cow and her calf must have laid down next to each other, awaiting the inevitable. The cow probably died first, since her back was turned toward the north, the direction from which the wind and snow were blowing.

Pa was wrong about finding two mounds of snow. There was only one mound.

IX

Pa told me the truck would arrive in the morning to take Tug to the slaughter house. I stayed in the barn with Tug until close to midnight. I stroked his head and told him what a good horse he was for saving our lives. He must have liked the compliments, because he nudged me playfully with his head while I fed him small handfuls of hay. Finally, I knew I had to go inside or Ma would have a fit. But every time I tried to walk out of the barn, I would turn around for one last look at Tug.

I stayed awake most of the night, thinking how much I despised Pa for doing what he was doing. Tug deserved better treatment. He lost his eyesight doing for us what we could not do for ourselves. Without him, we would have died. I just couldn't accept Pa's decision.

Pa must have been awake most of that night, too, because I could hear the coffee pot clinking against the stove downstairs. I finally fell asleep a couple of hours before daylight, but I woke up when I heard the front door swing open and close. I looked out the upstairs window as Pa strode across the yard with a spade in one hand and a rifle in the other.

Pa entered the barn and exited a few minutes later, leading Tug by a bridle. Pa had roped together the rifle and the spade, and tossed them over Tug's huge back. They swung back and forth as Pa led Tug across the yard and around the corner of the barn. They moved slowly toward a part of our property where the soil was soft and there weren't many rocks.

A few minutes later, I heard a single rifle shot ring out and reverberate across the prairie. Much later, when Pa walked back into the yard, he was carrying the rifle in one hand and the spade in the other. The bridle was draped over his shoulder.

As Pa leaned the rifle and spade against the barn door, the slaughterhouse truck pulled into the yard. Pa said something to the driver, and then he waved him off with Tug's bridle. The truck drove slowly out of our yard.

I heard the front door open and close. I walked downstairs to where Pa was sitting. The bridle was lying on the kitchen table in front of Pa, and tears were flowing slowly down his cheeks. It was the only time I ever saw him cry.

Pa never told me why he changed his mind about sending Tug to the slaughter house. He just hung Tug's bridle on a nail in the barn. I never saw him use it on another horse. As the bridle hung there year after year, it became to me a memorial to a "dumb animal" who had sacrificed his own life for three human beings who probably didn't deserve to live as much as he did.

Windmills and Wells

I

One day that spring, I was walking with Buster near the mound of dirt where Tug was buried, when I heard something behind me. As I turned around, Ivar was standing there, holding his cap in both hands. Since he had been gone for several months, I was somewhat surprised to see him there, paying his respects.

He had been south during our winter of blizzards and blindness, lost livestock and gallstones, but, somehow, he knew what had happened. He was offering silent homage to a beast of burden who, like himself, had been placed on this planet for one reason only: to work for weaker creatures.

After a few moments of silence, Ivar turned from the grave and walked slowly back to the barn. When I joined him, he was sitting on a bale of hay, polishing Tug's bridle.

II

Sometime in the late 1920s or early 1930s, we moved to a new farm three miles south and almost three miles west of Alberta. The farm was within walking distance of the Reque Church, the cemetery, and the country school. A drainage ditch, teeming with pheasants and other wildlife, snaked across the entire length of the farm and emptied into Lake Hattie about a mile farther north.

Pa did not purchase the new farm. As always, he rented from banks and insurance companies that had foreclosed on other farmers. For some reason, Pa did not believe in owning the land. No one could convince him that he would have a better chance of prospering as a farmer if he did.

Nonetheless, the new farm was an improvement over the old one. Like the old farm, it had a two-story farmhouse, a big barn, a chicken coop, a granary, a big hog house, and a calf pen. But the buildings were newer and in better condition. The land was blessed with rich black soil. Pa could have been successful on this farm—if he had worked at it. The problem was that the new farm was located much closer to Alberta. So Pa spent even more time in town playing cards, when he should have been working on the farm.

As a result of his malingering, his marriage to Ma became even more unstable. Pa's failure to work the land in a responsible manner also eventually contributed to our complete financial ruin. Still, for a few more years, we managed to survive.

III

The country school I attended after we moved to the new farm is very vivid in my memory. I enjoyed reading books in the school library, which was a small alcove near a pot-bellied stove in a corner of the one-room country schoolhouse. But I didn't especially like my classes. I liked to learn things on my own. I was much too shy and self-conscious to interact with the other students in classroom drills and instructions.

I missed more school days than I attended. Whenever Pa had something for me to do around the farm, he simply told me to stay home. At other times, he showed up at my classroom door, hat in hand, and told my teacher I had work to do on the farm. I suspect he figured that an education might ruin me as a hired man.

Whenever I made it to school, I would feel terribly self-conscious about the way I talked and looked. Plus, at times, I had to put up with some pretty vicious teasing about the fact that I was adopted. So school was not a pleasant experience for me.

One day Delores and I were eating our lunches outside, behind the school, when a group of boys surrounded us, creating a rotating circle. They held hands as they teased and taunted us.

"You were adopted because no one wanted you!"

"Your mom and dad probably didn't even know each other's names!"

Always more self-confident than I was, Delores got to her feet and marched toward the boys. She planted her hands on her hips and stared directly into the eyes of each of our tormenters as they passed by.

Seeing her courage, I thought surely *some* of the schoolyard bullies would wither into whimpering fools right on the spot. But before Delores could be tested as my protector, Raymond Kolden roughly pulled two of the boys away. The circle was broken. The teasing stopped. The bullies did not want to mess with Raymond Kolden. He was the oldest and biggest boy in the schoolyard. The bullies quickly scattered.

From then on, whenever Raymond made it to school, nobody dared tease me. Unfortunately, Raymond didn't make it to school very often. His pa kept him home. Some days when he went to school, I didn't, because my pa kept me home. When we both managed to meet up in the schoolyard, I felt an immediate boost in my confidence.

I often wondered what Raymond got from me. Friendship should give each person a better sense of himself. Raymond did this for me. But what did I do for him?

Eventually, we served on the same threshing crews together. We were the youngest members of those crews. So we naturally ate our lunches together and swapped stories during the breaks in the threshing activities. But there was more to it than that.

I can only speculate that Raymond saw something of himself in me. We were both raised to be hired men. And there is a code of honor among hired men. Since no one else looks out for them, they look out for one another. Maybe it's as simple as that.

IV

I made my first real friend that spring. Except for Buster and Minnie, and sometimes Delores, I had been pretty much isolated and alone on the old farm. But I didn't consider Buster and Minnie to be my friends. They were much more important to me than that. As I've explained, I considered them to be my real adoptive parents. Ma and Pa were just people I had to live with.

Except for Raymond Kolden, who I didn't see very often, I was never around any boys who wanted my friendship. So when Marcus Reece and I started doing things together, it was a special treat for me. We would meet on the same corner by the Reque Church and walk to school together. On the weekends, we would explore some of the abandoned farms in the area. We would dream up all kinds of stories and adventures and mysteries regarding the people who had once lived in the abandoned buildings. We shared those stories, and worked and reworked them, until we believed every detail.

One of our enchanted places was an old abandoned windmill in the middle of a field about two miles southwest of Pa's farm. Although it was dangerous, and I knew Pa would kill me if he found out, Marcus and I would climb the windmill and sit for hours gazing out over the grain fields. I had never been aware of how immense the Minnesota prairie was until I viewed it from on top of that windmill. From forty feet up, the prairie flowed uninterrupted, touching the horizon and the blue sky beyond. It was a beautiful, breathtaking sight, and Marcus and I shared many an inspired storytelling session on top of that windmill.

At times we would pretend that we were on top of a castle or watchtower, while our enemies were attacking us from all sides. But they could never get to us. Their arrows could not reach the top of the windmill. We dropped imaginary boulders on the ones who tried to climb the ladder to attack our fortress. It was great good fun. I was constantly amazed by how easily Marcus and I escaped into our imaginary world.

Another wonderful feature of my friendship with Marcus was more tangible. He owned a beautiful bronco pony. And that's not all. He owned a saddle, a bridle, and cowboy boots. That a boy my age should own all of this seemed impossible. No one was that rich. The only thing I remembered owning was the cap Clyde Roberts's wife had sewed for me. So I was a little in awe of Marcus and all of his wealth. To his credit, Marcus was an unpretentious young fellow, and he shared his wealth in a way that would probably make most Christians hide their heads in shame. I also think Marcus felt a little sorry for me. I say this because he let me ride his pony as much as I wanted to—which was just about every time we got together.

Sometimes, I would ride the pony alone. Other times Marcus would ride his pony, and I would walk alongside of Buster, pretending I was leading my horse by its bridle. In retrospect, I guess it must have been a pretty comical sight: one boy on a horse and one boy pretending that his dog was a horse. Sometimes, Marcus would have me sit behind him on his pony, and we would gallop off in search of high adventure, with Buster running alongside of us.

Freedom and the means to explore the world—what a wonderful way to live. I enjoyed my friendship with Marcus Reece enormously.

V

Marcus's father was the minister of the Lutheran church in Alberta, and he also preached at the Reque Church. For some reason, he didn't like me at all. I suspect it had something to do with the fact that I was adopted and, therefore, illegitimate in his eyes. Or maybe it had something to do with the fact that Ma, Pa, and I were from a much lower social class. Perhaps Reverend Reece didn't want his son associating with me for fear it would taint his own reputation.

Whenever Reverend Reece would see Marcus walking with me to school, he would drive up to us in his shiny new car. He would open the door and order Marcus to get in. He never offered me a ride. I heard him tell Marcus that I was dirty, and he didn't want me to mess up his car. Of course, I probably *was* dirty. But I still felt bad when Reverend Reece drove away, leaving me standing alone in a cloud of dust. Sometimes, I felt so hurt I just turned around and walked back home. That was fine with Pa.

In spite of his father's displeasure, Marcus kept sneaking away to play with me. One day, we started playing a game that Marcus had invented. The idea was to stand about twenty feet apart and throw a rock at the other person's shoes. The person whose rock came the closest, without hitting the shoes, was the winner.

I was getting pretty good at this game, when one of the rocks I threw ricocheted off something in the road, caromed in a different direction entirely, and hit Marcus right above the eye. The rock cut a gash on his forehead. Blood streamed down his nose and cheek.

I was upset by what had happened, but Marcus told me it wasn't my fault. He acknowledged that it was an accident. Besides, he said, it had been his idea to play the game in the first place. I wanted to walk Marcus home. But he said he would walk home by himself and have his father take him to Dr. Cumming to have the cut stitched up.

I didn't dare tell Ma and Pa for fear of what they would do to me. Later that night, Reverend Reece drove into our yard. When he came up to our front door, he was steaming mad. Pa let him into the kitchen.

"Did you tell your parents what you did to my son today?" Reverend Reece demanded, pointing an accusing finger at me.

I shook my head meekly and said, "No, I didn't."

Reverend Reece turned his back to me and directed his next comments to Ma and Pa. "What kind of a hooligan are you raising here?" he demanded. "He threw a rock at Marcus today, and it hit him right above the eye. Dr. Cumming had to put in two stitches to close the wound. An inch lower, and Marcus would have lost that eye. What kind of animal are you raising here?"

"It was a game," I tried to explain, somewhat tearfully. "It was Marcus's idea. We were throwing rocks as close as we could to each other's shoes. My rock glanced off something on the road. It was an accident."

"Marcus would never throw rocks at anyone," Reverend Reece insisted. He was so angry he was shaking. "Marcus was raised to know better than that."

He continued to berate me. He also threatened to talk to the members of the school board and have me expelled from school. Then he stomped out the door. Ma and Pa stared angrily in my direction.

"It was an accident," I repeated meekly. "We were playing a game."

I don't know if Pa believed me.

I certainly knew that Ma didn't. "You're no good," she said spitefully. "We never should have brought you into our home."

I was to hear that many more times in the months and years ahead.

VI

When Delores came over to visit Ma, I met her in our front yard and told her what had happened. "I'm probably going to be expelled from school," I said dejectedly.

"Why?" she asked.

"I threw a rock at Marcus Reece, and it hit him in the head," I explained.

"Why did you do that?"

"It was an accident. We were playing a game Marcus invented. My rock ricocheted off something in the road and cut him above the eye."

"If it was an accident," Delores counseled me, "then they can't expel you."

"His pa is going to tell the school board I did it deliberately."

"Why is he going to do that?" she asked.

"He doesn't like me. He didn't want Marcus to play with me in the first place."

I could tell that Delores was getting angry about what I was telling her—and not at me, either. She was a strong-willed young woman, who was fully capable of standing up to anyone who treated her or her friends unfairly.

For a moment, I thought I had seen that same angry look in someone else's eyes. But I couldn't remember who that person was.

"Lloyd, you've done nothing wrong," she said. "You tell the school board the truth about what happened."

"Do you think they'll believe me?" I asked.

"Yes, I think they'll believe you," she reassured me.

I hoped she was right, but I was terrified of what would happen to me if I had to appear in front of the school board to defend myself.

VII

True to his word, Reverend Reece talked to every member of our school board. He said that I had maliciously thrown a rock at Marcus's head. He advised them that I should be expelled before I seriously injured—or killed—someone. Reverend Reece insisted that I had committed an unprovoked attack on Marcus. I was told that he described me to the school board members as a violent, dangerous hooligan who should be locked up and kept away from other children.

On the basis of Reverend Reece's accusations, I was suspended from school. A hearing was scheduled. Reverend Reece, Marcus, Ma, Pa, and I were all expected to attend—along with all of the members of the school board and other interested parties.

The day before the hearing, I visited the abandoned windmill. I was feeling pretty discouraged and needed to be alone to think things over. The sun was setting as I climbed the forty feet to the top of the windmill. I sat down and listened to the wind groaning through the rusty metal blades.

Given my life thus far, the last thing I needed was a room full of adults who would be telling the world what a dangerous and terrible person I was. My ego wasn't big enough to sustain me through that kind of assault. I knew that I would probably just start crying and make a fool of myself. How could I say the things that needed to be said to prove my innocence? I had never felt so lost and alone—not even in the cellar, not even when Mr. Jensen moved away.

I thought about my birth mother. Why had she given me up for adoption? Certainly, life would have been better with her than it was with Ma and Pa in Alberta, Minnesota. *Any* life seemed better than the one I was living at the moment.

I became so depressed that I began to understand why some people decided to take their own lives. I wondered how Ma and Pa would feel if I jumped. Would anybody say nice things about me at my funeral?

I was so lost in my thoughts that at first I wasn't aware of a beautiful sound floating on the breeze, drifting lazily across the prairie. Unlike any music I had ever heard before, it seemed to be created by the wind itself.

The melody became more passionate and inspired as the sun disappeared into the horizon. The last notes lingered for a few more minutes as the sunlight turned to pink the underbelly of the clouds, washing the horizon reddish-orange. As the brilliant colors faded, and darkness settled across the western horizon, the last faint notes of the song reached my ears, and then faded away.

VIII

Ma said she wasn't feeling well, so Pa and I hitched up a team of horses and rode in the wagon to the country school, where we were to face the school board. Pa let me take Buster along for moral support, although he said Buster would have to sit in the back of the wagon during the hearing. I stroked Buster's neck all the way over to the school.

Pa didn't say very much. He only talked once, and that was when we passed another wagon coming down the road from the opposite direction. Two men, both dressed in grimy bib overalls, were sitting in the wagon. Their faces, hands, and clothing were so dirty the men looked like they had been dipped in mud minutes earlier.

Pa nodded at them as we passed. "Those are the Sanders brothers," he explained. "They're a couple of bachelors who live north of here. They dig wells and build windmills for a living."

To me, they looked like a couple of old bears that had just finished wrestling with each other in a muddy creek. The Sanders brothers, mud men, were unrecognizable as human beings.

When Pa and I entered the schoolhouse, several members of the school board were sitting around a large rectangular table at the front of the room. Except for the chairman, who I recognized as someone who lived close to town, they were husky, weathered farmers who seemed out of place in a schoolhouse. Reverend Reece and Marcus sat together on one side of the room. Pa and I sat on the other side. A handful of people were scattered around the center of the room.

Near the back of the room, I saw Delores. She was looking in my direction. She smiled broadly at me, trying to lift my spirits and build my confidence. I was too frightened to do much more than grimace.

The chairman of the school board made some opening remarks, and then he said, "The purpose of tonight's meeting is to decide whether or not Lloyd Clausen should be expelled for throwing a rock at another student, Marcus Reece."

I saw Marcus look down as the school board chairman said his name. Marcus's refusal to look in my direction convinced me that his father had persuaded him to change his story. Still, I found myself feeling even more sorry for Marcus than I did for myself. And I was feeling plenty sorry for myself.

Reverend Reece spoke first. He gave a long-winded sermon, which he concluded by pointing a finger in my direction and declaring, "This young man deliberately set out to injure my son. He threw a rock at Marcus that opened up a gaping wound in his forehead. Only through the grace of God did that rock miss my son's eye. Another inch lower, and my son would be sitting here today unable to see out of one eye. I urge you to expel Lloyd Clausen so he can do no further damage to any more of our students."

The chairman asked me to respond to the allegations, and I stood up to address the men at the front of the room. "We were playing a game," I said nervously. "We were trying to see who could throw a rock closest to the other person's shoes. Marcus threw first—"

Reverend Reece jumped to his feet and interrupted me. "Marcus did not throw a rock. My son does not—"

"Sit down, Reverend Reece," the chairman said. "Let Lloyd finish, and then we'll hear your son's version of the story."

I nervously gulped some air and continued, "After Marcus threw a rock at my shoes, I picked up a rock and—"

Once again, Reverend Reece leaped up and said, "Marcus did not throw a rock—"

"Sit down!" the chairman demanded impatiently.

"My rock glanced off something on the road," I explained. "It was an accident—"

"It was no accident," Reverend Reece insisted.

"Reverend Reece," the chairman admonished him, "we are trying to get to the truth behind this matter. And you are making it impossible for Lloyd to tell his side of the story." Then he turned to Marcus. "Marcus," he said, "since it seems that the school board's decision in this matter will largely depend on whether or not you threw a rock at Lloyd first, perhaps we need to hear your side of the story. Can you tell us what happened, in your own words? Then we can return to Lloyd."

Marcus swallowed hard as he slowly stood up to address the school board. He looked nervously for a moment at his father and then at the school board. He started out by reciting what appeared to be a prepared speech. "I was standing in the middle of the road," he began in a halting and nervous tone of voice, "when Lloyd threw a rock at me—"

As he spoke, Marcus looked in my direction. For the first time since this whole mess began, our eyes met. I don't know what he was thinking, but I know I was thinking about all the fun we had together, and how I didn't want to lose him as my friend. But I'm sure I also looked a little sad because I realized, whatever might happen during the hearing, those good times were over, and we would be going our separate ways.

Marcus continued to look in my direction for several seconds, staring directly into my eyes. Then he looked back at the school board. "No," he said,"That's not the way it happened at all. Lloyd and I were playing a game. It was my idea—"

"It was *not* your idea!" Reverend Reece shouted. He started to stand again, but several members of the school board glared at him, and he sat down.

"It was my idea," Marcus repeated emphatically. "I threw a rock at Lloyd's shoes. He threw one back at my shoes. We did this several times. Then one of his rocks hit something in the road, flew up, and hit me above the eye. It was an accident. We both knew it was an accident. And Father knew it was an accident."

"He's trying to protect his friend," Reverend Reece yelled, starting to stand up again. "That's all he's trying to do—"

"Reverend Reece," the chairman said firmly, "I really think you had better sit down." Then he glanced at the other school board members, all of whom nodded in his direction. "I don't think we need to hear from anyone else regarding this matter."

The members of the school board huddled together briefly at the front of the room. They returned to the table. "Lloyd," the chairman said warmly, "the members of the school board apologize that you were suspended because of vicious rumors one member of our community created to discredit you. You are innocent of the charges brought against you, and you are immediately reinstated in our school."

Then he turned to Reverend Reece and said, "As for you, Reverend Reece, if the school board ever again hears that you have tried to blame this incident on Lloyd, we will go to your church council, and we will tell them the whole story. You tell people the truth about what happened to your son, or you will be looking for a new parish."

Reverend Reece yanked his son by the forearm. Marcus glanced briefly in my direction before his father pulled him through the door.

I knew we would never again ride off together into the sunset in pursuit of high adventure. But Marcus Reece had defied his father to stand up for me—and I was proud to call him my friend.

IX

Later that evening, as Pa, Buster, and I rode home beneath the stars, I was feeling pretty good about myself. It was a beautiful spring night. As we passed Reque Cemetery, the wind whispered through the trees, and the moonlight played across the old gravestones. The sound of an owl echoed across the night air, intermingling with the panting of the horses and the crackling of their leather harnesses.

I probably felt better about my life than I had at any time previously. My faith in human nature, which had been pummeled by Reverend Reece's actions toward me, had been elevated to new heights by the members of the school board who had defended me against false accusations. They had seen to it that a powerful adult member of their community could not destroy the life of a young boy, who could offer nothing in his own defense except the truth.

I had just about come to the conclusion that most people are good and decent, when a black car passed us, coming from the opposite direction. The dirt road was so narrow that both Pa and the driver of the car had to slow down as they eased past one another. I recognized the car's driver, and I knew Ma's company was once again prowling the country roads, searching for our new home.

X

The next day, toward twilight, I took Buster and Minnie and went for a walk over to the abandoned windmill. I was feeling bad that Marcus and I would never again climb the windmill together. I guess I just needed to say good-bye to our enchanted spot—and to my first real friend.

I thought about the way Marcus stood up to his father. I'm not sure I would have had the courage to stand up to Pa under similar circumstances. But Marcus had the courage to publicly defy his father to do what was right for a friend. That was the most remarkable thing anyone had ever done for me.

I think about Marcus to this very day. I hope he went far in life. I'm sure that he did. He was certainly off to a very good start. But even if his life turned out to be a hopeless failure, I hope he knew that there was always one person who valued his friendship and treasured his loyalty to the truth.

I was about a hundred yards from the windmill, when I suddenly heard music. Again, it seemed to be music created by the wind itself. I looked in all directions for the source of such a beautiful, unearthly sound. As I listened carefully, the music seemed to be coming from a grove of trees about a quarter-mile farther south. So I headed out in that direction.

As I approached the grove of trees, the music grew louder. In a clearing in the middle of the grove of trees, I saw two mud-caked men sitting on the back of a wagon, which was parked next to a huge pile of dirt. The two men were playing violins with so much concentration they didn't even see me approach. Nearby, I saw a deep hole in the ground—a new well.

It was the Sanders brothers, the two men Pa and I had passed on the dirt road the previous evening. These two mud-caked men, who were barely recognizable as human beings, would build windmills or dig wells all day, and then, around twilight, they stopped everything and played soft, beautiful music on their violins.

The Sanders brothers lived at the windswept top of the world, or at its muddy core. Anything in between was of little concern to them.

I Lose My Parents

I

Pa attended a farm auction and bought another horse to replace Tug. The auctioneer tossed in a gasoline-powered electrical generator and a radio, neither of which had worked for years. They laid around our barn, collecting dust, until one day Ivar took them apart and put them back together in working order. Then he hooked the generator up to the radio and two small lights, one in the kitchen and one in the living room. The kitchen light was hooked up right above the shelf where Ma kept the jar containing her gallstones. Visitors to our new farm had an even better view of the grayish-green slime floating around inside that jar.

For the first time in my life, we had electricity—although not very much of it. Fuel for the generator was fairly cheap, but still too expensive for our meager budget. So we ran the generator for only an hour after dusk, while we played the radio. Even Ivar was allowed into the house to listen with us.

II

With the radio, I was connected to a much larger world. Up until that point, my life had been confined to the farmlands south of Alberta. From my earlier travels with our mailman, Clyde Roberts, I knew a little bit about Stevens County. From the books I read at school, I had a vague sense of what the rest of the state of Minnesota might look like. But I knew absolutely nothing about the rest of the country.

The United States of America might as well have been our whole solar system as far as I was concerned. In my mind, Washington, D. C., was as far away from Alberta, Minnesota, as the planet Jupiter was from the planet earth. In time, I came to realize the comparison probably wasn't fair to the planet Jupiter. During the early years of the 1930s, there was probably more intelligent life on the planet Jupiter than there was in Washington, D. C.

Some of my most vivid memories of my early life on the Minnesota prairie involve the months and years after the stock market crash in October of 1929. Every night, after chores, we would all gather around the radio to listen to the latest bad news. Sometimes, a few neighbors would join us. None of us knew at the time how the crash would affect Minnesota farmers. Little did we know that political and economic forces were shaping the defining event of our lives—the Great Depression.

The stock market crash didn't bother farmers too much at first. In fact, we were convinced that Wall Street was deserving of a little misery. The prevailing opinion on the Minnesota prairie was that Wall Street speculators got rich by manipulating grain prices to cheat farmers out of the fruits of their labor. We didn't rejoice when we heard that bankers and investment brokers were reduced to selling apples on the streets. We just figured it was their turn to share in the economic misery that was a fact of life for most working-class people.

Things took a turn for the worst, however. We soon realized that Wall Street's problems reflected much bigger problems. The country was broken. It needed to be fixed. But the politicians seemed incapable of fixing it.

As we gathered around the radio, we listened to President Hoover tell the American people that we should not worry because things would soon be getting better. Remember, he was the president who promised, "There will be a chicken for every pot, and a car in every backyard."

The farmers in our living room would inevitably greet his predictions with derisive laughter and deep cynicism. They had no faith whatsoever in Republicans. Most farmers believed the Republicans were largely responsible for the sad state of the nation's economy.

After hearing President Hoover offer his familiar shallow reassurances on the radio, one farmer scornfully said, "The Republican Party is a shrine to human greed."

Another farmer agreed, but added, "The Democratic Party is a shrine to human stupidity."

Those opinions probably reflected the general distrust of all politicians at the time. For the farmers, the two choices seemed to be a government controlled by human greed or human stupidity.

Almost all of the farmers became staunch Democrats.

III

For a time, Prohibition was a bigger issue than the stock market crash in our part of the county. Just about every farmer made homebrew in his cellar. It was generally recognized, however, that Pa made the best homebrew in the area.

One Saturday, Ma and Pa took me to Alberta with them, leaving Buster to guard the farm. We were gone most of the afternoon, and when we drove the team of horses and wagon back into the yard, Buster was barking and growling next to the cellar door.

I called Buster to me. Pa slowly approached the cellar's entrance. We saw the door rise slightly off its foundation, and a man's head poked out. He looked around apprehensively. But as soon as he saw Buster, he dropped the door and retreated back into the cellar. Pa told me to hold Buster.

He lifted the door. "Who's down there?" he yelled into the darkness.

Three of his card-playing friends from Alberta quickly scrambled up the cellar stairs. They were so drunk they could scarcely stand up as they stumbled out into the daylight. They explained that they had come over to steal some of Pa's homebrew, but Buster had trapped them in the cellar. So they just decided to sit down there until we got back home. To keep from getting bored, they kept sipping away at Pa's homebrew.

When Pa heard their slurred explanations, I expected him to be furious. But for some reason, the thought of Buster trapping his card-playing friends in the cellar after they'd tried to steal his homebrew, struck Pa as hilarious. And for the one and only time that I can remember, he laughed until the tears streamed down his cheeks.

Pa then joined his friends down in the cellar for one last sip of homebrew. When the four men came out a couple of hours later, Pa, too, was roaring drunk.

During the time they were in the cellar, Pa must have entertained his friends with stories about our just-purchased, bad-tempered buck sheep. It was always attacking people. Pa's friends demanded to see it.

He explained to them, as they staggered over to where the buck sheep was penned up, "The thing you have to do when you walk past a buck sheep is simply ignore it. Just pretend it's not even there. If that buck sheep knows you are concerned about its presence, it'll attack you every time. But if you ignore it, it'll leave you alone."

Well, Pa's drunken friends didn't think too much of his advice. They challenged him to prove his theory. If Pa had been sober, he probably wouldn't have taken up the challenge. But he was too drunk to exercise good judgment. So he threw a sack of grain over his shoulder and walked casually into the pen—right past the buck sheep—as though it were something he did all the time.

The buck sheep had been munching on some hay, but it looked up rather nonchalantly as Pa sauntered past. But once Pa was well within the pen, the buck sheep got this wild look in his eye, as though he had taken offense that Pa hadn't acknowledged him. The buck sheep lowered his horns and charged across the pen, hitting Pa right smack dab in the rear end. The sack of grain flew into the air. Pa did a backwards somersault and landed on his belly. The buck sheep immediately made a quick turn and proceeded to bear down on Pa from the other direction. Meanwhile, the sack of grain hit the ground, split open, and poured out onto the mud and sheep dung.

Pa scuttled toward his friends, who were laughing at him from the other side of the fence. With a little help from the buck sheep, who once again smashed into his rear end, Pa rolled under the fence. He came to rest at the feet of his card-playing friends.

"So that's the *proper* way to walk past a buck sheep?" one of his friends snickered good-naturedly as he looked down at where Pa was lying on the ground, covered with mud and sheep dung.

"Now, can you demonstrate the *wrong* way to do it?" another one chortled.

Pa sold the buck sheep a couple of days later.

IV

Minnie disappeared one day, shortly after we moved into our new farm. That morning she simply failed to greet me at the front door. I wasn't too worried. I figured she had found some excuse to explore the near-by fields and groves of trees. But when she failed to show up by noon, I started to figure that something was terribly wrong.

Buster was more concerned than I had ever seen him. He sniffed every square inch of the farmyard, looking for Minnie. Then he paced, pausing only to stare out into the fields.

I locked Buster up in the barn that night so he, too, would not dis-appear. I was fearful that there might be something dangerous out in the prairie, another animal or terrible hazard that was attacking or killing domestic animals.

The second day that Minnie was missing, I got up very early to see whether she had returned during the night. But she hadn't. When I opened the barn door, Buster raced out and sniffed the air in all direc-tions. Once again, he paced across the yard, pausing to stare out into the prairie.

Buster must have scented something in the wind, because he raced around in circles before streaking across the prairie in a southwesterly direction. I didn't even bother to follow him. I knew I couldn't keep up with him.

For the rest of the day, as I did my chores, I checked in the direc-tion where Buster had disappeared, hoping I would see him with Minnie, walking back to the farm. But the day ended without any sign of either one of them.

I slept very fitfully that night. Several times I stepped outside into the moonlight to see whether Buster and Minnie had returned. Near morning, I fell into a deep sleep. I was awakened by the loudest bark-ing I had ever heard. From the upstairs window, I could see nothing. I threw on my clothes and ran downstairs. Buster greeted me with fran-tic barking by the front door. Behind him, lying on the ground, was Minnie. Covered with so much mud and with so much fur missing, she was almost unrecognizable as a dog. She must have been in some terrible fight with a wild animal or pack of wild dogs. Somehow, Buster had found her and guided her back to the farm.

I poured some water into a bowl and held it close to Minnie. I fed her scraps of food from the kitchen. I then washed the mud off her. As I suspected, she had been in a terrible fight. She had cuts and welts all over her body. Eventually, she recovered from her ordeal, but she never again left the yard unless she was with Buster—or me.

To this day, I have no idea what happened to Minnie, or how Buster found her. Obviously, he smelled something in the air that day. But what it was, or how it led him to Minnie, is a complete mystery.

V

One of my favorite farm events was a blanket-weaving party. The farm families got together once a year, sometimes for several days in a row, to weave winter blankets. Cars and horse-drawn wagons arrived at one of the neighboring farmhouses, and women set up an ancient loom in the living room.

The women took turns working the handles, and somehow, as if by magic, the contraption would produce blankets. I found the loom to be as fascinating in its own way as the cream separator and the steam-powered threshers. It was beyond my powers of comprehension to understand how human beings had ever invented such marvelous gadgets.

While the women loomed blankets, the men went fishing, played cards, or sat around the farmyard swapping stories. The children played softball, kickball, or other games in the nearby fields. Since Pa had me working on the farm most of the time, a blanket-weaving party was one of the few occasions when I could play with the other children. I looked forward to it every year.

One of these parties was held in a neighboring farmhouse a few days after Pa had been upended by the buck sheep. I played kickball with the other boys and girls, while some of the women and smaller children watched us. Between games, one of the boys who had heard about Pa's run-in with the buck sheep asked me to repeat the story.

"Well," I said, "Pa bought this bad-tempered buck sheep—"

"What's a buck sheep?" another boy asked.

"It's a male sheep," I explained. "It breeds with the females."

"Why do they call it a *buck* sheep?"

"Many male animals are called *bucks*. I guess because males buck."

"Do they have antlers?"

"They have big horns. They fight with them."

I vaguely heard two other boys exchange wisecracks about my description of the buck sheep. A small girl cocked her head slightly and looked up at them. She appeared to be puzzled and confused by what they had said. Then she ran over to her mother and gestured excitedly in our direction.

I recognized the little girl's mother because Ma had a falling out with her over some church project. But I always sensed the problem went much deeper than that. During church services, I often saw her glaring at Ma with a stern look of disapproval. I don't know why, but I sensed that the woman knew something about Ma's relationship with the man whose black car was so often parked in our yard.

The animosity was mutual. Ma accused the woman of being too snoopy for her own good, and said she was always prying into other people's business. Ma's anger toward her went deep—too deep. It reminded me of the anger I felt the day she confronted me about the man I had seen in her bedroom window.

The little girl suddenly pointed her finger in my direction. Her mother glared at me with the same stern look I had seen in church when she stared at Ma. Then she grabbed her daughter's arm and marched her over to the farmhouse. I sensed trouble, but I didn't see how it could have anything to do with me.

When we started another kickball game, I pretty much forgot about the incident. A few minutes later, Ma marched across the field and over to me. She grabbed me by the ear and hauled me off the field and over to our wagon. Not only was it very painful, but it was also very embarrassing: the kickball game stopped while Ma dragged me away.

"You will not shame me with that kind of language," Ma insisted angrily.

"What kind of language?" I asked.

She muttered something about me using foul language. From what I gathered, the mother of the little girl had stormed into the living room and announced to the women working around the loom that I had used a dirty word to describe Ma.

"What word?" I pleaded.

"You know what word!" Ma insisted.

"No, I don't."

"Maybe if you sit out here for the rest of the afternoon, you'll remember it!"

"I didn't use a dirty word," I protested.

"Don't leave this wagon," she threatened, "or Pa will take his belt to you right here."

Normally, Ma would have waited until we got home to punish me. But this time she had been publicly humiliated. She was struggling mightily to control her anger. It mattered little to her that I might be innocent. To Ma, I was always guilty, always deserving of punishment.

For the rest of the afternoon, I sat in our wagon, beneath the hot sun. I watched the other children play kickball. The one day I had looked forward to so much, as a welcome relief from grueling farm work, had been turned into just another day of punishment.

When the other children were called inside to eat, no one came out to get me. I sat there, hot, thirsty, and miserable. I wished Buster were there with me. I knew the time would go by a little faster—and I wouldn't feel quite so isolated, unhappy, and alone.

When Ma and Pa came out later that day, they both sat on the driver's seat as we drove home. They made me sit in the rear of the wagon box, like some dirty little animal. I could hear bits and pieces of their conversation. I knew I would be beaten when we got home, and I expected the worst—the leather strap.

Much to my surprise, I wasn't punished that night. Instead, I was sent upstairs as soon as we arrived back at the farm. I hadn't eaten all day, so I didn't sleep very much. I lay awake wondering about the terrible price I was going to pay for the false accusations.

I tried to figure out what had happened. I considered the possibility that the little girl had misidentified me as the boy who had used the dirty word. The more likely explanation was that her mother knew it was not me, but she had seized the opportunity to retaliate for the things Ma had been saying about her to other people. It was a perfect opportunity to publicly humiliate and, possibly, expose Ma as an immoral woman who had raised an immoral child. I just got caught up in their personal feud.

VI

In the morning, I tried to sneak downstairs before daybreak. Pa was working in the fields. I did not want to face Ma alone. So I carried one shoe in each hand as I crept quietly down the stairs.

But I was too late. Ma was sitting by the kitchen table with a bar of homemade soap in her hand. She grabbed me and tried to force the soap into my mouth. It was a very strong soap, made of lard and lye and other chemicals and ingredients. She had used the same soap on me before, and it had left my mouth raw and blistered. I defended myself, keeping my jaws locked and my lips pressed tightly together.

"I never want you to use that word again," Ma screamed, struggling to force the soap in my mouth.

Because of the work I had been doing on the farm, I was much stronger and I was able to break away from her grasp. Ma blocked the front door. I retreated from the kitchen into the living room, and from there into the bedroom, where I slid under the bed.

Ma tried to pull me out from under the bed. I watched her feet. I rolled over to the other side of the bed, avoiding her searching grasp. I was successful for some time. Then she tried another strategy.

"Lloyd," she coaxed me, "I won't punish you if you come out. But if you don't come out, I'll tell Pa, and he'll take the leather strap to you when he comes home."

I had learned not to trust anything Ma said. But my memories of the leather strap were still painful. I decided to take a chance. I saw where Ma's feet were planted, and I rolled out from under the other side of the bed.

At first, Ma seemed fairly calm. "What did you say to that little girl yesterday?" she asked.

"I didn't say anything to her," I replied nervously. "I didn't even talk to her. She must have heard some other boy use a dirty word."

"That's not what her mother said," Ma insisted. She started to move slowly around to my side of the bed. "She said you used a dirty word in front of her daughter. She said you used it to describe me."

"That's not true. I told the story about Pa's encounter with the buck sheep," I explained. "That's all."

Ma suddenly grabbed me around the head. Again, she attempted to force my mouth open with the soap. I struggled free from her grasp and ran toward the front door.

Once I was outside, I realized I had dropped my shoes sometime during my scuffle with Ma. Rocks and debris tore into my feet. I could not run very fast. When I glanced over my shoulder, I saw that Ma held a frying pan. She waved it in the air as she pursued me across the yard and into the fields.

I had never seen her quite like this before—not even after I told Pa I had seen a man in her bedroom window. She was completely out of control. Whatever word the woman said I had used to describe Ma, it had sent her into a frenzy.

My heart was beating wildly. My feet throbbed as they were cut, torn, and punctured by the sharp field stubble. I wanted desperately to stop running, but every time I glanced over my shoulder, Ma was still coming, waving the frying pan in the air.

Finally, I fell to the ground. Behind me, I could hear Ma's galloping footsteps. I looked up, waiting for the worst, but I saw a gray streak tearing across the field. Buster raced to my side. He planted himself squarely in front of me. As a low rumble echoed deep in his throat, he bared his teeth, defying Ma to try to get around him.

She halted a few yards in front of Buster. Her face was bright red and she was panting. She raised the frying pan over her head. Then she brought it down to her side. She struggled to control her rage.

Ma was no match for Buster; she knew it. Defeated, she turned and stomped back to the house. Buster watched her disappear before he lay down on the ground next to me.

VII

With my friend Marcus no longer around, and Ma on the rampage, I started to go for long walks with Buster and Minnie. On one of our trips, I came upon a group of gypsies who had set up camp in a remote corner of Pa's property. Pa had told me to watch out for gypsies because he said they could not be trusted.

An elderly gypsy approached me. In slightly broken English, he asked, "We camp here tonight. Okay?"

I thought about Pa's warnings. He would be mad enough if he learned that I hadn't told him I had seen gypsies in the area. He would be furious if he learned I gave them permission to camp on our property.

"My pa probably wouldn't approve," I said.

"The children. They are tired," he replied.

I noticed that several mothers were sitting on the ground, nursing babies next to wagons loaded with their life's belongings. Small children napped on the ground next to them.

"Pa would be upset," I said. "I'm sorry."

"We be gone in the morning. We clean up. You not know we were here."

One of the mothers started to doze off as she leaned against a wagon wheel. I could tell that they had traveled for many miles. The women were so exhausted they did not have the strength to care for their children. I decided to take a chance and let them camp on our property for one night—so long as Pa didn't find out they were there.

"Do you plan to build a campfire?" I asked. I was worried that Pa might see the flames at night and check to see who was there. "My pa probably wouldn't want a campfire on his property."

"You say no campfire, we build no campfire," the elderly man promised.

"I guess it will be okay, then," I replied.

"Thank you," he said, grasping my hand in his two weathered palms. "You be very kind."

The next morning I walked back to that same spot. The gypsies were gone, and the area was clean as a whistle. No one would ever have known that anyone camped there the night before. I decided that Pa was wrong about the gypsies. They were honorable people. They could be trusted to keep their word.

That night, Buster started barking and growling from the barn, where he was locked up. A terrible commotion soon broke out in the chicken house. It was obvious that something or someone was in there. I rushed downstairs to join Pa.

Pa was pulling up his pants as he walked toward the door with his double-barrel shotgun. He stepped out into the yard and immediately fired a shot in the direction of the chicken house. We heard fleeing footsteps. It sounded like several people were running toward the dirt road. Pa fired the shotgun in that direction.

When we ran down to the chicken house, we found an empty chicken crate the thieves had left behind. They were obviously planning to fill it with chickens and flee into the night. Buster's barking had foiled their plans.

"Archie Flanagan said he saw a group of gypsies traveling through the area the other day," Pa said as he inspected the crate. "This looks like it might be their work."

"Would they steal chickens?" I asked.

"They'll steal anything that isn't tied down," Pa replied. "I'll leave Buster outside for a few nights, in case they decide to come back."

I felt betrayed. The gypsies I had allowed to camp on our property were merely setting me up so they could steal our chickens. Pa was right. Gypsies could not be trusted.

VIII

The next day I herded some cattle over to the rich green grass that grew by a slough near our farm. It had been raining off and on for about a week, and the dirt road was muddy and covered with puddles. I was walking next to Minnie. Buster was walking about thirty feet ahead of us, alongside the road. From the west, I saw a pick-up truck moving in our direction. When it approached our property, I saw that the hood of the truck was rusted and tied with rope to the bumper. The truck slowed down to avoid the mud puddles in the road.

I saw something sticking out the window on the driver's side of the truck. The truck came to a complete stop in the middle of the road. There was a moment of silence. Then I heard a rifle shot ring out, and Buster tumbled into the ditch. I rushed over to him as the truck sped away.

Buster was panting slowly and gasping for breath as I knelt by his side. A thin streak of blood was spreading slowly across the fur on his chest.

In my panic, I tried to pick him up. But he was too heavy for me to carry. I had to leave him there while I ran back to the farm to get Pa.

I found Pa standing next to the barn, working on one of the horses. "Pa," I screamed, pointing toward the slough, "someone in a pick-up truck just shot Buster."

Pa mounted the horse and rode off in the direction I had pointed. I ran back toward the ditch to see what I could do for Buster. In the distance, I could see the truck trying to accelerate, but the rutted, puddled road made traction difficult.

The truck turned south onto another dirt road. Pa immediately rode off across the field to try to head it off. I watched as Pa's horse and the truck converged near a grove of trees at the other end of the field. The truck got there first. Pa directed his horse into the grove of trees.

By the time I made it back to the ditch, Minnie was trying to comfort Buster by licking his snout. I looked down at the red blood that was seeping out of a wound and matting the fur on Buster's chest. I knew that he was badly wounded, probably even dying.

I leaned close to Buster's ear and whispered to him, "As soon as Pa gets back, we'll fix you up as good as new."

Buster responded with that same gentle whimper I had heard many times through the crack in the mortar—all those times when Ma had locked me in the cellar. He had tried to reassure me when I sat alone in all that darkness.

Now I was trying to reassure him as he lay bleeding, and probably dying, on the side of a dirt road. "You're going to be okay, Buster," I whispered to him through my tears. "You've *got* to be okay!"

IX

I learned later that the reason Pa rode the horse into the grove of trees was because there were some neighbors living there who owned a car. He quickly explained to them what had happened, and the neighbor, his brother, and Pa set off in pursuit of the man who had shot Buster. About two miles down the road, they caught up to the pick-up truck and ran it into the ditch.

They caught the man dead to rights. He had a rifle in his truck with a spent cartridge still in the chamber. The neighbor and his brother had all they could do to keep Pa from killing the culprit. As it was, Pa still gave him a terrible beating before the neighbor and his brother could pull him away. Then Pa asked the neighbor to drive him back to where Buster was lying in the ditch.

When Pa returned, he stepped out of the car, took one look at Buster, and yelled back to the neighbor, "Send a veterinarian out to our house right away."

Pa picked up Buster easily in his powerful arms and carried him back to the farm. He placed him on a blanket near the kitchen stove.

The veterinarian came out about an hour later. He examined Buster carefully, and then he leaned back on his knees. "There's nothing we can do for him," he said softly. "I'm sorry. If we try to get the bullet out, we'll kill him. All we can do is make him comfortable."

"What does that mean?" I demanded. "What's going to happen to Buster?"

The veterinarian looked up at Pa, as though asking permission to reply to my question. Then he looked back at me. "He's not going to make it, son. I'm sorry."

Pa let me sleep on the floor next to Buster for the next three nights. Each day Buster grew weaker, and his breathing grew shallower. Each night I threw my arm over his stomach and fell asleep next to him, while he whimpered gently beneath my touch. Outside, Minnie pressed her nose against the screen door and whined.

Late in the afternoon on the fourth day, Buster kind of turned and looked up at me with his big brown eyes, as though to say, "Okay, Buddy, I got you this far in life. But you're going to have to make it the rest of the way on your own." Then he laid his head down and closed his eyes.

I placed my hand on Buster's chest to see if there was still a heartbeat. But I could feel nothing.

X

Pa let me bury Buster next to the oak tree with the split trunk. I wanted him to be buried in a place where he could hear the prairie wind song. So we loaded Buster's body in a horse-drawn wagon and took him back to the area where he had spent most of his life.

Pa was also very attached to Buster. As we traveled down the dirt roads, I thought for sure he was going to cry. He even helped me dig the hole in the rich prairie soil beneath the oak tree. Then we stood together in silence for several minutes, staring at Buster's grave.

Minnie pined away for Buster. She stopped eating and died a few weeks later. Pa and I loaded her in the wagon and buried her next to Buster beneath the same oak tree.

The man who shot Buster turned out to be one of the chicken thieves who had broken into our chicken house. Pa and I both had it wrong: the gypsies had nothing to do with it.

When the judge asked the man why he shot Buster, he replied, "I was tired of that damn dog barking up such a fuss and making it impossible for me to get into the chicken house and steal those chickens."

The judge fined the man fifty dollars and put him in jail for thirty days. That's all he got for killing a beautiful dog who had been my constant companion from the day Ma and Pa brought me back to the farm to live with them. That's all he got for making Minnie so sad that she gave up on life.

For many years afterwards, when I sat on the pile of rocks near the oak tree, I felt like I was sitting next to the graves of my parents. God never put a more devoted couple on the planet earth. Buster and Minnie were devoted to each other. And they were completely devoted to me.

No boy ever had a better set of parents than Buster and Minnie.

FAMILY SECRETS

I

After the deaths of Buster and Minnie, Pa seemed to lose his spirit—and all of his interest in farming. He started going to Alberta nearly every day to play cards with his friends, leaving Ivar and me to do the chores.

Ma also went back to her old ways. Her company started coming by almost every day after Pa left for town. As for me, I became more withdrawn and lonely. Always before, I had Buster and Minnie to turn to whenever my spirits had completely bottomed out.

I spent some time talking to Reilly, the other horse that had teamed up with Tug to pull us safely through the blizzard. But for the most part, except for Ivar, I was on my own.

II

One day that summer a group of town boys pulled up to our house in a pick-up truck. They asked me if it would be okay if they used one of our groves to play a game they called "Capture the Flag." When I told them

I thought it would be fine with Pa, they asked me if I would like to join them. I thought it was very nice of them to ask, and I told them so. I was thrilled that some boys my own age had taken an interest in me as a friend. So I jumped into the back of the pick-up truck.

There were seven boys in all, counting the driver, who was somewhat older than the others. He drove the pick-up truck down the dirt road and parked not too far from the grove of trees where they planned to play the game.

Once we were in the grove of trees, the boys explained to me how the game worked. They said there would be four boys on each team, and each team would have a flag they would have to defend. The two flags, which were dirty rags the boys pulled out of the truck, would be tied to trees at opposite ends of the grove. The idea was to defend your own flag, while at the same time you tried to capture your opponent's flag. But if you were captured in your opponent's territory, you would be arrested and you would be out of the game. The winner would be the team that captured their opponent's flag, and returned it to their own territory before their flag could be captured.

I was assigned to one of the two teams, and we proceeded to move to opposite ends of the grove of trees. Then we slowly and stealthily crawled through the bushes and vegetation toward each other's flag. I tried to be the stealthiest player of all, and pretty soon I hid myself so well that I couldn't see any of the other players on my team. Eventually, I could see our opponent's flag tied to a tree approximately twenty feet away, and no one seemed to be guarding it. I moved quietly from bush to bush until I was only a few feet away from the tree. I quickly reached up, untied the flag, and disappeared back into the bushes to make my way back to our territory.

When I reached my team's territory, I raised the flag triumphantly in the air and yelled, "I've got it. I've captured their flag."

Much to my surprise, I wasn't greeted by the cheering voices of the other players on my team. Instead, I heard the sound of the pick-up truck's motor starting over by the dirt road. When I walked out of the grove of trees, I saw all of the town boys, including the members of my team, sitting in the back of the pick-up truck. They were laughing hysterically as they pointed at me and the dirty rag I was holding.

I immediately felt embarrassed and foolish. I realized the town boys had come out to the farm for only one reason. They weren't there to be my friends. They were there to play a practical joke on me—and I had played right into their hands. As I had crept silently through the bushes and trees, they had snuck back to the pick-up truck and waited for me to walk out of the grove waving the flag triumphantly. I guess they got a big chuckle out of their practical joke, for I could hear their laughter reverberate across the fields as they drove away.

But I learned a lesson that day that was probably different than the one they had been planning to teach me. I had enjoyed sneaking through the grove as I tried to capture my opponent's flag. I had enjoyed the anticipation of capturing that flag. It didn't matter one bit to me that the other players had snuck back to the truck. I just enjoyed playing the game—even if I was playing it by myself. I realized then that the thrill of the game was what you made it out to be in your own mind. Nothing else mattered. Not even if you were the only player left in the game.

So after the pick-up truck was gone, I walked back to the other end of the grove and tied the flag to the same tree. For the rest of the afternoon, I crept through the grove, capturing one flag after another, and having a jolly good time. I created imaginary opponents lurking behind every bush, and imaginary friends sneaking through the grove alongside of me.

I was grateful to the town boys for introducing me to the game. Without their invitation to join them that afternoon, I would never have known what a marvelous experience it can be just to go into a grove of trees for a few hours, and let your imagination run wild. I had gone into that grove with a good imagination, but I came out with a real world beater.

I also learned that when you're the last player in the game—and winning and losing are no longer important—you might just as well keep right on playing. And you might as well keep right on enjoying the game.

III

Next to playing cards, Pa's favorite pastime was fishing. At least once a week, he went fishing with his friends on Big Stone Lake or Big Pelican or any of the other sport fishing lakes within reasonable driving distance. I begged and pleaded with Pa to take me with him, but he always found some excuse why I could not go. So I was left behind with Ivar to do the chores and run the farm. Even when Ivar asked Pa if he could take me fishing with him, Pa refused to allow me to leave the farm. Pa told Ivar, "The boy has too many chores to do to go fishing."

I wasn't even a teenager yet, but I had already been doing a man's work for several years. Every day, Ivar and I would feed and milk the cows, herd the cattle out to the pasture to graze, haul wood in the winter, water the livestock, gather up the eggs in the chicken house, and do a variety of other chores. At night I would have to repeat most of those same chores all over again. Normally, I would start my chores as the sun was coming up, and sometimes I wouldn't be done until the sun was going down. So I was well on the way to becoming a champion hired man.

One day Pa planned an overnight fishing trip with some of his friends. I overheard them talking about all the walleye and northern pike that were biting on some lake up north. Those were the best game fish of all, and so once again I begged and pleaded with Pa to take me along. And once again, he found some excuse to leave me behind.

The day Pa went on his overnight fishing trip, I did my morning chores as usual. But I was a little bit angry with Pa, so I didn't do all of my afternoon chores. I only did the ones that couldn't be put off until the next morning. Then I walked over to Lake Hattie, which was within easy walking distance of our new farm.

If Pa wasn't going to take me with him to the northern lakes, I would just sit on the shores of Lake Hattie and imagine what it might be like to catch a walleye or northern pike. There were some game fish in Lake Hattie, but closer to shore on our end of the lake, it was filled primarily with bullheads. Those are just about the ugliest fish on the planet earth. Bullheads have slick smooth skin, like the texture of a lizard's skin, sharp spines sticking out of their backs, and small beady eyes. Not too many people fished for bullheads on Lake Hattie. Those who did generally fed them to the hogs.

As I approached Lake Hattie, the gypsies who had camped in Pa's field were gathered along the shoreline. Several of the men were teaching their children to fish with willow poles. The women were caring for the babies in the campsite. They recognized me from our earlier meeting, and they were very friendly.

The old man who had asked for permission to camp in Pa's field came over and greeted me. He must have seen me staring enviously at the men and children fishing along the shoreline, because he asked me if I would like to join them.

"You fish with us, okay?"

"I don't have a pole," I said.

"We fix," he smiled as he led me over to some willow trees.

He selected a straight, slender willow branch about fourteen feet long. He used a hatchet to cut it off the tree. He trimmed off the smaller twigs, and then he cut two feet off the thicker end of the branch. About two inches from the narrow end of the branch, he used a sharp knife to whittle a small groove into the bark. He attached some twine to the groove, made a bobber out of a small stick, and created a hook out of a thick piece of wire he cut at a sharp angle with a pliers. I was ready to fish.

I joined the gypsies down by the shoreline, and fished alongside of them until nightfall, using angle worms as bait. I don't know how many bullheads I caught. As I said, the lake was filled with them. The first one I brought in stung my hand pretty good with the spine on its back. But after a while, I learned how to take the bullheads off my hook without getting stung. I threw all of the fish I caught into two huge buckets the gypsies had placed there.

What a great time! I loved the excitement and anticipation of watching the homemade bobber twitch gently in the water, then suddenly plunge beneath the surface of the lake. It didn't matter one bit to me that I was catching bullheads—and not walleye or northern pike. I was hooked on fishing. I knew it was going to become one of my life's obsessions.

Later, as the gypsies hauled their catch over to the campsite, the old man approached me. "You join us for supper?" he asked. "We cook the fish we caught."

"I can't," I replied. "I have to get back to the farm."

"Then, you take some fish with you," the old man insisted. "They are yours."

I knew that Pa would probably be coming home with several stringers of fish from his trip up north, so I told the old man to keep the bullheads. I also knew that the gypsies would probably eat the bullheads, whereas Pa would just feed them to the hogs.

I held my willow fishing pole out to the old man as I was about to leave.

"No, you keep," he said. "My gift to you."

I thanked him and walked down the dirt road, carrying my willow pole. It was the first fishing pole I'd ever owned. It made me feel proud and important.

IV

It was dark by the time I got home, and I could hear the generator pumping away behind the house. When I walked into the yard, I saw the black car parked over by the fence. Normally, Ma's company was gone by this time, but then, of course, normally Pa wasn't one hundred miles away.

I knew Ma would be furious with me if I set foot in the house, so I went to the barn. Ivar was inside, rubbing oil into a leather harness in his tiny cubicle, which was illuminated by a single kerosene lantern. I could tell that Ivar knew there was something very wrong with the fact that the black car was parked in the yard whenever Pa was away. But Ivar never said anything about it.

As soon as Ivar saw me, he smiled broadly and pulled out his checker board. Ivar and I played checkers until almost midnight, while the sound of the generator pulsated in the darkness outside the barn. Finally, I stood up to leave. But when I walked outside, I could see that the black car was still parked in the yard.

I remembered well what had happened to me the last time I saw Ma's company in the bedroom window. Still, my curiosity got the better of me, especially since there was a dim light glowing in the living room window, and I could hear soft music intermingling with the crackling sound of static coming from our radio.

As quietly as I could, I snuck up to the house and peered into the living room window. A dimly lit kerosene lantern illuminated a table in the rear of the room, but the rest of the room was shrouded in shadows. Ma was dancing in slow circles with a mustached man who was wearing a black suit. I could not see very much of the man's face.

As they danced to the staticky music drifting out of the radio, it looked to me like Ma was wearing a cream-colored dress similar to the one she wore in the photograph taken the day she was married to Pa.

I had no idea what was going on in our living room. I wasn't too sure I wanted to know. But I was extremely tired, so I walked back to the barn and fell asleep on a pile of straw next to Ivar's cubicle.

In the morning, when I woke up, I was covered by two blankets. When I looked into Ivar's cubicle, I saw that he was asleep on his bunk bed. He did not have any blankets. He had given them both to me.

When I walked outside, the black car was still parked in the yard.

V

Ivar decided to take me with him when he went to Alberta that morning. He probably knew it was best that we both get away from the farm in case there was some kind of blow-up between Ma and Pa when Pa returned from his fishing trip.

It was a very uneventful trip to Alberta. Ivar and I rode to town in silence, as we always did. But for some reason, Ivar took a different route. I think he was just trying to kill some time. He was obviously in no hurry to get back to the farm.

After a time, we stopped and waited for several minutes by a train crossing. I had seen trains before, of course. But I had never seen one carrying the cargo this one carried.

Unshaven, thin, poorly dressed men were sitting on top of the cars or dangling their legs out the open doorways. Their faces showed no emotion. They were listless and bleary-eyed, gazing vacantly at the countryside as the train rumbled past.

Even in the depths of our poverty, Ma, Pa, and I never looked as defeated as the men who were passing in front of me. They were a breed apart. I realized these men had been cast out to wander across the country, looking for odd jobs, any jobs. As I watched the train disappear in the distance, I knew I had just seen a glimpse of the future.

VI

One day Delores's parents sent her over to stay with us for the night. They were going someplace, and for some reason they didn't want to take Delores with them or leave her home alone.

There was no place downstairs for Delores to sleep, but there was an extra cot upstairs on the opposite side of the room where I slept. Ma decided to have Delores sleep on that cot rather than set up a bed on the floor downstairs.

In the middle of the night, I was awakened by Delores's voice. "Lloyd," she said as she pressed her fingers against my shoulder, "do you have any extra blankets up here. It's kind of cold."

I told Delores that we didn't have any extra blankets, but she was welcome to take one of mine. She didn't answer me. I heard soft footsteps padding across the floor, and the next thing I knew Delores was dumping her blankets on my bed. She crawled under the covers and cuddled close to me to warm herself up.

Delores and I had slept together several times when we were kids. But Ma decided that wasn't proper as we got older. Still, it was all pretty innocent on Delores's part. She just wanted to sleep in a warm bed— that's all.

As she cuddled up, she threw her arm around me, and we started whispering back and forth in the darkness. I have to confess it felt real good to have someone hold me like that. I had never been held like that in all my life.

"Lloyd," Delores whispered, "I've been meaning to tell you something."

"What's that?" I asked.

"Remember, years ago, when you asked me to try to find out whatever I could about your natural mother?"

"Yes, I remember," I said.

"Not too long ago," Delores said, "I overheard your Ma say, 'He was born not too far from here.'"

"What did she mean by that?" I asked.

"I don't know."

For another hour or so we whispered back and forth in the darkness. I told Delores how very much I wanted someday to find my birth mother. She told me she was not at all interested in such things. She was happy in her adoptive home. Eventually, we fell asleep together, and we did not wake up until morning. I went downstairs while Delores got dressed.

VII

Nothing unusual happened for the rest of the day. Then, toward evening, Ma and Pa told me to get ready because we were going over to visit a neighbor. When I asked who we were going to visit, they did not answer my question.

The wagon and team of horses headed out with Ma and Pa in the driver's seat, and me sitting in the rear. I wasn't paying much attention to where we were going. I kept thinking about what Delores had said the previous evening about me being born not too far from here. I knew that little bit of information about my birth mother was probably going to drive me crazy. From that point on, I knew I would probably look at every middle-aged woman in the county and wonder if maybe she was my birth mother.

I began to speculate that maybe I had already met her and didn't even know it. Maybe I had been around her many times before, but she had been too embarrassed about my being illegitimate to say anything. Or maybe she didn't want me to know who she was. All kinds of possibilities kept running through my head.

Pa pulled up to a two-story farmhouse. It was a beautiful farm, probably the nicest one I had ever seen. Green grass surrounded the house. The barn and other buildings looked as though they had been recently painted.

"Who lives here?" I asked.

But Ma and Pa remained silent as we walked up to the front door.

A small, fragile, somewhat unfriendly middle-aged woman came to the door and escorted us into a kitchen. Four chairs had been set up along one wall of the kitchen. A single wooden chair had been placed in the middle of the room. I was told to sit in that chair.

A tall mustached man walked into the kitchen and over to the area where Ma, Pa, and the other woman were already sitting. He, too, sat down. As he looked at me, I knew immediately that he was the same man that I had seen several years earlier standing in Ma's bedroom window. He was also the man I had seen dancing with Ma in the living room when Pa was on his overnight fishing trip. He was Ma's company.

But what were we all doing in his house? And why was the other woman, who I assumed was his wife, here with us? It made no sense to me. I was completely baffled.

"Lloyd," Ma said slowly and calmly, "we know that you slept in the same bed with Delores last night."

"How did you know that?" I sputtered. I knew immediately that I had been lured into some kind of an informal trial. But why in God's name was Ma's company a part of it?

"Never mind how we know," Ma replied sternly. "We've asked two of our friends to help us decide whether or not you should be sent to a *reformatory.*"

The word sent a cold shiver down my back. For the rest of my trial, I was forced to listen to Ma give an exaggerated account of everything she thought Delores and I had done the previous night. I was described as a child of the devil who did not know the difference between right and wrong. Ma also said I was dangerous to girls and should never be left alone with them.

I was not allowed to say a single word in my own defense. When I tried to explain that Delores was cold, and there were not enough blankets upstairs, Ma cut me off. I do not remember the mustached man saying anything during my trial. He just stared in my direction. His eyes betrayed no emotion.

I took all I could take of Ma's relentless accusations. Without even knowing what I was doing, I bolted out of the room and ran outside. I hid behind a shed for a few minutes before I decided to walk home.

I had never been down that road before. But I was vaguely aware of how we had gotten out to the farmhouse. So I set off in the general direction of our farm. Somewhere along the way, I heard the clopping of horses' hoofs behind me. I jumped into some brush and hid. Ma and Pa drove by in our wagon.

After they were gone, I continued down the road, watching the moonlight playing across the ground. I tried to figure out what had happened that evening. When I arrived back at the farm, I did not go inside the house. I walked over to the pasture, sat on a fence rail, and talked to Reilly.

The events of that evening made no sense whatsoever. Why would two families, one unknown to me, conduct such a trial? If any other family was to be involved, why not Delores's family? If I was guilty of some terrible crime, then Delores was equally guilty. But Delores wasn't on trial. Were those people trying to protect her? She probably didn't even know what was happening to me that night, or what a terrible price I was paying for the sin of keeping warm.

The only explanation seemed to be that Ma and Pa, for whatever reason, did not want Delores and her family involved in my trial and punishment. But why? Why involve the man Ma had been seeing on the sly? If a decision was to be made regarding whether or not I should be sent to reform school, he was the least likely candidate to exercise good judgment.

My imagination started to run a little wild. Was it possible that these two families held some deep secret that they did not want to share with anyone else? But what was that secret, and how was I involved? Was my birth mother also somehow involved?

As I ran my hand through Reilly's thick mane, I pledged to find my birth mother and ask her about my past. Nothing was going to stop me!

VIII

The next morning, Ma and Pa were unusually quiet. They offered no explanation for what had happened the previous evening. They dressed for church the way they did on any other Sunday morning, and we hitched up the team of horses and drove the wagon over to the Reque Church.

Reverend Reece was no longer our pastor. The word got around that he had made a fool of himself in front of the school board. Eventually, he lost the support of his congregation for his heavy-handed ways, and the church council sent him packing. I never talked to Marcus again. I felt bad about that because I wanted to thank him for standing up for me at the school board hearing. But I never got the chance.

Every Sunday, the members of our farm community continued to gather in the Reque Church for services with our new pastor. A few of them gathered there to praise the Lord. Some gathered there to atone for just about everything they'd done the previous week. Most gathered there to impress their neighbors.

The church was located about three-quarters of a mile from the cemetery. No one ever told me why the early pioneers kept the church and the cemetery separate. I just kind of surmised that they had the good sense to keep the living separated from the dead, perhaps so the Almighty would not allow the on-going weekly activities of the former to prejudice him against the spiritual destinies of the latter.

Ma, Pa, and I made it to most of those Sunday services. I would dress up in my one pair of wool dress pants, which had worked their way through several generations of neighbor boys before Pa picked them up at some rummage sale. The wool was very coarse, about the texture of burlap, and it itched something terrible. As a result, Sunday church services were for me one long scratching session.

Seemingly everyone was in church the Sunday morning after my trial. The farmer who stole hay from his neighbors—he was there. Some of the boys who lured me into the game of capture the flag—they were there. Some of Pa's card-playing friends—they were there. Farmers who abused and underpaid their hired help—they were there. Just about everyone who had done something outrageous to their neighbors during the week was there.

About the only person I never saw in church was Ivar. And, of course, the gypsies. They weren't there, either. I guess they weren't good Christians.

IX

A few weeks later, Pa and I found Reilly struggling to get to his feet out in the pasture behind the barn. Reilly was panting. His massive chest heaved. Saliva ran out of his mouth and puddled on the ground.

Pa took one look at Reilly and said, "Go get my rifle. He either ate some poisoned grain, or else his huge heart is giving out."

I ran to the house, grabbed Pa's .22, and headed back out to the pasture. By the time I got there, Reilly's chest was no longer heaving up and down. He was lying on his side.

"Take the rifle back to the house," Pa said softly, "and bring me my spade."

For the rest of the afternoon, Pa dug a hole. When the hole was deep enough, Pa managed somehow to roll Reilly's massive body into it. Then he filled the hole with dirt and walked back to the barn.

As I stood alone in the pasture next to Reilly's grave, I realized I had just lost the last of the animals that connected me to my childhood. After the deaths of Tug, Buster, and Minnie, I thought I had become hardened to the awful reality of death. But I hadn't. Once again, I found myself thinking about the old oak tree with the split trunk. The prairie wind that sang so sweetly at that spot had become my only consolation in a life grown increasingly lonely.

Ivar, King of the Hired Men

I

By the early 1930s, the Great Depression had tightened its grip on Minnesota. Many farmers had gone under. Others would soon go under. In certain parts of Stevens County, there seemed to be more abandoned farms than functioning ones.

Before abandoning his property, one farmer staked a wooden sign in a weed-covered field. In huge red letters, the farmer had written, "Hoover's Legacy: no chickens, no pots, no car, and no backyard."

Without Ivar, Pa would have been one of the first farmers to fail. Ivar's hard work enabled Pa to make a profit on his farm—in spite of the fact that he was gone most of the time. Ivar also taught me how to shoot a rifle, stalk ducks in a slough, hunt pheasants, and snare gophers for the bounties. Since the county was overrun with gophers, and they were a menace to the crops and livestock, the county authorities paid a bounty of three cents for each striped gopher, and five cents for each pocket gopher.

Ivar showed me how to make a snare to put around the gopher hole. Then I laid out about fifteen feet of line, stretched out on my belly, and waited for the gopher to stick its head out of the hole. When the gopher stuck its head out, I pulled hard and fast on the line. Presto, I had another gopher, another bounty. Some people drowned them out with buckets of water poured directly into the hole, but I preferred the snare. I didn't like the idea of drowning any animal, even destructive pests like the gophers.

I was a very successful gopher hunter. The first year I trapped gophers, I snared about two hundred of the little pests and earned about seven dollars. I hid it in a jar in the barn. It was the first time in my life I had any money. Ma and Pa provided me with room and board, but they gave me very little in the way of spending money. So with my seven dollars, I felt like the richest king on the face of the earth.

Ivar never tired of teaching me the skills I would need to survive as a hired man. Without those skills, I probably would have ended up on the streets, unemployed. With them, I have always managed to survive.

I am also convinced America would never have survived the Great Depression without laborers like Ivar. What Ivar did to rebuild everything on our farm, America's workers did to rebuild the nation. The politicians didn't get us through the Depression. America's workers did. Their hard work and indomitable spirits not only mended the nation's broken economy. They mended its broken spirit.

But Ivar became much more to me than Pa's hired man. Other people broke things. Ivar repaired them. Other people destroyed human lives. Ivar helped put those lives back together again. Other people thought they were superior to Ivar. Ivar was superior to all of them. Yet, he was the most unpretentious person I ever met.

There was only one King of the Hired Men—and that was Ivar.

II

I often begged Pa to take me fishing with him. I wanted to go out in a boat. He started slipping out of the house earlier and earlier, so I wouldn't be there to badger him. I did keep the willow pole the old gypsy had made for me, and I frequently fished Lake Hattie. But I desperately wanted to fish from a boat.

One Sunday, there was a big community picnic over by Big Stone Lake. I thought for sure that this would be an opportunity for me to go out fishing in a boat. I didn't see how Pa could turn me down in front of all of the neighbors. I was so excited that I tested my willow pole and stored it safely in the wagon. In the morning, I jumped out of bed and rushed downstairs. I don't think I have ever anticipated anything quite so much in my entire life.

When we arrived at Big Stone Lake, all of the boys started to get into the rented boats with their fathers. But as I started to get into one of the boats with Pa, he grabbed my arm and set me back on the dock.

"The water's too rough," he said as he sat down in the boat. "You stay with your Ma."

"The waves aren't even a foot high," I pointed out tearfully.

"The water's too rough," Pa insisted.

He obviously did not want to be bothered by a young boy who might occasionally need his help or advice. His comment that the water was "too rough" was just another excuse. He wanted to fish alone.

I was crushed. Every boy went out in the boats, except me. I sat on the shore by myself for the rest of the day and watched the boats out on the lake. Every time I heard one of the men or boys in the boat yell, "I've got one," I stood up and tried to see what kind of fish they were catching. But they were too far away.

III

Archie Flanagan and his brother brought over a horse they couldn't break. They asked Pa if he would help. Pa had a reputation as a pretty tough fellow with animals as well as people. If anyone could break that horse, the Flanagans knew it would be Pa.

Pa and the brothers took turns trying to ride the horse. It bucked each one off repeatedly. While they were taking a short breather, I asked Pa if I could take a shot at it.

"Break a horse?" Pa scoffed. "You? He'll throw you in two seconds."

"Ah, let him try it," Archie Flanagan said. "It'll be a good lesson for him."

"Okay," Pa said with a shrug. "Why not?"

What Pa didn't know was that during the times he and Ma were away from the farm, I would ride the cows and some of the calves, too. They gave me many a wild bareback ride across the pasture. I didn't think this horse would be any tougher to ride.

Archie's brother put a blindfold over the horse's eyes. I climbed on and grabbed ahold of the rope attached to the horse's muzzle. When I was ready, off came the blindfold, and that horse went wild.

It reared up on its hind legs. When that didn't throw me, it made a mad dash for the granary. It threw its full weight against the granary, trying to brush me off. I pulled my leg up just in time. The horse raced over to the barn and tried the same maneuver against the barn door. But, again, I pulled my leg up before it was crushed against the wood slats.

The horse careened from building to building, but nothing it did could shake me off its back. In the center of the yard, it bucked and jumped. Still, I held on.

Suddenly, the horse stopped bucking and began prancing gently around the farmyard. The horse was broken—and I was the one who broke it!

I was pretty proud of myself. Pa and the Flanagan brothers couldn't quite believe what they had just seen. I dismounted, acting as though breaking horses was something I did every day. Then I looked into the horse's eyes. They were the saddest eyes I had ever seen.

"What're you gonna use that horse for?" Pa asked as the brothers prepared to leave.

"I need a good work horse," Archie replied. "I think he'll be one of the best."

As the two men led the horse away, Pa walked into the barn. I was left standing by myself. I had been awfully proud of my accomplishment, but I was starting to have second thoughts about what I had done. Maybe that horse wasn't meant to be broken. Maybe that horse wasn't meant to pull a plow or wagon. Maybe it was meant to be a free spirit—not just another beast of burden.

The more I thought about what I had done to break that horse's spirit, the more ashamed I became. Wasn't that exactly what Ma and Pa had tried to do to me? Weren't they trying to break my spirit so I would meekly accept my role as their unpaid laborer—someone who didn't need love, encouragement, and understanding?

I just knew, if I had to do it all over again, I would have let that horse throw me.

IV

Pa heard Ma badmouthing him in front of our neighbors. He slapped her in front of everyone. Ma immediately packed up her things and moved over to Delores's house. With Ma gone, Ivar took over as our temporary cook. He turned out to be a very good one, which kind of surprised me. But then nothing Ivar did should ever have surprised me. He was the King of the Hired Men. Now, it seemed, he was equally adept at work requiring a woman's skills.

With Ma gone, and Pa playing cards in Alberta, I had the house completely to myself. This was even better than the time Ma and Pa stayed in Graceville, when she had her gallstones taken out. Then, I had to contend with the elderly grandmother who was looking after me. Now, except for Ivar who stayed in the barn or worked outside unless he was cooking, I had the run of the house. Ma's departure created the ideal time for me to search every nook and cranny for any records concerning my birth and adoption.

Ever since Delores had shared with me what she knew, I found myself looking closely at every middle-aged woman. When Ivar and I went to the Alberta creamery, I would look at all the windows on Main Street and wonder if, maybe, my mother was behind one of them. I just about drove myself crazy speculating about the phrase, "He was born not too far from here."

I searched every room in the house. I started with the living room and the kitchen. Finding nothing of significance, I tried the bedroom. It still seemed like the most logical place to hide important family papers. I found Ma and Pa's wedding photograph again. Ma looked like she was trying to force a meek smile, but her eyes were sad. There was also something strangely familiar about her eyes, something I had seen before. But I could not quite put my finger on it.

From what I could surmise from postcards and letters I found in the bedroom closet, Ma and Pa must have broken up a couple of times before. I guessed that Ma had gone off to live with a friend in Montana for a time, and, from there, to live with another friend in Minneapolis. Eventually, she came back to Pa, but I do not know precisely when or why. I was only able to gather bits and pieces of information from the items I found in the bedroom. I was not able to put the whole story together.

The only certainties were that Ma and Pa had spent time apart during the early years of their marriage. Also, from what I could gather, it was always Ma who left Pa—not the other way around.

Having found nothing in the house relating to my adoption, I remembered that someone had once told me people from Ma and Pa's generation liked to hide important documents behind the matting of framed photographs. So I proceeded to dismantle every photograph in the house.

I had just about given up my search, when a piece of writing paper slipped out from behind the matting of one of the framed photographs that had been hanging on the wall ever since I could remember. The paper looked like it had been used to provide a little more thickness to the matting, a tighter fit between the glass and the photograph.

The piece of paper, which apparently had once been attached to some other document or item, had the three words, "For Baby Edward," written on it in beautiful, carefully scripted handwriting. I briefly studied the writing, then put the piece of paper back behind the frame. I reassembled all of the framed photographs I had dismantled.

Once again, my search had produced nothing regarding my birth records. If Ma and Pa still had those records, they had hidden them well.

V

Ma moved back in with Pa one month to the day after he had slapped her. Life went pretty much back to normal, although Pa stayed home more often. I think he was trying to figure out some way to live with Ma without the two of them fighting and arguing all the time. Still, I don't think they ever made up after that. They hardly spoke to one another. They seemed to exist in two separate worlds. They were certainly candidates for a divorce. But not too many people got divorced in those days. Divorce was considered almost as bad as giving birth to an illegitimate child. Besides, neither of them had anywhere else to go, except, perhaps, to join the migrant labor force that was moving across the prairie states looking for food and work. So Ma and Pa remained married to one another—in spite of their insurmountable differences.

Every day, after my morning chores, I would generally go out to the fields to spend an hour or two snaring gophers. My little treasure chest of coins was growing larger with each new gopher tail I turned in to the county authorities. While lying on the ground, holding my snare, I thought a lot about the three handwritten words I had found on the piece of paper behind the picture frame. Whoever had framed the photograph, which was a fairly typical picture of a setting sun descending into a wheat field, had used the piece of paper to add a little more thickness to the matting—nothing more. The piece of paper was probably lying around at the time the picture was framed. If another discarded piece of paper had been lying around, it probably would have been used instead.

I didn't even know whether Ma or Pa had framed the picture. It might have been framed several decades earlier. The timing was important. I had never heard either Ma or Pa refer to anyone by the name of "Edward." Sure, it's a fairly common name, but there were no Edwards in the Clausen family—at least not that I knew of.

VI

Midsummer, while I was lying on the ground next to a gopher mound, I became aware that dark clouds were building in the southwest. The air that day had been deathly still, hot, and humid. The temperature had exceeded one hundred degrees.

I sat up as strong winds started to blow off the prairie. Soon thunder crashed and boomed in the distance, and brilliant lightning ripped seams across the horizon.

I gathered up my gopher snare and headed back to the farm. Ma and Pa were in the yard, looking apprehensively at the dark clouds. Ivar had gone to town earlier. He was not back yet.

"What is it?" I asked.

"I don't know," Pa said, not taking his eyes off the clouds.

Strong, cold winds whirled the dirt around the yard. An even stronger, angrier wind moved toward us from the southwest. Then we saw it: a dark, twisting funnel cloud snaking across the fields and heading straight for the farm.

"Get into the basement!" Pa yelled.

As we hurried to the cellar door, the fierce winds tore branches from the trees and hurled them across the yard. Gravel, kicked up by the winds, pelted us and stung our exposed skin. Ahead, the cellar door was flapping, banging open and shut with every burst of wind.

Pa pushed Ma and me into the cellar. He struggled to close the door. But the winds wrenched the door out of his hands and tore it away from its metal hinges. The heavy door, similar to the one that had kept me imprisoned so many times on our old farm, flew out into the yard like a flimsy piece of cardboard. Pa fled into the safety of the cellar. We huddled together in the southwest corner, hoping and praying that the mortared stone walls would protect us.

We could hear the sounds of the tornado splintering lumber, breaking windowpanes, and wrenching metal from concrete foundations. Above our heads, the house lifted off its stone foundation, hovered there for a few seconds, and settled back down. We heard an enormous explosion, and we knew that one of the buildings on the property had just been smashed by the fierce winds.

We cowered together as the rains pounded down on the farmhouse.

VII

Mother Nature did a pretty good job of rearranging our farm that day. The barn no longer had a roof. The tornado had lifted it, broken it into two sections, and deposited it a few feet away from the house. The barn walls were reduced to a twisted pile of lumber, except for the section that housed the cows and calves. That part was relatively undamaged. The livestock stood in the middle of the twisted wreckage, munching on hay and straw, neither comprehending nor caring very much about what had just happened.

Except for a handful of chickens that were still seated on their nests, most of the others, and the chicken house itself, had vanished. We never found any sign of them. The granary, which was located twenty feet away from the chicken house, was untouched by the tornado. Ma's wash tubs, with the wringers and scrub boards intact, turned up in the front yard of the church a half-mile away, ready for the next load of wash. The house was in fairly good shape, although it had been moved four inches off its foundation. The horses were okay, but the forty-foot straw pile was gone, sucked up into the black funnel cloud. In the yard, a single piece of straw had been driven through a six-inch-thick wooden fence post.

When all is said and done, I suppose there's a lesson in everything we experience, even tornadoes. I don't suppose the missing chickens

Above. Lloyd and Pa with the horses.

Right. Lloyd, wearing his "mailman's cap," sitting on Tug.

"Pa was not a good farmer and everyone knew it. He stuck with horses when everyone else was switching to tractors. He seldom got around to planting crops on all of his acreage. He never timed the harvest the way he should have. He was a good worker, but he would rather play cards than work. It was inevitable that he would fail as a farmer—but only after years of futile struggle." (page 31)

Top. Lloyd, Jessen Cudrio, and Buster. "Minnie liked me, but Buster loved me. He and I became inseparable." (page 12)

Bottom. From left to right, Chris, Lillie, and Jessen Cudrio, with Delores. "Pa's sister and her husband, who farmed a few miles northeast of us, had adopted Delores. But from everything I could tell, they treated her as a member of the family." (page 19)

Top. Lloyd and Delores at opposite ends of the front row.

Bottom. A more typical grouping, with Lloyd and Delores together in the middle of the front row.

"We two adopted children were kindred spirits, and we stood up for each other in all kinds of ways." (page 19)

"Threshing season was a festive time. Farmers, their wives, and the migrant threshing crews worked together until all the crops in the area were harvested and sold, or safely stored away for the winter. They would finish one farmer's crops and move the steam engine and thresher to another farmer's fields." (page 51)

"Jack Schultz carried just about all of the farmers in the area for several months.... Rather than squirrel [his money] away someplace, or use it just for his own family, he had used it to keep his store stocked with food for the area farmers." (page 133)

Courtesy of Stevens County Historical Society Collections, Morris, Minnesota.

"Pa made it very clear to Ma that he regarded their relationship as primarily a marriage of convenience. He needed someone to cook, clean, and care for his house. So in a way, Ma, as Pa's wife, and I, as Pa's hired man, merely provided services for him." (page 233)

"Dr. Cumming pronounced me cured. Pa handed him two jars of preserves as payment for his services. And then Dr. Cumming was out the door and down the road to attend to the other children in the county who were sick or dying from whooping cough." (page 52)

Courtesy of Stevens County Historical Society Collections, Morris, Minnesota.

"Sometime in the late 1920s or early 1930s, we moved to a new farm which was located three miles south and almost three miles west of Alberta." (page 72)

Pa (far left), Lloyd (center, with bandanna), and some of the hired men. "Under Ivar's watchful eye, I had served my apprenticeship as a hired man. Now I had achieved journeyman status." (page 150)

Top. Lloyd (far left) and fellow soldiers at Camp Haan in Riverside, California.

Bottom. Lloyd in full uniform.

"We were teenagers who had been released from our Midwestern schools and farms. We gave little serious thought to the war. We were much more concerned about news from back home, which we shared with everyone who would listen.... We were just pretending to be soldiers. None of us had any idea what it meant to be a real one. In spite of the long hours we spent training to become anti-aircraft gunners, fighting in a war was the farthest thing from our minds." (page 212)

Top. Lloyd and Arlene Clausen in their 1942 wedding photograph. "I married your mother on the rebound. Your mother deserved better." (page 234)

Bottom left. Delores Cudrio. "Ever since we were kids, growing up together as adopted children on the Minnesota prairie, that love was always there. It was and always will be a deeper love than most married people share." (page 235)

Bottom right. "I searched through all the dresser drawers to see if I could find my adoption papers or anything else that might yield some information about my birth mother. I found a number of old photographs, including one of Ma and Pa on the day they were married." (page 65)

would agree with me on this, but maybe tornadoes just tell us—in a pretty loud voice, I might add—that when we're in trouble, the best thing we can do is find a safe spot, huddle together, and hope for the best.

VIII

Since Pa was renting our farm from an insurance company, which owned the property through an earlier foreclosure, he wasn't responsible for repairing the buildings. He was, however, responsible for the lost livestock and damaged farm equipment.

The tornado set in motion a series of decisions that drove Ma and Pa deeper into debt and despair. After sinking several thousand dollars into repairs, the insurance company expected its investment to show a greater profit. Up until that point, the owners had never put much pressure on Pa to turn a large profit. They seemed satisfied that he was willing to farm a property that would otherwise be vacant and unproductive.

They now expected to recoup their investment. So Pa was under pressure to make the farm much more productive. Unfortunately, he was not the kind of farmer who could labor effectively under any pressure. He worked to put food on the table. After that, his mind turned to leisure: fishing and playing cards.

The tornado also forced Pa to take out a loan from a local bank to replace the destroyed farm equipment. With the loan payments hanging over his head, he had to either produce as a farmer or face foreclosure. The middle of the Great Depression, with prices for grain crops and other farm commodities at an all-time low, was no time to be saddled with additional debt. Still, Pa had no choice. It was either take out the loan, which would be secured by everything we owned, or join the thousands of unemployed men and women crossing the prairie, looking for work and food.

Pa took out the loan.

IX

The insurance company sent out a team of carpenters to repair our buildings. Ivar worked alongside of them. While they were putting a new roof on the barn, I thought maybe they would like some apples. I picked a bucketful from a tree behind our house and climbed the huge extension ladder up to the carpenters. I had no sooner started across the roof, when my foot slipped on a loose shingle, and I slid. Apples bounced from my bucket as I tumbled to the lowest section of the barn roof.

Somehow, I managed to catch hold of some shingles. While I hung on to those shingles for dear life, I heard one of the carpenters yell something. I could tell he was trying to reach me. But the pitch of the roof was too steep. There was nothing he could do short of falling to the ground with me.

Then I heard a loud scraping sound. Ivar appeared, standing still and strong on the extension ladder. He was a fairly old man. I have no idea how he did it. But somehow he had picked up the ladder, which had required two carpenters to lift earlier, and carried it to the side of the barn where I was clinging to the shingles.

Ivar grasped me with one hand, while he held onto the ladder with the other. He guided me to the ladder. He placed his body over mine so I couldn't possibly fall. Then he escorted me down the ladder, my entire body shaking with fear on every step.

Once I was safely on the ground, Ivar walked away as though nothing had happened. To any onlooker, it appeared as though Ivar had just brought a paint can down from the roof. He never paused for one moment to accept praise for saving my life.

X

Although Ivar taught me how to shoot a shotgun and a rifle, he didn't hunt much himself. He understood that duck and pheasant populations had to be thinned each year, or else all would perish from the lack of food. But Ivar preferred hiking the sloughs, studying the birds, animals, and wild vegetation.

On one of his trips out to the sloughs, he found two baby ducklings whose mother had either abandoned them or been killed by a predator or a poacher hunting out of season. In either case, the ducklings were clearly starving and helpless. Ivar brought them back to the farm and raised them.

He built a pen out of old wire and boards that were lying around the farm. He even gave the ducklings names: Gus and Charlie. When they got a little older, Gus and Charlie waddled after Ivar as he did his chores. He fed them handfuls of corn from a pouch he had strapped to his waist. Sometimes, he would flip individual kernels over his shoulder. Gus and Charlie became very adept at catching the corn.

Even though Ivar treated the two ducks as if they were members of his family, he always planned to release them back into the sloughs— after the hunting season was over and they were fully grown. However, Ivar never got the chance to follow through on his plans. One day, when he returned from Alberta with food and supplies, he found the wire cage had been blown apart by a shotgun blast fired at point-blank range.

Gus and Charlie were gone. All that was left were blood-stained feathers at the bottom of the cage. Some hunters had apparently wandered into the farmyard and, having seen two ducks in the pen, had decided to add Gus and Charlie to their game pouches.

Ivar was more angry than I had ever seen him before. He climbed back into the horse-drawn wagon and drove toward the nearby sloughs in pursuit of those hunters. A few hours later, he found Gus and Charlie's blood-stained bodies lying in the back of a pick-up truck. Ivar confronted two men who were sitting in a duck blind near the water's edge. Convinced that they had killed Gus and Charlie, Ivar tore the shotguns out of their hands and threw both weapons into the water. The two hunters made no attempt to stop him. He made them understand that after what they had done to Gus and Charlie, they were lucky he didn't turn their weapons on them.

Afterwards, I stood solemnly in the distance as Ivar gave Gus and Charlie a decent burial in the field behind our barn.

XI

Ivar left us that fall, after the barn was rebuilt, and I never saw him again. I don't know where he went. But, then, I never knew where he had come from, either. He didn't even say good-bye. One day, I walked into his tiny cubicle in the back of the barn, and all of his things were gone. Left behind was a freshly painted, reconditioned metal fishing pole, reel and all. Ivar must have picked it up at some farm auction, taken it apart, and put it back together. At the tip of the pole, he had attached a small piece of paper with "Lloyd" printed in crude letters. I knew then that the fishing pole was Ivar's final parting gift to me. He was saying good-bye in the only way he knew how—with something he had made new again with his hands.

Pa's hired man left a lasting impression on me. He taught me how to hunt, snare gophers, and repair just about every piece of farm equipment on the property. He also taught me the value of hard work and how to live without hurting the world too much. I can't say, however, that I have always lived up to his example. Ivar was the most unpretentious soul I ever met. He was unassuming, kind, and generous in ways you don't see in very many human beings.

I admired Ivar. But I also knew I did not want to live the life of a hired man. Ivar was completely alone in the world. He had no past and no future. He had no dreams and no goals. He was disconnected from the rest of the human race. He accepted what came his way and did his best with it. He wandered from county to county, and from state to state, completely alone. His was the life of a hired man, the life Ma and Pa had chosen for me at the time of my adoption. But I wanted more than that. I wanted the very things that Ivar didn't seem to need or want. I wanted to *belong* somewhere.

I missed Ivar terribly and always wondered what happened to him after he left us. How much longer did he live? How many more families did he join before he died? Did anyone attend his funeral? Was he buried in some quiet country cemetery or in a big city plot surrounded by a sea of strangers? Was there a last name on his gravestone, or was the single word *Ivar* engraved there?

Whatever was carved on his gravestone, I know that I would have added: IVAR, KING OF THE HIRED MEN.

WE ALMOST STARVE TO DEATH

I

During the early years of the Great Depression, Minnesota farmers lost all faith in anything that was associated with the government. They also lost all faith in the banks. Farmers who had any money left—and there weren't too many of those—stashed it in cream cans and buried it in their yards. To the farmers, all institutions—the government, banks, insurance companies, big businesses—were owned by the rich and greedy.

But when we heard the voice of Franklin Delano Roosevelt over the radio, and he told us that all we had to fear was fear itself, we believed in him. When he became President, Roosevelt restored the farmers' faith in government; to many out on the prairie, FDR was God. There were a few more years of tough times and economic depression, even under his administration, before farmers saw any significant improvements in their lives. But our faith had been restored.

II

When the insurance company started making demands, Pa stopped going to town to play cards. He became a more responsible farmer. As a result, I saw less of the black car in our yard. Ma and Pa seemed— once again—to have arrived at a truce. They were always able to pull together in the aftermath of a crisis or life-threatening experience. During good times, they often could not tolerate one another.

When I wasn't working, I continued to explore the nooks and crannies of our new farm. I knew all of the pheasants' favorite hiding places, and I liked to sneak up on them. Five or six rooster pheasants can make quite a commotion when they explode from the thick prairie grass and underbrush. I tired of that game, however, after I startled a hen pheasant with a brood of little chicks. I felt terrible when I saw the little chicks, who had not yet learned how to fly, scurry off in different directions across the prairie, while their mother soared into the sky. I never again tried to startle another pheasant, except during hunting season when the roosters had to be thinned out to keep the entire pheasant population from starving to death. There just wasn't enough food to keep all of them alive during the winter season.

III

During one of my explorations, I encountered Delores near the Reque Church. I had not talked to her since her overnight stay at our house. She had matured considerably since our last meeting. The night she slept upstairs with me, she still had a childlike, girlish innocence about her. But during the months since I last saw her, she had matured into an attractive young teenager. I'm sure she still saw me as a gawky adolescent, which I was.

We talked for only a few minutes because she was late for some church function. It was obvious she knew nothing about the trouble she had caused me. She also knew nothing about Ma's accusations. Clearly, Ma had not said anything to Delores or to her parents.

The fact that Delores had not been reprimanded confirmed my suspicions. The purpose of the interrogation seemed to be to frighten me into a state of blind obedience. Never again should I aspire to be anything more than a farm hand. I believe Ma and Pa wanted to humble and shame me so I would never rebel against my appointed destiny. The purpose of the trial was also to put some kind of a wall between Delores and me, without Delores knowing there was a wall there.

After Delores left and I was again alone, I remembered something that had bothered me during my search through Ma and Pa's bedroom when I was looking for records of my birth and adoption. What had bothered me was Ma and Pa's wedding photograph. Not only were Ma's eyes sad in that photograph, but they had reminded me of someone else's eyes. Now I knew who that person was. In Ma's eyes, I saw Delores.

IV

Whatever I might have imagined at the time, I soon realized it would be months, perhaps years, before I could even began to investigate my suspicions. Shortly after I talked to Delores, we had another crisis in our home. After my chores one day, Pa was sitting by the kitchen table with his face buried in his hands. Ma stood nearby, her arms folded, her face somber. Pa looked the very portrait of human failure. Ma studied him with a look of concern, but with her characteristic detachment.

"What happened?" I asked.

Pa rubbed his hands across his forehead. "We have to move," he said.

"Why?"

"The owners have broken the rental agreement," Pa explained. "They've found someone else to farm this place."

"Can they do that?"

"It's their farm. They can do what they want with it."

"Where will we go?" I asked. "It's almost winter."

"I'll start looking for a new place," Pa replied. "We have a few weeks before the first snows."

With that brief conversation, Ma, Pa, and I were to begin a new odyssey into the very depths of human poverty and despair. We did not join the nation's homeless labor force. But in time we came to understand the utter despair of those people who have nothing in their lives except the clothes on their backs.

V

Pa did not have as much time as he thought to find us a new place. The nights were already terribly cold. The first winter snow was only a few short weeks away. Fortunately, there were many abandoned farms in Stevens County, so Pa was able to enter into another rental agreement with one of the banks that had foreclosed on the property.

The new farm was located one mile east and two miles south of Alberta. I was still within walking distance of Lake Hattie. We were also within walking distance of Alberta.

The farm Pa rented was 360 acres in size, although a huge slough covered about forty of those acres. Even on the acreage that could be farmed, the topsoil was thin and rocky. Not very good farm land. Any strong breeze would send the topsoil drifting across the prairie.

The day we were to move, some of the neighbors brought over their wagons, and we loaded everything up. It took three or four trips, but finally everything we owned was hauled over to the new farm. Only it could hardly qualify as a "new farm." The place had been abandoned for years. It was one of the most run-down properties in the area. The buildings had weathered beneath the sun until they turned a pale gray. The house appeared to be unfit for human habitation.

Furthermore, the granary, hog house, and barn were overrun with rats. It was impossible to walk anywhere on the property without stirring up a mess of them. You could see their long wiry tails disappearing into every crevasse in every wooden or stone structure on the property.

As soon as our furniture and other belongings were moved into the dilapidated old farmhouse, Pa borrowed a rat terrier. His name was "Spike." The dog's owner was another area farmer who had hit bottom. He couldn't afford to feed his family, much less the dog. Pa also handed me his .22 rifle and told me to start rat hunting.

Spike was an excellent ratter. He could catch one and snap its neck in a flash. I must have killed a hundred rats with the .22. Between Spike and me, and some poisoned grain we spread around the property, we soon had the rat population under control. Unfortunately, we had to give Spike back to his owner. We couldn't afford to feed him, either.

We learned later that Spike's owner killed the dog rather than allow it to starve to death. There were rumors that the farmer and his family were so low on food that they ate Spike. But I don't know whether or not those rumors were true.

VI

Another tough winter. The wind leaked through the old farmhouse. The only way to stay warm was to huddle around the wood-burning stove in the kitchen. Even then, the parts of your body that were turned away from the stove would get cold. You'd have to shift your chair around to warm up the other side of your body. When we went to bed, we wore all of our clothes, including our coats. Most nights, we wouldn't wear our shoes. But there were some nights our feet got so cold, we'd wear our shoes to bed, too.

After the tornado, Pa had sold all the remaining livestock, because we had no way to house and feed them until the farm buildings were rebuilt and repaired. He'd only kept two of the cows for milk. So when we moved to the new farm, food was scarce. There was so little money.

I remember that period of time in my life as several months of sitting in a chair next to the kitchen stove, trying to ignore my hunger. Periodically, we ventured out to the barn and milked the two cows. But since we couldn't feed them properly, they produced very little milk. Pa considered butchering one of the cows, but only as a last resort. Without the cows, it would be difficult, if not impossible, for us to get the farm up and running in the spring.

My other vivid memory of that winter was when Pa and I chopped up one of the old out-buildings for firewood. The wood was stored in a shed out back of the house. Several times a day, I trudged through huge snow drifts to replenish our supply of firewood.

The only topic of conversation I remember, while we all sat around the stove, was which building we would chop up next. I guess I must have let my imagination roam free during that long, bitterly cold winter. I don't know how else I would have survived.

I thought a lot about the pheasants nesting beneath the snowdrifts in the nearby fields. I knew some had to die so that others could survive and start reproducing all over again in the spring. I wondered if maybe nature periodically weeded out human populations the same way. Maybe the purpose of harsh winters and poverty was to separate the weak from the strong, so that the strong could start all over again in the spring. I didn't like that idea very much.

I also wondered how many new graves would have to be dug in Reque Cemetery once the spring thaws released the frosts from the ground. During some of the howling blizzards that shook the walls the old farmhouse that winter, I was convinced that Ma, Pa, and I might be three of the new additions.

But, once again, we managed to survive.

VII

Spring came and we waited for the fields to dry. At least fifty people stopped by the farm, looking for food and work. They came alone. They came in pairs. They came on foot, on horses, in pick-ups, in cars, in horse-drawn wagons, and even on bicycles.

On our previous farm, we would have maybe three or four people a month come by looking for food or work. Now, we were visited nearly every day, sometimes several times a day. The Great Depression had definitely found its way into Stevens County.

Entire families pulled into the yard in pick-up trucks or horse-drawn wagons. Most of them had lost their farms and homes through foreclosures. Many slept in their vehicles or underneath the stars. Displaced farm families were America's new migrant labor force. Whatever they owned, they carried with them. All they wanted was work, something to eat, and a place to sleep. They had no dreams.

All of these people needed help. Little children suffered the most. It was difficult for me to look into their eyes, knowing they hadn't eaten in days. It was even more difficult to know we could do very little to help them. Our supply of food was greatly limited.

Still, Ma and Pa did what they could. They were extremely selfish toward one another, and toward me, but they could be surprisingly generous with complete strangers. I think it was part of the farming tradition on the Minnesota prairie. People tried to look out for one another. Our collective survival depended on it.

I remember one family in particular. The father knocked on our door. Pa and I walked outside to greet the stranger. He was politely holding his hat in his hands. Behind him, his wife was holding a small boy in a wagon that was hooked up to a single horse. All of them were gaunt, thin, and undernourished—even the horse.

"Can you spare some food?" the man asked. "We haven't eaten in days."

"I'm sorry," Pa said. "We've already given away everything we can afford to give away."

"My son probably won't live unless I can find something for him to eat," the man said. Tears pooled in his eyes.

When Pa saw the boy wasting away in his mother's arms, I could tell that he was deeply moved by this family's predicament. "Wait here a minute," Pa said. He walked toward the barn. "I'll be right back."

Moments later, Pa walked out of the barn, carrying a small bucket with a little warm milk he had just gotten from one of our two cows. The cows themselves were so undernourished that they weren't giving out enough milk to feed us, much less to bring to the market. I knew Pa was being very generous with this family.

The man took the bucket from Pa and held it up to his son's lips. The boy drank the milk slowly, as though he did not have the energy to swallow. The boy finished the milk. The man handed the bucket back to Pa.

"God bless you for your kindness," he said, joining his wife and small son on the wagon.

Ma suddenly appeared next to us. She handed the woman a jar of vegetables she had canned the previous year. "Please, take this with you," she said.

The woman smiled at Ma as she reached for the jar. She was too weak to talk.

"Thank you again," the man said, tipping his cap.

To this day, I still see that little boy's eyes staring over the top of that bucket of warm milk. And I still wonder if he survived the Great Depression.

VIII

We had no sooner dug out from the winter snows, and were making plans to plant some kind of crop in the spring, when Pa received a notice from the bank that his farm equipment, livestock, and other personal property would be put up for public auction. During the cold winter months, Pa had missed two loan payments. Pa begged and pleaded with the local banker to carry us through the planting season.

Without any farm equipment, we couldn't put a crop in the ground. If we couldn't put a crop in the ground, we had no source of income. And if we had no source of income, we would starve.

Nothing Pa said to the banker made any difference. The banker had already foreclosed on numerous other area farmers. Many farmers believed he deliberately loaned them money, knowing he could soon foreclose. Pa believed that bankers made more money this way than they could from the interest payments on the loans themselves. He said that foreclosures also put bankers in complete control of human lives and human destinies—which probably pleased them as much as the financial rewards. The fact that human beings were left destitute didn't seem to bother them in the least. According to Pa, bankers enjoyed destroying people.

During the Great Depression, there would undoubtedly have been some hardships under any circumstances. Human greed, however, made the situation much worse. Our banker was one of those people who amassed a huge personal fortune, while simultaneously driving many area farmers out across the prairie without food or shelter.

IX

The day of the public auction, I saw a spectacle unlike any I had ever seen before, and I hope never to see again. Up and down the dirt roads that passed by our property, a small, weary army of farmers trudged toward our farm. There were at least a hundred farmers in all. Many of them had been victims of previous public auctions conducted by this same banker. They arrived on foot.

The auctioneer was there, along with the banker, who must have weighed at least two hundred pounds. There were the gaunt, weary-eyed farmers shuffling into the farmyard like convicts yoked together by some invisible chain. The more prosperous farmers from other communities, who arrived in wagons and sometimes pick-up trucks, came looking for bargains. In some cases, entire families were there, including wives and children. There were rumors at the time, although I do not know if they were true, that some of the prettier farm wives sold their favors to the area bankers in order to prevent foreclosure.

The auctioneer stood on top of a wagon. The banker leaned against his shiny convertible. A makeshift table was set on the ground. Into a wooden box, the banker deposited the coins and dollar bills as each item was auctioned off. Directly in front of the auctioneer, but facing away, a small army of homeless farmers stood with their arms crossed, glaring at the more prosperous farmers who were bidding.

Farmers who had already been sold out knew that Pa's worldly possessions would be sold no matter what they did. They also knew the banker was going to pocket every dime. The only way these farmers could affect the outcome was to keep the bidding as low as possible. That way, the banker would not reap as much profit. As a result of their efforts, some pieces of farm equipment sold for as little as fifty cents.

Throughout the day, I sensed a growing restlessness in the crowd. Tensions heightened as each new piece of farm equipment was sold. Farmers, whose possessions had been sold at previous auctions, remembered, and the anger registered on their faces. Finally, there were only the two cows left for sale.

Pa stepped forward and addressed the banker. "Could I please keep one of the milk cows?" He gestured towards Ma and me. "For the boy and my wife."

The banker paused for a moment. He looked at us, as though trying to determine how much we might be worth. He shook his head. "Everything has to go," he insisted. "Those are the bank rules."

"Just one milk cow?" Pa pleaded.

"Everything goes," the banker repeated.

I noticed that several of the farmers standing in front of the wagon had pulled a rope off a pile of smaller auctioned items. The group approached the banker, while the other farmers stepped aside.

Pa saw them coming. He knew what they had in mind. He grabbed the banker by the arm and pushed that huge bulk into his shiny convertible. Pa tossed the box containing the money into the back seat. "You best get out of here," Pa warned, "or you'll be swinging from one of those trees over there."

The banker's eyes bulged wide as he saw the men surging toward him with the rope. He started his car and sped out of the yard. Pebbles and dust spit up behind his rear wheels.

The auctioneer brought down his gavel and announced that our two cows sold for two dollars apiece. The auction was over.

X

We had no cows, no machinery, and no way to make a living or raise a crop. We had a small store of potatoes, vegetables, and canned goods that Ma had rationed us during the winter months. Pa and I scraped up whatever little piles of grain that were left in the corners of the granary. I had already given Pa most of my gopher-snaring money to buy groceries. I had fifty cents left. Pa bought some dried beans with it. Ma rationed the beans by handfuls.

Before the auction, Pa had hidden some hand tools and his ax in the cellar so they wouldn't be sold. He planned to use them to plant a garden, but it would take months before a garden could produce anything for us to eat. I still had my six traps, which I could use to trap pheasants and other wild game. But other than that, we were only a few weeks away from starvation.

We managed to get the garden planted, but there was little rain. The few sprouts that poked through the parched soil soon withered beneath the hot sun. Without adequate rainfall, the lakes dried up and the fish died out. The wildlife also died out or went into hiding. My traps came up empty. Soon we were down to our last few potatoes. Then those were gone.

We hadn't eaten for two days. Pa searched around the farm for anything that was edible. He found some sprouts of green grass growing in a shady area near the barn. He cut and washed some. Ma boiled the blades in order to break down the tough fibers. She found a few teaspoonfuls of some kind of cooking oil that had been stored away in the pantry. She rubbed the oil onto cooked grass, and we tried to eat it. Even with the oil, it was too bitter, and we ended up gagging and spitting it out before we could swallow.

We lasted another day without eating. The next morning Pa said to me, "Get your cap. We're going to town."

As Pa and I walked together past the dry, barren fields toward Alberta, I knew that this was one of the most important journeys he and I would ever make. Somehow, at the end of our journey, we would know whether we were going to live, or die like the decaying pheasants and other wildlife whose carcasses littered the ditches and parched fields.

Once we were in Alberta, Pa and I walked over to the Schultz grocery store. Jack Schultz, the owner, was standing in the rear of the store, wearing a white apron stained with blood. He looked up as Pa and I shuffled through the doorway. I think he must have known, by looking at us, what we were going to ask him.

"Jack," Pa said softly as he took off his cap, "the boy and I, and his Ma, we haven't eaten for three days. I was wondering, is there any chance you could carry us for a while? I'll pay you back, when my crop comes in."

"How are you going to plant a crop?" Jack Schultz asked. "Weren't you auctioned off?"

"I'll find a way," Pa said. "But in the meantime, we got nothing to eat."

Somehow, I knew that this balding man in the blood-stained white apron held the power of life and death in his hands. For the moment, he was God, and whatever he decided, we would have to accept. If he turned us down, we would just have to go back home and face death by slow starvation. There were no other options left.

He studied my face and Pa's face for what seemed like an eternity. Then he nodded and said, "Okay, I'll carry you. Pick up what you need. I'll set up the account when you're ready to leave."

Pa kept his eyes down. Jack Schultz recognized that Pa was near tears, and he tried to lighten things up a bit with a smile in my direction. I was too hungry to think of anything except my stomach. But I got the distinct impression that he did not want to see Pa humbled any more than he had already been.

"Here," he said, handing Pa and me each a piece of beef jerky. "Eat this while you're doing your shopping."

To this day, that piece of beef jerky is the finest meal I have ever eaten.

XI

Jack Schultz carried just about all of the farmers in the area for several months. He had been smart enough to protect his money during the Great Depression. Rather than squirrel it away someplace, or use it just for his own family, he had used it to keep his store stocked with food for the area farmers.

For a long time, he gave food away. He did not sell it. He kept accounts, but he made no threats to collect. He knew area farmers could not have paid him anyhow. But when times got better, every farmer who had an account with Jack Schultz paid him back. And for several generations thereafter, the farmers' sons and daughters, and their grandchildren and great grandchildren, bought their groceries at that little corner grocery store. In its own way, that little store became a shrine to human decency.

XII

One day, a neighbor drove Pa and me to another small town a few miles west of Alberta. While I waited for them on Main Street, I saw an attractive young woman in her mid-twenties exiting the door of a bank. I recognized the woman as the wife of a farmer who had attended Pa's public auction earlier that year. She had come to the auction with her husband and children in a horse-drawn wagon.

The woman's clothing was patched and somewhat wrinkled. She paused briefly to adjust her skirt and straighten her collar. Then she saw me looking at her, and she managed a very nervous, awkward smile. She walked quickly down the side street in an easterly direction.

Perhaps she was uncomfortable seeing me because her husband was one of the farmers who had bid on some of Pa's equipment. Or, perhaps, she felt embarrassed because her worn clothing revealed that her family had also fallen on hard times.

When I looked back at the bank building, the banker who had foreclosed on Pa stepped into the open doorway. He smiled as he leaned against the door jamb and watched the attractive farm wife join her husband and two small children, who were waiting for her in a wagon at the end of the street.

DIRT, DROUGHT, AND DEATH

I

Drought came to Stevens County. When water was plentiful, we took it for granted. Now that we had no water, we understood its true value. Water is life itself. Without water, nothing is possible. Without water, this small planet becomes one vast, shifting desert.

The winds blew hard each day, sucking up the loose soil and scattering it hundreds of feet into the air. Nothing grew in the barren ground except tumbleweeds. The water evaporated out of the lakes and sloughs. For a time, dead animal carcasses rotted in the fields and ditches. Drifting soil slowly buried the remains, as it eventually covered everything. The unrelieved monotony of the landscape was unbearable.

Soon the winds plucked the tumbleweeds out of the dry soil and drove them along the ground or tossed them high into the air. Many of the tumbleweeds lodged against barbed wire fences. The dirt piled up against the tumbleweeds, slowly sifting and building six-foot-tall mounds of powdery black dirt everywhere across the prairie.

II

Pa decided to visit one of his card-playing friends who had been paralyzed in a farm accident. I was surprised when he asked me to go along.

As we walked the two miles to the man's house, Pa told me that his friend had no movement in his body. He was able to talk a little and move his eyes, but nothing more. He just lay in bed all day, staring at the ceiling or out the window. Friends and neighbors took turns stopping by to cheer him up.

We caught a ride with a farmer for the last mile. He dropped us off next to a farm that was half-buried in dirt and tumbleweeds. Everywhere you looked, dirt had drifted. One side of the house had a huge five-foot dirt mound that was building steadily toward the bottom of the window sills.

Pa's paralyzed friend must have thought that he was slowly being buried alive under all that dust and dirt. What, I wondered, had he done that was so awful that he had to remain completely motionless in the middle of a world of dirt, drought, and death?

The man's wife opened the door and invited us into the house. Her dress was faded and torn in several places. She moved without much energy and spoke with little emotion.

Pa motioned for me to sit down in the kitchen. He walked into the bedroom to visit his friend. The man's wife disappeared into another part of the house, leaving me alone.

I could hear Pa and the man talking in the next room. Several times the man's voice rose, seemingly in anger. I could hear Pa trying to calm him down.

Some family photographs hung on the wall on the other side of the kitchen table. In one of the photographs, a young woman was smiling next to a muscular farmer who was dressed in a plaid shirt and bib overalls. I recognized the woman as a much younger version of the wife. I assumed the farmer in the photograph was the person Pa was talking to in the next room.

A few minutes later, I heard what sounded like some muffled cries.

Pa walked out of the bedroom and into the kitchen. "It's time to go," he said, putting his cap on his head and walking toward the door.

I followed closely behind.

"Will he be paralyzed for the rest of his life?" I asked Pa as we passed by the rotting carcasses of dead sheep half-buried in the dirt drifts.

"Yes," Pa replied. "There's nothing the doctors can do for him."

"How long can he live like that?"

"He doesn't want to live. He wants to die."

"Is that what he told you?"

Pa nodded. "He's been asking his friends to kill him. When we refuse, he starts to cry."

III

During the drought and the Depression, we went to church more than usual. Which is to say we spent an awful lot of time in church. All of the farmers did. No one wanted to offend the Almighty any more than He had already been offended.

Reverend Sandager, our new pastor, was a tall, homely man who was stern and unemotional on the surface, but he had a deeply felt compassion for the poor. After one Sunday service, he asked me if I would like to join the choir because they needed more male voices. Ma and Pa weren't too happy to give me up for choir practice. But they could hardly say no to Reverend Sandager.

The only problem was that my voice was changing. Sometimes, I was a tenor. Sometimes, I was a baritone. And sometimes, I sounded like a banshee rooster. There were times, I'm sure, when the congregation must have thought they were witnessing some kind of exorcism, and that demons were escaping out of my mouth. But once my voice changed, I was definitely a tenor. I improved enough so that Reverend Sandager asked me to sing some solos. Everything we sang, of course, was gospel music.

In addition to going to church more often, we also started saying grace over every meal. There's nothing like a little starvation to make people more religious. We said grace many times over a few crusts of bread. And I never took food for granted ever again.

If there's anything positive I can say about the drought and the Depression, it's that Ma and Pa treated me better. I guess starving people, unless they have resorted to cannibalism, seldom have the energy to do much damage to their fellow human beings. Starvation reduces everyone to the level of the weak and the infirm. Life is no longer a test of strength. It is a test of will.

IV

The wind blew so hard, the dirt blotted out the sun. The blue sky, a distant memory, was replaced by a brownish-gray darkness. The air was dangerous to breathe. It tore up our lungs until we spit blood. Sometimes, we could not see for more than a hundred feet through the dark, thick haze. We did not dare stray too far from the farm buildings because we could get lost, breathe in too much dirt, and be buried in the drifting soil.

With the wildlife dead, there was nothing to hunt or trap for food. Nothing grew in the parched earth. We hoarded our meager rations of food until we ate less than a handful of bread crumbs each day. Jack Schultz carried us and the other farmers as long as he could, but eventually his resources gave out, and the food supplies on his shelves dwindled. Before the drought ended, Jack Schultz was in the same shape as the rest of us.

In the midst of all this human misery, some people shared what little they had. Others hoarded their share and tried to get other people's shares as well. Rumors of human cannibalism spread like the winds tearing away at the prairie soil.

To add to our agony, heavy clouds formed almost daily on the southwestern horizon, and loud thunder rolled across the prairie. Every day promised rain, but rain never came. Through the loud, scornful voice of the distant thunderheads, nature mocked our efforts to survive. The clouds would dissipate and disappear without shedding a single drop of rain. The clouds reminded us that we could not survive for long in a waterless world. They only added to our daily torture.

Dirt was everywhere. You walked through black piles of it as high as snow drifts. You breathed it. You slept in it. Everywhere you went there was dirt. But there was no water.

V

The Great Depression and the drought years unleashed a crime wave in Stevens County. In one respect, Ma, Pa, and I were lucky. We didn't have any personal property to protect. Our local banker had already taken everything we owned that was worth anything. There was precious little for other thieves to steal from us. But that wouldn't stop them from trying.

With nothing growing in the ground, and most of the livestock either dead or sold off at the bank auction, I didn't have much in the way of chores. About all I had left to do was milk one sickly old cow that one of Pa's friends had given him after the auction. Pa's friend had also brought over enough hay so the cow could eat and produce some milk for us to drink.

When it was time to feed or milk the cow, I would cover my nose and mouth with a rag so I wouldn't breathe in too much dust. I would tramp through the swirling dust and piles of dirt from the house to the barn.

One day, as I stepped into the barn, I heard a strange sound in the rear of the building. Where we kept our cow, I saw a wooden milking stool lying on its side next to a small bucket with a little milk at the bottom. Someone other than Pa or me had been milking our cow. We had an intruder in our barn.

As I reached for the milking stool, a small, thin man leaped out from behind a wooden partition. He pointed a pitchfork at me as he slowly backed out of the barn. Then he dropped the pitchfork and ran out the back door into the dust storm. I guess my adrenaline must have been pumping pretty hard, because I gave chase.

Bursting through the open doorway, I almost ran into an emaciated woman who was standing with two starving children. They clung to her skirt. The man I had confronted in the barn took up a defensive position between his family and me.

He was no common thief. He had been trying to feed his starving children.

The memories of how Ma, Pa, and I had almost starved to death were still too fresh in my mind for me to feel anything except empathy for this family.

But before I could invite him to go back into the barn and get the milk, the woman and her two children walked into the dust storm. The children, clinging to their mother's skirt, were swallowed up by the swirling dust.

The man, looking more defeated than defiant, eyed me for a few seconds, before he, too, disappeared into the dust storm.

VI

The thunderheads, rumbling on the distant horizon, moved closer to our farm. A cool, damp breeze blew from the southwest. I dared not look in that direction for fear I would be disappointed, as I had been disappointed so many times before. I had tried to convince myself that perhaps it was possible to survive in a world of dirt. Once I sensed water, my spirit longed for more.

The first random raindrops were sucked up by the parched soil. But more came. And still more. Finally, it was raining and pouring in torrents. Pa and I took off our shirts and jumped and yelled like lunatics who had just been released from an insane asylum. We felt the raindrops splash against our faces and splatter against our exposed skin. The heavens opened up with still more rain.

The drought was over.

VII

Regular rainfall restored the normal cycles of life and death on the prairie. The rain cleansed the brownish-gray haze. White clouds and blue skies reappeared. The fields sprouted green vegetation, and little puddles collected in the bottoms of the lakes and sloughs. Jack rabbits returned. Then came pheasants, foxes, and skunks. Soon the land was teeming once again with wildlife. Before long, seeds that had lain dormant in gardens and fields burst to life, and new sprouts pushed through the soil.

With my traps and the .22, I replenished our exhausted food supplies with fresh game. In time, these food sources would be supplemented by garden and field crops.

We had survived.

VIII

Good news came in waves. President Roosevelt announced that every man who wanted work would be offered a job constructing a new highway through Stevens County. Others were offered work in the northern Minnesota forests. Pa, as well as most of the farmers over the age of thirty, chose the highway over the forests. To make sure they were on time to start work, they got up early and left home while it was still dark.

The promise of work was greeted with the same unabashed excitement and enthusiasm that people had greeted the first rain. Work meant food. But it also meant pride. Work was to the farmers' spirits what the rain had been to the parched soil. It restored a sense of purpose and lost dignity.

An army of farmers marched out one morning down just about every dirt road in Stevens County. Some carried picks and shovels. Some walked alongside horses and scrapers. All were put to work on the highway project. At the end of the first week, Pa got paid five dollars. With one dollar, he bought food at Jack Schultz's grocery store. He paid an additional two dollars on the account we had run up over the drought months. Pa kept the remaining two dollars in reserve.

Throughout that afternoon and into the next day, formerly unemployed farmers stopped by the grocery store and paid one or two dollars against their accounts. Each farmer wanted to shake Jack Schultz's hand and thank him for coming to the aid of their families in their hour of need. Jack Schultz didn't know how to accept all the gratitude. Pa said the grocer, seeing the line of thankful farmers, hid in the back of the store and told his wife to accept the money. The farmers, however, would have none of that. Every one of them sought out Jack Schultz in the back of his store, personally handed him their payments, and shook his hand.

In the small town a few miles to the west of Alberta, farmers were expressing their feelings in a much different way. One of the farmers, who had lost his place through foreclosure, decided to walk over to the bank to tell the banker off for the way he had treated farmers during the drought and Depression. The banker, sensing trouble, locked the door and hid in his office.

Realizing the door was locked, but knowing that the banker was still inside, the farmer figured out another way to express his displeasure. He pissed on the bank's front door.

Seeing what was happening, other farmers decided that this was about as good a way as any to let the banker know what they thought of him. Lined up in front of the bank like men at a ballgame waiting to use a urinal, one after another relieved himself on the bank door. Some farmers drank as much water or beer as their bladders would hold, walked to the end of the line, and had another go at it.

IX

President Roosevelt convinced Congress to pass legislation allowing farmers to receive low-interest loans for farm equipment and livestock. Pa was approved for one. He used the money to buy cattle, horses, feed, seed, and farm equipment. Included in Pa's purchases was an old rebuilt tractor.

The problem was that Pa had never driven a tractor before. The first time he got it started, he couldn't get the tractor out of second gear. He drove from one field to the next, down one dirt road after another.

Hearing the straining engine, the neighbors waved at him as he passed by. Pa was too embarrassed to ask any of them for help. Finally, the tractor ran out of gas, and Pa walked back home. The tractor set out there in the field for the rest of the planting season. Pa went back to plowing with horses.

X

I had become a pretty good shot with the .22. When I wasn't doing chores, I spent much of my time hunting. Having almost starved to death, I was determined never to go through that experience again. I hunted wild game almost every day so we could fill the cellar with canned meats.

I was returning from one of my hunting trips near our slough when I saw the black car parked in our yard again. I suppose I should have been expecting it. Things had been going so well for us that Ma's company was long overdue. He always seemed to come back into our lives at the very moment when Ma and Pa settled down. He always arrived, just like clockwork, to set them at each other's throats again.

I was older, stronger, and not as afraid of Ma as I used to be, but I still avoided the house when her company was there. I decided to stay in the barn and clean the pheasants I had shot. But an hour later, the car was still parked in the yard. I snuck up to the house and peeked through the kitchen window.

Ma wasn't with her company. She was sitting next to the kitchen table with his wife, the unfriendly middle-aged woman who had participated in my trial. The woman was doing all the talking. Ma sat there passively.

The first thought that came to my mind was that they were deciding that I should be sent off to reform school. But that incident had taken place so long ago, and so much had happened since, that it didn't seem reasonable that they would still be holding that sword over my head. Something else was at stake.

After lecturing Ma for a few more minutes, the woman stood up to leave. Ma, who had been stoic up until that point, calmly watched the woman walk out the door. Then she lowered her head and started to cry.

Somehow, I knew that the woman had figured out what was going on between Ma and her husband. She had come over to put a stop to it. I could almost read Ma's mind as she sobbed by the kitchen table. For better or worse, she would now have to spend the rest of her life with Pa. Her company was gone for good. Her last joy had just been taken away from her.

XI

Delores's confirmation took place that summer. It was a tedious affair—confirmation was always the longest church service of the year. The young people who were being confirmed were publicly grilled about various passages from the Bible. They had to recite these passages to the congregation without missing a single word. When they missed even one, they had to go back and start all over again. By the time the service was over, I doubt that any of them had a bit of religion left.

For me, as I sat with the choir, the service was an endurance contest. I hated to sit still for that long—even under the best of conditions. Wearing those coarse, scratchy wool pants, while the sun beat down on the church, and feeling the room grow intolerably hot and stuffy, was my version of hell on earth. I tried to preoccupy myself with other thoughts. When that didn't work, I studied the people and the faces in the congregation.

The church, which held about a hundred people, was packed. Ma and Pa were sitting in a pew not too far from where Reverend Sandager was grilling the young people on their catechisms. Ma's company and his wife, although they normally attended another church, sat near the back of the room. Other farmers and their wives and families were wedged so closely together in the narrow pews that some of them looked like their ears were touching.

In all my life, I have never seen so many people pretend to be so interested in something they cared so little about. Everyone wanted to flee outside, into the fresh air. That was obvious to me as I listened to Reverend Sandager's tedious questions about bible passages.

Finally, it was Delores's turn. She was wearing a cream-colored confirmation dress that contrasted nicely with her dark hair. I watched Ma smile proudly as soon as Delores stood up. In the back of the room, Ma's company seemed to sit up a little straighter and pay more attention. Almost everyone else had a frozen look of boredom on their faces.

As I listened to Delores recite the catechism, I had the strange sense that something like this had happened before. In my mind, I saw Ma's wedding picture. Ma had worn a cream-colored dress in that picture, just as Delores was wearing a cream-colored dress at her confirmation ceremony. I was struck by how much Delores resembled Ma. I had noticed the similarities before. But now that Delores was a few years older, she looked even more like Ma—and not just her eyes.

After the service, as people gathered outside on the front lawn, Ma walked over to congratulate Delores. I noticed that Delores, now that she was a young woman, was the same height as Ma. Furthermore, Delores had a dimple in exactly the same place that Ma had hers.

XII

A few weeks later, Delores gave Ma a copy of her confirmation picture. I waited until Ma and Pa were away from the farm visiting friends before I compared it to their wedding photograph.

It took me a while to find the wedding photograph, since everything had been moved around a bit in the new farmhouse. When I placed Delores's confirmation picture next to Ma's wedding picture, there was no question about it. They could pass for sisters, or at least first cousins. In person, most people would probably not notice the similarities, because Ma was thirty years older than Delores. Still, in the photographs, the noses, eyes, mouths, and body shapes were close to identical. Even their arms were the same shape and length. The major difference seemed to be in the hair, but that was more the result of style than color.

I studied some of the postcards and envelopes from Montana and Minneapolis more carefully. They were postmarked from 1918 to 1919. The envelopes were addressed to Pa, in Ma's handwriting.

That could only mean that Ma had been separated from Pa for several months—during the time that Delores was born in 1919. Ma was in a position to have a child without Pa—or anyone else in the community—even suspecting that she was pregnant.

XIII

I must have contemplated the meaning of what I found in that bedroom for the next six years—maybe I still do. I felt like there was another completely different reality coexisting alongside the one I thought I had been experiencing for the first twelve years of my life. Events and experiences, which I had come to understand one way, seemed to contain a whole different set of implications that had never even occurred to me. I set out to revisit many of these events and experiences in order to determine what new insights they might reveal.

At no point did I tell Delores about any of my suspicions. She had never expressed any interest whatsoever in learning about her birth parents. She was quite content to be a part of her own adoptive family. I felt I would be doing her a great disservice, and perhaps even hurting her deeply, if I told her what I suspected.

What *was* really going on with respect to Delores's birth and adoption? Here were some of the possibilities. I say "possibilities" because I couldn't verify anything without having access to public records and documents. Still, as you get older, sometimes you start to feel in your bones that many things in life might be different than you have been led to believe. Understanding that, the following is my alternative reality, the one that might have been coexisting alongside the life I thought I was living with Ma and Pa.

Earlier in the century, Ma and Pa had entered into a marriage that was—for Pa, at least—a marriage of convenience. Apparently, they could not have children together. That much I already knew. But Ma might have been capable of having a child with another man. Ma's company was coming over to our house from the time that I was a very little boy. In fact, his presence in our home was one of my first memories. It seems conceivable that he was coming over before I arrived at the farm, perhaps even before I was born. If so, he could have fathered a child. Could he possibly have fathered Delores?

If Ma had become pregnant with Delores, and Pa could not have been the father, Ma would have had no choice but to leave the community and give birth elsewhere. She would have to contrive some reason to be away from home for several months. Maybe she would even have to manufacture some kind of temporary separation from Pa.

Ma's letters to him from Montana and Minneapolis did not appear to be particularly angry. She wrote mostly small talk about people and places she had visited. If she had left Pa because they were having marital problems, it seems strange that the letters would not discuss those problems in some detail. Even though the letters were not affectionate, they did not reflect any serious rifts in the marriage at that time.

Once Delores was born, could Ma have tried to bring her back into the family through a private adoption to a close family member—in this case, Pa's sister? Ma was very close to Pa's sister, who didn't think much of her own brother. They could easily have worked out the details of that arrangement together. Ma understandably would have wanted to be close to her only child. What better arrangement than to have Pa's sister adopt Delores?

Clever? Yes! Ingenious? Yes! True? Who knows!

Perhaps Ma's frustration with me was caused in large part because I was a poor substitute for the daughter she could never acknowledge as her own child. If so, my trial in front of Ma, Pa, the mustached man, and his wife was staged in front of Delores's mother and father—although Pa and the other man's wife probably did not know that to be the case.

The purpose of the trial was not to threaten me with reform school. I was a good hired man. Ma and Pa didn't really want to get rid of me. They only wanted to scare the hell out of me and keep me away from Delores. Or, at least, Ma did.

I believe Ma wanted Delores to marry into a better class of people. She did not want to chance for one minute that Delores might someday fall in love with a hired man who was destined to work for room and board for the rest of his life. So Ma had to throw up a wall between the two of us to minimize whatever contact we might have with one another.

The final piece to the puzzle? The mustached man's wife could have figured out that her husband had fathered Delores with Ma. Perhaps that was the reason she drove out to our house that day. She may have even threatened Ma. She might have told Ma if she ever again suspected that her husband was sneaking over to our house on the sly, she would tell everyone who Delores's real mother was.

Such public humiliation would have shamed Ma forever in the eyes of our small community, not to mention the damage it would have done to Delores. Whatever the case, I never again saw that black car parked in front of our house.

Ma became more human to me that day. I did not forgive her. I was not ready for that yet. But if Ma *was* Delores's mother, she must have truly loved that baby to conspire with Pa's sister to bring it back into the family through a private adoption. Still, she could only love that child from a distance, and without Delores knowing. When Pa brought me home from the orphanage, she was forced to accept an adopted son she could not love, to replace a daughter she could not acknowledge.

If I was wrong, my imagination had just created a whopper of a story. But if I was right, I was beginning to understand many of the things about the people in my life that had never made any sense before.

There were only two possibilities: Delores was either Ma's daughter, or the fates had conspired to place in Pa's sister's family an adopted daughter who bore an uncanny resemblance to Ma. I don't know which of those possibilities was the more improbable.

XIV

In the fall, Delores was sent away to live with a couple in Morris. I was told that her parents had decided that Morris had better schools. She would get a better education there. I suspected that part of the motivation was to get Delores away from me. I also wondered if perhaps Ma was concerned that some people south of Alberta might watch Delores grow up, notice the physical resemblances, and put two and two together. Perhaps, if Delores grew to young womanhood in Morris, a community a few miles east of Alberta, the chances of discovery would be lessened somewhat.

Whatever the reasons, Delores was leaving Alberta. We met near Reque Cemetery to say good-bye. I toyed with the idea of telling her what I believed. But she seemed so genuinely excited and enthusiastic about her new adventure in a bigger school that I didn't want to ruin it by telling her about Ma and the mustached man.

Before we parted, she kissed me on the cheek. Then she ran across the fields to catch a ride back to her home. I stood there for a long time as I watched her blend into the horizon. I listened to the winds sweep the autumn leaves across the ditches and empty fields.

Once again, I felt very much alone.

XV

Shortly after Delores left to attend school in Morris, Pa's paralyzed friend died of pneumonia. He made it through the drought years, lying flat on his back, watching through his window as the drifting dirt crept steadily across his farmyard. Maybe that wasn't the worst part of his agony. Maybe—after the rains came, and he noticed the green trees and fields of grain reborn—maybe, then, he understood that he could never join all that new life. Maybe that was more painful than all the dirt and drought and death he had grown accustomed to. Whatever the case, news of his death added another sad voice to my prairie wind song.

At the End of the Field

I

I attended an auction for a farmer who had decided to give up farming, sell out, and head south. When everything that was worth anything had been auctioned off, the farmer gave away many of the things he didn't want to take with him. Among the things he gave away was an old framed oil painting he said had been painted by a distant relative who once farmed in Stevens County.

It was a painting of an elderly farmer standing behind a plow and a team of horses in the middle of a freshly plowed field. The farmer's weathered hands rested on the wooden plow handles as he paused from his labors to gaze at the horizon. In the distance, a flock of birds was flying toward a thin beam of sunlight shining through a seam in the cloudy sky. One bird, its wings spread wide, was flying ahead of the other birds toward the light. In the lower right-hand corner, the artist had written the words, "At the End of the Field," in thin black brush strokes.

I took the painting home with me and hung it on the wall of my bedroom. For years it hung there, fading and gathering dust. I never thought very much about what the artist was trying to say in the painting. I just liked the colors.

II

By the mid-1930s, rain was plentiful and the growing seasons were long. The drought continued to ravage farmlands farther south, and migrant farm families continued to move through our area, but we were spared. We were not, by any means, affluent. But we were able to make a living on the farm, which was more than we had been able to do for many years.

Pa earned enough money to buy a used Model-T Ford. Although it was seldom in running condition, the car gave us a status we had never experienced before. Running or not, Pa parked the car on the edge of the yard, close to the driveway, so everyone could see we owned it. The fact that we frequently had to push the old relic to its parking place was of little concern to Pa. He just wanted everyone to recognize our arrival at a new and enhanced economic status.

I had repaired the abandoned Ford tractor that had taken Pa on such a merry ride around the countryside. I used it for some of the lighter farm work. But it didn't have the power to pull the hat off your head. Heavy field work was still done the old-fashioned way—with horses.

Under Ivar's watchful eye, I had served my apprenticeship as a hired man. Now I had achieved journeyman status. I had been doing a man's work ever since I was eight years old. By the time I was fourteen, very few men could have maintained my daily schedule.

I milked the cows, fed the livestock, harvested our garden, and pitched silage. I could hitch a team of horses or drive a tractor. I plowed and disked the fields in the spring. In the fall, I pitched hay and hauled the massive bundles from the fields to the barn.

Since Pa knew almost nothing about farm equipment, I was also responsible for repairing and maintaining all the machinery and equipment. I finished with my chores about nine at night. I rose at four in the morning to start the whole routine all over again.

III

Ma became a somewhat different person. After she lost the one relationship that had sustained her throughout her unhappy marriage to Pa, I expected her to become even more angry and bitter. She didn't.

Instead, Ma was softer, more mellow. Hers wasn't a complete conversion by any means. She was still unpredictable. But I noticed a change in her attitude toward me. She was less aggressive. She seemed to have retreated into her inner world of lost dreams, a world where her company visited often and romanced her while Pa was away from the farm.

Ma spent much of her time staring out the window, gazing across the prairie. I became sensitive to her quiet moods, and I did not intrude. In return, she left me alone.

After the death of his paralyzed friend, Pa also changed—but not in the way that either Ma or I might have wanted. He went back to his old ways. He did not get all of his land planted, preferring to spend most of his time fishing or playing cards. If there was work to be done, I had to do it.

I remember Pa working hard only once that year, when he and Hans Kolden bought a threshing machine together. They kept very busy during the threshing season. I worked on those crews, alongside my good friend Raymond Kolden. After the threshing season, Pa went right back to the smoke-filled card rooms in Alberta.

Our lives fell into a pattern: Pa played cards; Ma gazed sadly out the window; I farmed our land.

Pa's plans for my future became very clear. Little by little, he had me take over the farm so he could live a leisurely, semi-retired life. Anything that got in the way of those plans was discouraged, or forbidden.

IV

I started school in Alberta. In the fall and spring, our school bus was a horse-drawn wagon. In the winter, the horses pulled an enclosed bobsled. When the weather was nice, I preferred to run across the open fields to school, a distance of almost three miles—as the crow flies.

School, however, continued to be an insignificant part of my life. For every six weeks that I should have been in school, Pa kept me home a minimum of four. During the two weeks that I attended classes, Pa often showed up at school and told my teacher he needed me. Most afternoons, I was back on the farm doing chores and working in the fields. Only Raymond Kolden, who had been held back several grades because he had missed so much school, was absent more than I was. Other boys were allowed enough school time to receive some kind of an education. But Pa wanted his hired man at home, working. That was all there was to it.

Because I didn't attend classes on a regular basis, I wasn't sure what was expected of me during classroom drills. I felt embarrassed, frustrated, and eventually isolated from the other students. Some of my teachers recognized my distress. They were kind and sympathetic. But the teachers couldn't force Ma and Pa to send me to school. The laws didn't protect children in those days.

When the other students were doing drills, the teachers would sometimes tutor me for a few minutes. I could tell they were surprised that I caught onto some things so fast. I think they were expecting that I didn't have the ability to learn, and that's why Pa kept me home. I remember one of my teachers shaking her head in astonishment when I did some math problems the other students had been struggling with for several days. I don't know how I solved those problems. I just kind of played around with them until the answers popped into my head.

I could tell that some of my teachers were upset with Pa for the way he was treating me. They couldn't change it. But I knew they felt sorry for me, especially when they realized I had abilities that Ma and Pa should have encouraged me to develop. Some of my teachers even shared their lunches with me when Ma had thrown nothing but a couple scraps of bread into my lunch pail. I was very lucky to have those teachers in my life. Without them, I would probably still be pitching hay on someone's farm—and working for a few scraps of bread and a bed in the barn.

V

Lewis Billars, one of my teachers, was a man I will never forget. He had heard me sing in the church choir, and he told me that I had a very good voice. He explained, however, that even a good voice needed training. He recommended a series of exercises I could do at home to strengthen my voice, including breathing and diaphragm control exercises. He also taught me to sing with a pile of books or a cream can on my stomach, so I would learn to breathe properly. Under his guidance, I learned more about music than I ever thought it was possible to know.

I practiced my singing when I was plowing or doing the chores. I had a very strong voice, and the sound carried for some distance. Many people who drove by our farm said they could hear me singing while I herded the cows in from the pasture.

In the process, music—like fishing—became one of my life's obsessions. I could not get enough of either one of them. When I die, I hope heaven turns out to be a fishing boat on a big lake stocked with walleye or northern pike, with plenty of breathing room for me to sing while I fish.

Nothing I've ever heard about the hereafter compares in the slightest to my vision of it: a big lake stocked with fish, some good music, and not a single bale of hay to haul into the barn.

VI

The biggest problem I had in school was that I stood out so much that I was the target of an awful lot of ridicule and teasing. My clothes were always hand-me-downs in need of patching. Plus, my bottom teeth desperately needed dental work. So I tried never to smile. My ears also protruded rather prominently from my head, due to Ma's constant beatings when I was young. I guess there are good reasons why I stood out. I was probably the strangest looking thing that ever walked into that schoolhouse.

Almost every day I was challenged to a wrestling match by one of the other students. I had to fight to get into the schoolhouse, and I had to fight again to get back home. If I didn't accept their challenges, they would call me a "sissy" or worse. Some of my classmates never let me forget that I was adopted, that I was their inferior. So maybe it was best that Pa didn't let me attend classes very often.

One spring day, I was surrounded by a group of boys after class. Most of them had lost to me in earlier wrestling matches. They were trying to get even by ganging up on me. They challenged me to fight two of them at once. I didn't want to have anything to do with that. I didn't have time to take on a group of them. I also didn't trust that I could win an unfair fight. But as they crowded in on me, I knew I had no choice.

As I was about to wrestle two of them, Raymond Kolden appeared from around the corner of the schoolhouse. I had worked on some threshing crews with Raymond, but I hadn't seen him in school for months. I assumed he had dropped out for good.

A sense of quiet awe settled over the other boys as soon as they saw Raymond. He was still regarded as the biggest, toughest boy in the county. No one wanted to mess with him. I figured between the two of us, we could do a pretty good job of taking on the whole group. But Raymond had something else in mind.

He gestured for the other boys to step back, and then he said, "I'll wrestle you, Lloyd."

I wasn't too sure that I had heard him correctly. "Wrestle? You and me?" I asked.

"*Just* you and me," Raymond replied.

There was a look on his face that I hadn't seen before. He glared at me, his jaw locked, but his eyes were still friendly. The other boys hoped that Raymond was about to destroy me right in front of them. I saw their delight. They pushed me toward Raymond. They laughed at my agony.

I had no desire to wrestle Raymond Kolden. Next to Delores and Marcus Reece, he was the best friend I'd ever had. Plus, he was much bigger and stronger than I was. I didn't stand a chance. The other boys were convinced that Raymond was out to get some kind of revenge. They couldn't wait to see me get what they thought I deserved.

Raymond knelt to tighten one of the twine laces on his work boots. Then he took off his shirt and assumed a standing wrestling position. Muscles rippled across his neck, chest, and arms. I reluctantly took off my shirt and squared off against him.

Raymond dove for my waist. I leaped away from his charge. We locked arms and the sweat poured down our bodies. We fell and rolled across the ground, our arms and legs interlocked. Dust clung to us. With each move, the boys cheered and goaded us to be even more aggressive.

Raymond was easily the strongest boy I had ever wrestled. I was quicker. I lunged for his knees and tried to flip him onto his back. It was not a smart move. Raymond suddenly had me in a hammerlock. I used every ounce of strength in my body to break his hold. Raymond was much too strong. He was wearing me down. I was close to giving up.

Then, much to my astonishment, Raymond's arms seemed to go a little limp. I escaped from the hammerlock and threw him to the ground. Too easily, I flipped him on his back. I threw one arm around his neck, the other around his leg. I pulled my hands together and locked my fingers.

He could not break my hold. Someone counted to three and that was the end of the match.

I could scarcely believe what I had just done: pinning Raymond Kolden, the strongest boy in the county. A hushed silence fell over the other boys. When I stood up, they stepped back, as though granting me the measure of respect they had so stubbornly withheld.

I helped Raymond to his feet. He had that strange look on his face again. His jaw was still locked, but his eyes were warm, friendly. He nodded, acknowledging his defeat, before picking up his shirt. The other boys looked at me as though they were staring at the new heavyweight champion of the world.

As I watched the strapping, muscular Raymond Kolden walk away, I concluded that he had given up too easily on that hammerlock. He was much too strong for me to break that hold—unless he wanted me to break it. He must have known all along that the boy who pinned Raymond Kolden was not to be messed with.

I don't remember ever seeing him at school again. I don't even know if he was officially enrolled, or just passing by the school, when he saw my predicament. Some of the other kids started the rumor that Raymond was too embarrassed to come back to school after I had "whipped him good and proper." But I knew the truth. Raymond decided to throw the match and smooth the way for me in school. He had found a way to be my friend without anyone else even suspecting what he was doing, without asking for anything in return.

He threw that wrestling match my way. I just know it.

VII

I didn't see much of Delores for the first year she was in Morris. Not only was she going to school, but working as a nanny as well. The next year, she sent word through a friend that she would like for me to come to Morris to see her. She had a Saturday off, and she said she wanted to show me around. She also indicated that she had a special treat for me.

I had been to Morris a few times with Pa. But we never did much except drive through, or skirt the edges of town. I had never spent much time in the town itself. Her invitation provided a new experience for me.

I thought about asking Pa if I could take the Model-T to town to visit Delores. I had been practicing in the farmyard. I could drive at least as well as he could. But I decided against asking. I thought Delores might be a little embarrassed if I drove up to her house in that old relic. Plus, I probably would have ended up walking back home anyhow. Once you turned off the motor of that Model-T, you paid hell getting it started again.

I knew Ma and Pa would kick up a fuss if I told them I was taking a Saturday afternoon off to visit Delores. They would have insisted that I stay around the farm and do more chores. For the most part, I didn't care what they expected from me. I certainly was no longer afraid of Ma. I felt more sympathy than anger toward her. Still, I decided I wouldn't say anything about going to Morris. Instead, I told them I was going fishing. I didn't want to get everyone all riled up again.

I got up extra early and finished my chores. I hitched a ride on Highway 28 with a farmer who was hauling a load of grain to the Morris elevators. I asked him about directions while we drove the six miles to town. He told me which streets to take to get over to the house where Delores was staying. He dropped me off near one of the grain elevators, and I was on my own.

I suppose, at the time, Morris was a town of about three thousand people, but to me it seemed like the biggest city on the planet. I had never seen so many paved streets and tree-lined boulevards. Main Street, which was about three blocks long, was, to me, a mind-boggling assortment of stores and shops. There were also railroad tracks that ran parallel to Main Street.

As I made my way through town, I pondered my earlier suspicions about Delores's birth and adoption. It had been a couple of years since her confirmation service. I had started to have some serious reservations about many of my assumptions. In spite of the physical resemblances, the thought that Ma might be Delores's real mother, adopted back into the family through Pa's sister, became increasingly uncomfortable to me. There were many things that pointed in that direction. Still, it was extremely difficult for me to believe that Ma and Pa's sister could have pulled off such a complicated charade.

But if what I suspected were true, I just couldn't believe that someone else hadn't figured it out earlier. Maybe someone *did* figure it out earlier, and the truth had become the great unspoken secret in our family. Once again, I decided I wouldn't say anything to Delores. Whether or not Ma gave birth to Delores, my suspicions would surely hurt her. It seemed best that I forget the whole thing—at least for the time being.

Delores was waiting for me on the front porch of a big two-story house. She bounded down the steps and gave me a big hug. "My, look how tall you are," she said affectionately.

"I'm fourteen," I explained awkwardly. "Almost fifteen."

"Funny," she teased, "I thought you were twelve."

Before I could protest, Delores grabbed my arm and led me back down the street. We explored Morris for probably an hour, visiting various places of interest. She took me by the community's small Carnegie Library and the Stevens County Courthouse. At our journey's end, we stopped in front of a small movie theater a block or so off Main Street.

"This is my treat," she exclaimed proudly as she pointed at a movie poster in the front window of the theater.

"What is that?" I asked.

"A movie, dummy. I'm taking you to a movie."

The poster was an advertisement for *Rose-Marie*, starring Nelson Eddy and Jeanette MacDonald. I had seen a few silent films before, when someone set up projectors in their homes in Alberta. But I didn't like the silent movies very much. Everyone watching was always talking and adding their own dialogue during the film. But now, thanks to Delores, I was about to enter a world unlike anything I had ever experienced before.

At first, *Rose-Marie* was a little boring, especially the parts pertaining to high society life. Luxury and leisure were impossible for me to comprehend. But when the action moved to the beautiful Canadian Rocky Mountains, and Nelson Eddy and Jeanette MacDonald sang songs like "Rose-Marie" and "The Indian Love Call" from distant mountaintops, I felt my spirit soaring with the music into some invisible romantic world: a world that lived in the darkness of the movie theater.

In my adolescent enthusiasm, I believed that I, too, could enter that world. I, too, could find the right mountaintop and sing the right song. I, too, could soar into that world in pursuit of the perfect love, the perfect life. Delores could accompany me. And the life that Ma and Pa had created for me on the farm, the world where I worked fourteen and sixteen hour days as a hired man, would cease to exist.

I could have sat through that movie ten times. Unfortunately, there was only one matinee that afternoon. I remember walking out into the bright sunlight and thinking what a boring thing reality is. The world I had just left behind beckoned me back into the movie theater. But Delores grasped my arm and led me to the two-story house where she was living and working as a nanny. She had to take care of the children again later that day, so she hugged me, kissed me, and bid me farewell. I walked alone back through the city streets to the highway.

The movie played in my head. It was intoxicating—more intoxicating than Pa's homebrew could ever have been. I had always loved music, but after *Rose-Marie*, music became for me a gateway into a whole new reality, a whole new way of life. I knew that Delores would always be waiting for me somewhere in that world—if only I could find the right mountaintop, and sing the right song.

VIII

I hitched a ride home with a farmer who was driving a tractor and empty trailer back to Alberta. As I gazed over the autumn fields, I was struck by the barren emptiness of the prairie. How could Marcus Reece and I have searched for adventure and excitement in those vacant fields, among those abandoned farms? Life and the promise of romance could only flourish elsewhere. It could not possibly survive on the Minnesota prairie. There were no romantic mountaintops.

That day, in a small-town theater, I had found the true meaning of romance. I was not about to lose it. I already had Delores, who was my Rose-Marie. I had the songs from the movie. All I needed was a mountaintop.

It was not, however, easy to find one in west central Minnesota. There were a few hills that achieved some elevation, perhaps fifty- to seventy-five feet above the flat fields that surrounded them. I knew I would have to improvise—and I did.

I hitched a ride with another farmer to the abandoned windmill Marcus Reece and I had climbed so often as children. Toward twilight, I climbed the rusty, forty-foot windmill. From that height, I pretended

I was in the Canadian Rocky Mountains. And I sang my heart out to my Rose-Marie as the sun gradually set in the west.

IX

A few days later, I was sitting by the kitchen table. Ma was dicing carrots on a nearby counter top.

"How was Delores?" she asked, without missing a beat with the knife as it sliced through the carrots.

"What do you mean?" I asked innocently.

"Someone saw you with her in Morris," Ma explained calmly.

"She was fine," I replied evasively.

"I thought you were going fishing."

"I changed my mind," I said. Then something inside of me decided to test Ma on what I suspected about Delores's past. "Ma, where was Delores born?" I asked.

"I don't know," Ma replied. "She was adopted. You know that."

Then I decided to ask the real question, the one that had been on my mind since Delores's confirmation. "Do you suppose anyone around here knows who Delores's real ma and pa are?" I asked.

I watched the knife hesitate ever-so-slightly above the carrot. But Ma didn't have a chance to answer my question. Pa came into the kitchen.

"Did you hear about Raymond Kolden?" he asked as he sat down in a chair on the other side of the table.

"What about him?" I asked.

"He was out plowing, and he breathed in too much dust." Pa paused. "He came down with pneumonia. He's in the hospital in Morris."

"Can we go see him?" I asked.

I knew that Pa was close friends with some of the Koldens, so I was hoping he would agree to take me to the hospital.

"We'll go tomorrow—right after chores," Pa replied.

In the morning, Pa and I got into the Model-T Ford and drove to the Morris hospital. It was nothing more than a bunch of single beds stuffed into the rooms of what had once been a large private residence.

An elderly woman was seated at a desk just inside the front door.

"Which room is Raymond Kolden in?" Pa asked.

She looked up. "Are you family?" she asked.

"Just friends," Pa answered.

The elderly woman stared past us, as though she didn't quite know what to say. "I'm very sorry to have to tell you this," she said gently. "But Raymond Kolden passed away earlier this morning."

"Are you sure?" Pa stammered.

"The doctor did everything he could," she said. "But Raymond had a very bad case of pneumonia. I'm sorry."

Directly behind the desk where the elderly woman was sitting, I saw two nurses in a room on the other side of an open doorway. One nurse was stripping the wrinkled sheets off a bed. The other nurse carried a pair of work pants and some work boots out into the hallway. The nurse discarded the clothing in a cardboard box that contained other trash she had collected from the room. I recognized the boots as the ones Raymond had worn the day we wrestled in the schoolyard.

I was too overcome to do or say anything. My good friend Raymond Kolden, who had stood up for me and shared his lunches with me for all those years, was gone, and I was still here. I was too stunned by the enormity of that to cry. I don't even remember Pa driving me back to the farm.

I didn't go into the house. As soon as Pa parked the Model-T, I walked out into the pasture. I had to get the cows for milking. I also needed to be alone with my thoughts. Raymond Kolden and I had both been raised to be hired men. He had accepted that as his destiny. Now he was gone. I was still here, still struggling with my life as a farm hand, working for room and board. I couldn't accept that. I didn't know if I was the lucky one for still being alive, or if Raymond was the lucky one for having died.

I felt overwhelmed by thoughts of Raymond Kolden: my good friend and fellow hired man, who was dead. I would never see him again. I was still too shocked and stunned to cry. I remembered how he had stood up for me the day the boys had jumped me in Alberta. After that fight, I noticed that his work boots were laced with twine. The work boots the nurse had dumped outside the hospital room where Raymond had died were also laced with twine. The image of those worn boots, lying on top of the pile of discarded trash, suddenly crowded out every thought I had.

I sat down in the pasture and cried like a baby.

X

Later that day, Raymond's mother asked me if I would sing a solo at the funeral service. I told her I didn't know if I could do it, but that I would try my very best.

Singing at Raymond's funeral turned out to be one of the hardest things I have ever done in my life. But I sang "Rock of Ages" with all my heart. I wanted the people in church to feel what I felt about Raymond. I owed my friend that much. At the end of the song, there were so many tears streaming down my face that I couldn't see the congregation. I heard people sobbing in the pews below me. I didn't know what to make of that. I just knew that I had sang that song with everything I had inside of me. I had done the best I could for my good friend.

Afterwards, I was one of the pallbearers who carried Raymond's inexpensive coffin into Reque Cemetery and over to a freshly dug hole in the prairie soil. As we lowered the coffin into the ground, Reverend Sandager said one last prayer over Raymond's grave. But I didn't hear the prayer.

As I stared at Raymond's coffin at the bottom of that black hole, I heard only my own thoughts: Raymond, I know you threw that wrestling match. I just know it.

XI

After the funeral, I laid in my bed and stared at the ceiling for hours. Toward evening, I finally went downstairs. As I walked past the oil painting I had hung on the wall, I paused to take a closer look at the elderly farmer who was standing behind the plow and team of horses in the middle of the freshly plowed field. In the distance, a flock of birds was flying toward a thin beam of sunlight that was shining through a seam in the cloudy sky.

One bird, its wings spread wide, was flying ahead of the other birds toward the light at the end of the field.

SKINNING SKUNKS

I

After the Depression, sabers rattled in a place called Europe. We didn't hear much of that noise in our remote corner of the Minnesota prairie. But we did sense that something important was happening on the other side of the Atlantic Ocean. No one thought it would affect us too much, however. Little did we know how events in Germany, many thousands of miles away, would eventually transform our insignificant lives. Little did we know that many of the people in Stevens County, those who had survived the Great Depression and the drought years, would perish in the next decade.

Throughout the 1930s, word drifted across the Atlantic Ocean about a fellow named Adolph Hitler who was making belligerent threats against his neighbors. The name meant very little to most of us, although some of the farmers figured out who Adolph Hitler really was long before people in the big cities had a clue as to what he was capable of doing. Minnesota farmers had dealt with tyrants during the Great Depression. They knew Hitler's type. They knew what these tyrants were capable of doing to innocent, hard-working people.

To me, Adolph Hitler meant nothing. He posed no more of a threat to me than the crazed farmer up north who started shooting a .22 at his neighbor's livestock, just for sport. I couldn't imagine that a mustached maniac would eventually change my life and the lives of just about everyone I had grown up with.

But I am getting ahead of myself again. There is much more to tell about the late 1930s, a time when getting my teeth fixed, swatting mosquitoes, and snaring gophers to buy myself a new shirt for school were much more important than anything that might be happening in a place called Europe.

II

I never traveled past Reque Cemetery without thinking about Raymond Kolden. Many times I would walk into the cemetery and stand by his grave to be alone with my thoughts. Reque Cemetery was one of the few places where I felt at peace with myself. I stood by Raymond's grave for hours and pondered the mysteries of life and death. I began to wonder if maybe my life's destiny had been written in the stars hundreds and thousands of years before I was born. Maybe some higher power had determined that I was to go through life alone, as punishment for something I had done wrong in a previous life. Maybe we all live many lives—and every one of those lives is God's attempt to teach us something we didn't learn in a previous existence. If so, I must have squandered the love of everyone I knew in some previous life. I must have taken every human being I knew for granted, for I seemed destined in this life to lose everyone who befriended me. I didn't want it that way, but it was the pattern of my existence.

I almost envied people buried in family cemetery plots, surrounded by grandparents and parents and sons and daughters. They had the connections to the human race that I wanted, but did not have. Still, if there are such things as guardian angels, I had more than my share: Buster, Ivar, Delores, Raymond, and others. Without them, I would never have made it into my teenage years.

If God was trying to teach me a lesson that I would carry into the hereafter, one of my classrooms was Reque Cemetery. For it was there that I felt most alone, and yet most connected to the rest of the human race. I hope, if I ever have another life to live, I will never take for granted the love of people who cared enough about me to walk through life by my side.

III

Later in the 1930s, we were invaded by insects and pests of every shape and species. Everything that crawled or flew visited our farm. Since there were few effective insecticides in those days, all you could do was wait the insects out, pray they wouldn't do too much damage, and hope they left quickly—which they seldom did.

The first insects to pay us a visit were the box elder bugs. They were more of a nuisance than anything else. In our grove we had a number of trees that were infested with billions of these little flying bugs. In a matter of days, the trees became a huge swarming mass of tiny insects. At night you could hear their wings beating in the darkness.

Once they were through with the trees, the box elder bugs started working their way over to the house. They covered the roof and all of the exterior walls until you couldn't see out any of the windows. You had to be careful that you didn't leave a window open at night, because you could wake up the next morning to find the walls of your bedroom, and perhaps even your bed, crawling with ugly little bugs.

On hot summer nights, with the windows closed to keep the bugs out, and the temperatures and humidity high, it was all but impossible to sleep. Sometimes you would soak a sheet in a cold bucket of water and throw it over your body to try to keep yourself cool. You didn't sleep—you just lay there, waiting for the sun to come up the next morning so you could go back to work.

Eventually, the box elder bugs grew tired of us, and they moved out of the area, only to be followed by swarms of blood-sucking mosquitoes. I am not talking about an occasional mosquito. I am talking about billions of mosquitoes, covering every square inch of the farm. All the standing water from the plentiful rains had created a breeding paradise for mosquito larvae. They sure took advantage of nature's generosity.

We started to notice what appeared to be low-flying white clouds hovering above the sloughs and other standing bodies of water. Within days, these white clouds of mosquitoes moved across the fields and settled on the farmyard. Sometimes the mosquitoes were so thick you couldn't see from the house to the barn. When I did the chores, I had to cover myself head to foot. Only my eyes were exposed. All that clothing made me sweat profusely, which seemed to attract even more mosquitoes.

Thankfully, the sun eventually destroyed enough of the mosquitoes so I could go back out into the fields without being eaten alive. But that respite lasted for only a couple of days. The next visitor we had on our farm was the most unwelcome guest of all: grasshoppers.

We had a bumper crop in the fields, almost ready to be harvested, and the grasshoppers arrived. Like a biblical plague descending from the clouds, a black swarm circled the fields and settled on our corn. Within days, they had stripped the fields clean. And there was nothing you could do about it except watch them munch away on all your hard work, until they had digested your profits for that year. Then one day, the grasshoppers were gone, moving on to areas yet untouched by their voracious appetites.

Through my experiences with these insects, I have learned something about life: human beings have been on this planet for only a short time—and we seem to have control of things right now—but insects, the tiniest creatures in nature's food chain, will again rule the world. They will be crawling over our graves long after the human race is a distant memory.

Maybe that should make all of us pause and think about how we're living our lives, and how we're treating one another. Unless, that is, we're too busy swatting mosquitoes, or fighting off grasshoppers, to have too much time to think about such things.

IV

Then came the skunks. They must have been breeding underground in Stevens County during the wet years, because suddenly everywhere you looked you would see a raised striped tail sticking out of the prairie grass, a kind of submarine periscope looking to unload its torpedo.

The skunks made for bountiful trapping. Any kind of fur pelt was worth money in those days—even skunk. It was a stinky business, to be sure, but since there was a market for skunk pelts, I starting trapping them in earnest. I was determined to do just about anything to raise the money I needed to get my bottom teeth fixed. If that meant trapping and skinning skunks, then that's what I would do.

The one thing you have to bear in mind about trapping skunks, and skinning them for the pelts, is that after a while you grow used to the smell. I suppose the human nose will adjust in time to just about anything, including politicians. However, after you've been around a truly wretched smell for a long period of time, you tend to forget that other people probably haven't become accustomed to those same odors. And there is some danger in that.

What I'm trying to say here, in sort of a roundabout way, is that after a few days of trapping and skinning skunks, you probably don't want to go over and court your favorite girlfriend. The time isn't right for romance to blossom. You need several days in between each skunk-skinning session before its safe to rejoin the human race, or at least the part of it that's worth rejoining. While waiting, you might want to do something like go into your bank and open up an account. I can assure you that you won't have to wait in line very long. They'll get right to you, and usher you back out the door quicker than you can say, "Skunk tail."

I also trapped weasel, mink, and muskrat. But those memories are not as vivid in my mind. Trapping skunks, however, is one of the most memorable experiences of my youth. It was also a great character builder. Once you have developed the will power to kneel next to a freshly trapped skunk, while its bladder leaks on the ground and its spray hovers in the air, you can put up with just about anything the government might ever decide to do to you.

V

Pa could not live with even a little prosperity. Even a taste of affluence ate away at him like a cancer. Every time the farm started to turn a small profit, Pa slipped gradually back into his old ways: sneaking off to play cards or out fishing with his friends. I say sneaking off because I still begged Pa to let me go fishing with him—especially when he went out on a boat. When his excuses wore thin, he started sneaking out the house long before I woke up.

One evening, I saw Pa making some sandwiches in the kitchen. Since he normally made sandwiches the nights before his fishing trips, I asked, "Pa, are you going fishing?"

"No," he replied, "I've got some work at the far end of the property. So I thought I'd take my lunch with me tomorrow."

I doubted him. He seldom did any kind of farm work anymore. If there was work to be done, I was certain he would have told me to do it. I knew something was up.

Early the next morning, while it was still dark outside, I awoke to the sound of a door opening and shutting downstairs. I bolted out of bed and rushed over to the upstairs window. I saw Pa hurrying over to a car that was parked in our yard. As I saw him put his fishing rod and tackle into the trunk of the car, I pulled on my trousers and rushed downstairs.

I threw open the front door and yelled, "Wait for me! I want to go fishing, too!"

I was too late. The car drove out of our yard and down the dirt road. I recognized the car as belonging to Hans Anderson, one of our neighbors who Pa fished with on a regular basis. Hans had a son, Erling, who also went fishing with them.

Ma had heard the commotion. She was standing in the kitchen when I turned around and walked back into the house. I was so angry I almost started to cry.

"What's wrong with you?" she asked.

"Pa's gone fishing again. I wanted him to take me along."

"Pa never takes anyone with him," she said, more to herself than to me. "He never has."

I knew Ma was not sympathizing with me. She was commenting on her marriage to Pa—and the many days he had left her alone on the farm. She didn't say anything more to me. She just walked over to the window and stared outside at the dark fields. I knew what she was thinking. It was times like this, when Pa was out fishing, that her company used to come by for a visit. But those days were over. I knew Ma would spend the rest of the day lost in her thoughts, dreaming about a love that no longer existed.

I was so hurt that I planned to walk over to Lake Hattie to fish for bullheads, leaving the chores for Pa to do when he got back. But I knew I couldn't do that. The cows had to be milked. I had no choice. I milked the cows, separated the cream, and took the tractor out in the field to do some light field work. By the time I was through with my morning chores, it was time to start my evening chores. I finished my evening chores about the time Hans, Erling, and Pa drove into the yard.

I had already practiced what I would say as soon as Pa got home. And I did—right in front of his fishing buddies. Pa was carrying a stringer full of walleye pike over to the barn when I walked up to him. "Why didn't you take me fishing with you?" I demanded.

"There wasn't enough room in the boat," Pa replied.

"You're a liar!" I hollered. "You just want to leave me here to do all the chores, while you're out having fun!"

I could tell that Hans and Erling Anderson were very puzzled by what was happening. "What's going on here?" Hans asked. "I thought you said Lloyd didn't want to go fishing with us."

Pa mumbled something incomprehensible.

"I never said anything like that," I said to Hans. I continued to look Pa straight in the eye. "I've been begging him to take me out in a boat ever since I was able to hold a fishing pole. But he refuses. He wants me to stay here and do the chores. That's all I am to him—a hired man!"

I could tell that Hans was greatly troubled by what I had said. "Is Lloyd telling us the truth?" he asked Pa. "Has he been wanting to go fishing with us all along, and you wouldn't take him?"

Pa didn't answer his friend's question. He just stomped off toward the barn with his stringer of fish.

VI

That wasn't the last I heard from Hans Anderson. Two weeks later, very early on a Saturday morning, a car pulled into our front yard. I heard a horn honk. When I looked out the upstairs window, I recognized the car as Hans Anderson's car. My first thought was, well I guess they're at it again. I figured they'd be driving out of the yard to go fishing. I didn't even attempt to get dressed.

Pa walked outside to meet Hans, who had stepped out of the car. They talked briefly. Then I saw Hans shake his head vigorously. He waved Pa back toward the house with a simple flick of his wrist.

Hans then looked at the upstairs window, and, seeing me there, he gestured for me to come down.

I had no idea what he wanted, but I quickly put on my shirt and trousers and went downstairs. As I walked through the kitchen, I could hear Pa talking to Ma in their bedroom.

"Lloyd," Hans said as I walked over to where he was standing by the car, "do you have a fishing pole?"

"Yes, I do," I replied awkwardly. I was still not quite sure what was going on. "It's in the barn."

"Go get it," Hans insisted.

"Why?"

"We're going fishing," he said. Then he raised his voice as he looked in the direction of the house. "You, me, and Erling. We're going fishing on Lake Minnewaska—just the three of us."

I was so excited I ran down to the barn to get the rod and reel Ivar had rebuilt for me. I jumped in the car and we were off.

I always thought that was a pretty decent thing Hans Anderson did for me that day. I had my first big adventure out on a boat, which remains one of the big thrills of my life. Pa had to stay home and do chores.

Actually, he never got around to doing chores. I had to do them when I got back from Lake Minnewaska. But as I walked past Pa and waved a stringer of fish right under his nose, I didn't care if I had to work all night to make up for the fun I had that day on Lake Minnewaska.

VII

Pa held a grudge against me for quite some time. He wouldn't even talk to me for several weeks. Then one day, he took me with him to Morris to pick up some extra hired men to help with the threshing. We drove the Model-T. It was big enough to seat four people—five, if someone was willing to sit in the open trunk.

For several years, men looking for work had been coming through Morris on railroad flat cars. They would travel to any part of the country that offered them work and something to eat. Most of them were honest, hard-working people, just like the rest of us. They were simply trying to make a few dollars to support themselves and their families during the tough times. But a hardened, borderline criminal element also migrated north from the still-struggling southern states. These men were not necessarily seeking an opportunity to earn an honest day's wages. They were looking for easy money. So you had to be careful what kind of people you hired as temporary field hands.

When we arrived in Morris, the streets were lined with men. All of them looked like they had been sleeping in their clothes for weeks. Pa parked the Model-T on Main Street and walked over to talk to a group who were waiting for local farmers to offer them employment. They would soon get back on the flat cars and move on to another county, looking for more work. It was not a good life. But as I knew all too well from my own experiences during the Great Depression, desperate men will do anything to feed themselves and their families.

I watched as Pa passed up what looked to me to be the most honest, hardworking men in the group. He paused to talk to two tough-looking men. As he talked to them, they glanced occasionally in the direction of the Model-T, where I was sitting.

Later, Pa gestured for the two men to walk with him back to the car. As they approached, I remembered thinking that these were not the two men I would have selected. If there were any hardened criminal types among the recent arrivals, I would have suspected they were the two men Pa was bringing with him back to our farm.

"This is Lou and Hank," Pa said as he slipped behind the driver's wheel.

The two men climbed into the back seat.

"They'll be working with us today," Pa confirmed.

I said hello, but they did not acknowledge my greeting. I don't remember either of them saying a word during the trip back to Alberta. Their faces remained expressionless. They stared straight ahead as the Model-T chugged down the road.

Once we were back at the farm, all four of us went out into the fields. As I was getting the thresher ready, Hank, the bigger of the two men, kept bumping into me. Each time he would grumble something under his breath, as though it were my fault. Each time, I would tell him I was sorry—even though he was clearly the one doing the bumping.

Finally, he bumped into me very hard. Then he put both of his huge hands on my chest and pushed me away from him. "What the hell's wrong with you, kid?" he taunted me. "Can't you walk in your own two shoes?"

"You've been bumping into me," I replied. "I've just been trying to get everything ready so we can start threshing."

"Are you trying to start a fight?" he said, pushing me in the chest again. "Is that what you want?"

"No, I'm not trying to start a fight," I replied. "If you stay out of my way, we can start work in a few minutes."

Lou suddenly joined in. "Looks to me like the kid needs to be taken down a notch or two," he said, smirking. "Looks to me, Hank, like he's begging for a fight."

I looked over at Pa to see if he was going to say something to put an end to this nonsense. But he just looked off in the distance and said nothing.

Hank suddenly charged, flailing away at my head with both fists. I saw him coming. I quickly dropped to one knee, grabbed his neck, and sent him flying over my shoulder. He came down flat on his back. He rolled over on his side, scratching his face something terrible on the sharp field stubble.

He leaped to his feet and charged again. I was ready for him. He took another swing at me. I caught him off balance and sent him flying into the stubble again.

This time, when he got to his feet, the other side of his face and neck were bleeding. Again, he lowered his head and came at me like a charging bull. I stepped aside at the last second and put all my weight on his back. He crashed face-first into the stubble. It was a miracle he didn't poke an eye out because the stubble was sharp as knives, and every bit as pointed.

He rose more slowly this time. He was winded, but he charged again. Exhausted as he was, it was very easy for me to throw him over my shoulder and back into the stubble. He struggled for a second or two to get back to his feet. Then he lay flat on his back, panting and struggling to breathe.

I glanced over at Pa, who was leaning against the threshing machine. "Why didn't you stop it?" I demanded.

Pa walked over to where Hank was on his knees. He put one hand on Hank's shoulder and said, "That's enough. Let's get to work."

For the rest of the day, I worked right alongside Hank and Lou. I had no more problems with either of them. They both turned out to be very good workers. After they were paid at the end of the day, Hank even walked over and shook my hand. "I'm sorry, kid," he said quietly and politely. "It wasn't my idea."

I knew, then, that Pa had put him up to it.

VIII

I never trusted Pa again. He had obviously decided to take me down a notch for embarrassing him in front of his fishing buddies. His full-time hired man had gotten out of line and needed to be taught a lesson.

What Pa hadn't counted on was that I had been doing a man's work for so long that I was already as strong as men ten years older than me. Plus, I was much more agile than Hank. And I had the experience of wrestling for my self-respect and dignity for all those years at school. Everything had backfired on Pa. Instead of getting even with me, he had been embarrassed once again—this time in front of hired men he considered inferior to himself.

Still, I lowered my guard one last time. Later that fall, Pa offered me ten dollars to hand-pick his last cornfield. The field was filled with nubbins—small, imperfectly formed corn cobs that had to be picked by hand. There was no other way to do it.

Everyone Pa asked to pick the corn refused. They knew that picking a field that big by hand, with just a hook strapped to your wrist, under an intensely hot August sun, would test a man's strength and endurance to the limits. Pa had no other means to pick the corn, short of doing it himself—which he would never do. He had to ask me. I agreed. For ten dollars of backbreaking work, under a blistering sun, Pa was getting a deal, and he knew it.

With that ten dollars, I would have enough money to go to the dentist in Morris and get my bottom teeth fixed. I had saved another fifty dollars by trapping skunks and snaring gophers. So I seized the opportunity to earn the last ten dollars I needed. I had been self-conscious about my smile for too long. I was desperate to look the way other people looked when they smiled.

I worked for almost six full days, twelve hours a day, picking that corn. I don't remember how many acres it was. I just remember that the sun was blistering hot, and there wasn't even a hint of a breeze.

Finally, after sixty-five hours of grueling work, I loaded the last wagon full of corn and drove it back to the farm. Pa was over by the barn when I drove up to him.

"This is the last load," I said. "I'm going to Morris to set up an appointment with the dentist. Can I have my ten dollars?"

"That'll have to wait until later," Pa said nonchalantly. "I don't have the money right now."

"When will you have it?" I demanded.

"That just depends. It could be in another week or two. Maybe a few months. It depends on what I get for this year's crop."

"You had no intention of paying me, did you?" I yelled at him. "You just made that promise so I would do work you didn't want to do yourself."

Pa walked away. I was shattered by his latest betrayal. The most important thing in my life at that moment was to get my teeth fixed. Once again, I was reminded that I was nothing to Ma and Pa.

Not knowing exactly what to do, but knowing I did not want to be around Pa for fear I might take a swing at him, I just walked down the road.

I hadn't walked very far when Hans Anderson pulled up in his car. He must have been able to tell that something was terribly wrong. "What's the problem, Lloyd?" he asked. I tried to wave him past, but he insisted on knowing what was wrong with me.

"Pa promised me ten dollars to pick the corn in one of his fields," I explained.

Hans leaned out the window of his car.

"I need the money to get my teeth fixed. I just finished picking the corn, but he won't pay me."

"He won't pay you!" Hans said. "Why won't he pay you?"

"He said he doesn't have the money."

"We'll see about that," Hans said. He opened the passenger door of his car. "Jump in. I'm going to have a talk with your Pa."

Hans turned the car around, and we sped back to the farm. Pa was standing by the granary. Hans parked the car and confronted Pa. "Did you promise to pay Lloyd ten dollars for picking the corn in one of your fields?"

Pa nodded.

"And now you've said you can't pay him?"

"I don't have the money," Pa replied. "Not yet."

"Well, I'll tell you something," Hans said, pointing an index finger in Pa's direction. "You'd better find that money. And you'd better find it fast. Because if you haven't paid Lloyd by tomorrow morning, I'm going to Alberta, and I'm going to tell everyone in town that your word is no good. I'll tell everyone that you've cheated your own son out of ten dollars. We'll see what kind of credit you get in the stores after that."

Hans turned to me and said right in front of Pa, "Lloyd, tomorrow morning I want you to come by my house and let me know whether or not your Pa has paid you that ten dollars. If not, he'd better never again show his face in Alberta. I will tell everyone that your Pa is a liar and a cheat."

That night, at the supper table, Ma and Pa didn't say a word to me. I could tell they didn't quite know how to deal with the situation. After we were through eating, I walked out to the barn to check on a cow that had injured itself in the pasture.

Later, when I walked into the house and upstairs to my room, I found ten crumpled-up one-dollar bills lying on my bed.

IX

I set up three separate appointments with Dr. Bernard Ederer, the dentist in Morris. He agreed to fix all of my teeth for a total cost of sixty dollars, a good price considering everything that needed to be done. Ma and Pa had never sent me to the dentist in all the years I had lived with them.

Dr. Ederer also agreed to accept twenty dollars at the end of each of our three appointments, rather than have me pay all the money up front. I got to know Dr. Ederer pretty well. I told him that I had been snaring gophers and trapping skunks for several years so I could get my teeth fixed. He was very impressed. He said he would make sure everything was done right.

"This bridge will last for the rest of your life, Lloyd," he promised.

Toward the end of our final appointment, he held up a mirror and told me to smile. I had always been self-conscious about my smile. At first, I was hesitant to follow his instructions.

"Go ahead, Lloyd," he urged me. "Just one little smile."

I managed a weak smile. But when I saw my beautiful new white teeth, my smile filled the mirror. I had been waiting most of my life to see my own smile in a mirror.

"Thank you," I said weakly, as the tears filled my eyes. "Thank you very much."

When it was time for me to leave Dr. Ederer's office, I reached into my worn trouser pockets for the last twenty dollars I owed him. I pulled out a crumpled array of dollar bills and coins. I counted them. When I had finished, I pushed the money in his direction. He scooped ten dollars of it into an envelope. He sealed the envelope. Much to my surprise, he placed it in my shirt pocket.

"I don't understand," I said.

"Use it to buy some clothes for yourself," he replied cheerfully.

"But why?" I asked. "Why are you doing this for me?"

"I don't think I've ever had a patient who worked so hard to save the money to get his teeth fixed," he explained. "Besides, I trapped a few skunks to get through dental school. I know that's worth a ten-dollar discount."

Dr. Ederer was true to his word. I've still got that bridge. Every time I smile, I remember that he was an excellent dentist—and a man who kept his word.

X

Leaving Dr. Ederer's office, I smiled at every glass window on Morris's Main Street. I think I felt better about myself than I had at any other time in my life. My new smile, together with my somewhat awkward attempts to imitate the hairstyle Nelson Eddy had worn in *Rose-Marie*, had boosted my confidence. I felt so good that I went into one of the clothing stores and bought a sport coat that was on sale. The coat reminded me of the one Nelson Eddy wore when he sang "The Indian Love Song" to his Rose-Marie. I wore the coat out of the store and hopped into the Model-T.

I decided to drive over to Delores's to show her my new smile. It was a real high point in my life; I had the right to show off a little. But as I approached the two-story house where Delores lived, I saw her walking down the sidewalk with a young man. He was wearing a gray suit. They were heading toward a new two-door convertible parked on the street.

Suddenly, I felt more self-conscious than I had ever felt in my entire life. I slumped down in the driver's seat, hoping Delores would not see me. She didn't. She was too preoccupied with the young man, whose arm she was holding, to notice me.

I glanced down at my worn work trousers. I realized how silly I must have looked with those trousers and my new sport coat. Plus, Pa's ancient Model-T no doubt completed the image of some country hick who had come to town for the first time in his life.

Having seen Delores with another man, especially one who was dressed in such an expensive suit and who drove such a beautiful new car, hurt my feelings.

At least I had my new smile. For that, I was grateful.

XI

A few days later, I was waiting in the Model-T by the railroad crossing where Ivar and I had watched the train load of migrant workers rumble by in the early months of the Great Depression. I had learned from that experience that I could sometimes predict future events by the cargoes trains carried through Stevens County.

I learned, for example, that railroad cars filled with grain reflected a good harvest and meant that prices would probably fall. Our own crops wouldn't be worth as much as we hoped. When the railroad cars did not carry much grain through our area, especially in the fall, I knew there had been a poor harvest throughout the Midwest. Our crops would be worth more; but everything we needed to survive would also cost much more. Farmers lost out either way. Still, it was kind of fun to try to predict *how* we were going to suffer. A railroad crossing is, in short, a place where you can see history in the making. I idled the Model-T, expecting, perhaps, another train load of migrant workers of the type Pa had hired. What I saw was something quite different.

The train, which was traveling east, did not carry a human cargo. It was filled with National Guard military cargo. Every car that passed by had jeeps, military transport trucks, large guns on wheels, and other such weapons of war.

I waited for almost fifteen minutes by the railroad crossing, as the cars kept rumbling by, each one seemingly more burdened with military cargo than the previous car. It was one of the longest trains that had ever passed through the area. As the train finally disappeared on the eastern horizon, I knew that I had seen the future.

I sensed that there were going to be a lot more skunks to skin in the years ahead. Only we wouldn't be skinning them in the sloughs outside of Alberta, Minnesota. We'd be doing it overseas.

Searching for the Past

I

Events of the late 1930s and early 1940s kind of run together in my mind, but I will try to sort them out and describe them as best I can. It was a very confusing time for me personally, and perhaps for all young Americans. The sounds of war were growing louder overseas. It seemed only a matter of time before America would be drawn into the conflict.

To those of us who grew up on the Minnesota prairie, and who were teenagers at the time, the prospect of war was both exciting and terrifying. We believed that we would be called to fight, and we knew that many of us probably would not survive. When war came, we would be uprooted from our farms and small towns and sent away to foreign countries and places we had only read about in books. Still, existing within the threat of war was the possibility of romance and adventure.

The one thought that ran through most of our minds was that we would probably be a generation who lived very short lives. There was an urgency to do the things that other generations might have put off until they were older. We took stock of our lives and made decisions that probably should have waited until we were wiser and more experienced.

To some young Americans, that meant getting married and having children before they were out of their teenage years. To others, it meant behaving with reckless abandon. The hope, I suppose, was that a short life could still be a full life. My sense of urgency rekindled a desire to find my birth mother and reconnect with my real family—before I was called away to fight, and maybe even die, far from home.

Every day carried with it a strange combination of worries and concerns, ranging from the commonplace to the profound. I was still struggling to run the farm and do my daily chores, while trying to get enough of an education to graduate from high school. At the same time that I was busy devising a plan to search for my birth mother, I was preparing myself emotionally to fight in a war overseas. I suppose, in retrospect, this is why it is so difficult to sort out the events of that period of time. My inner conflicts defy tidy explanations and descriptions. Those were confusing times for everyone.

II

During the Great Depression and the drought years, I had to put the goal of finding my birth mother on the back burner. Life was a daily struggle for survival. It was impossible to think ahead or think back.

Later, when the farm started to earn us a decent living again, I looked ahead as well as back. What I saw in either direction was not encouraging. I realized, if I did not break out of the mold Ma and Pa had established for me, I was destined to be their hired man, and nothing more, until the day they died. To change my destiny, I had to find my birth mother.

Once dedicated to this course of action, I faced several problems. Ma and Pa had always refused to discuss my adoption, except when they threatened to send me back to the orphanage. Of course, from these threats, area children who teased me about being adopted, and vague memories I had about my birth mother and the orphanage, I figured out very early that Ma and Pa were not my biological parents. Delores also knew I was adopted, and we talked openly about it. Ma and Pa, however, refused to answer even the most basic questions about my adoption.

So I knew they would not help me locate my birth mother, even though they undoubtedly had adoption records somewhere. In fact, they would actively work against my efforts to find her. They could no longer control me through physical beatings or threats of reform school. They tried to control me by keeping me in a state of poverty. Nonetheless, from my trapping activities, I did have a small source of income. Withholding information about my birth and adoption was the only weapon they had left to manipulate my life and control my destiny. If they released that information to me, I would no longer be their hired man. I would be someone else's son. I would have to find my birth mother with my own meager resources.

Another problem was that I knew absolutely nothing about adoption procedures and birth records. I would have to start from scratch. I had to educate myself in these things so I could devise meaningful strategies in order to began my search. At the outset, the search for my birth mother seemed like the proverbial quest for a needle in a haystack. All I knew was what Delores had overheard Ma say: "He was born not too far from here."

I did not know, however, precisely what Ma meant by that statement, or if it even applied to me. She might have been referring to some other child.

Since I was limited in terms of how far I could search for my birth mother, out of necessity I accepted that Ma's statement applied to me. It was more an act of faith than conviction on my part. If I had been born in another state, I did not have adequate resources to conduct a systematic search. I could only look within miles, in all directions, from Alberta. And even that would take some time and careful planning.

III

I started with the basics. I figured the public library in Morris might have some books or articles on state laws regarding adoption and birth records, so I started there. Pa had sold the old Model-T and used the money to make a down payment on a used Model-A. However, that car was seldom available because Pa was gone most days fishing or playing cards. So after I finished my morning chores, I sometimes rode to Morris on an old bicycle I had reconditioned, or I walked to Highway 28 and hitched a ride into town.

The librarian was a very nice elderly woman who showed me some old books containing information about the Minnesota statutes and laws governing births and adoptions. From the books, I learned that each county generally kept birth records in the county recorder's office, located in the county seat. Adoption records were generally kept by the state, although it was unclear to me as to whether or not copies of those records were given to each county recorder.

After several visits to the library to review the information in the old legal books, the elderly librarian asked me why I was so interested in adoption and birth records.

"I was adopted," I replied. "I'm interested in trying to find my birth mother."

"Do you think that's a good idea?" she asked sympathetically.

"It's very important to me," I replied.

"Then you should go up to the Stevens County Courthouse," she offered, "and ask the county recorder. The books we have are pretty old and probably out of date. Much has undoubtedly changed since these were published."

"Thank you," I said. "I think I'll do that."

"You might also ask the county recorder about the differences between private and public adoptions," she added.

"I don't understand."

"I suspect there are different records for private and public adoptions," she explained. "Do you know how you were adopted?"

"I was adopted out of an orphanage. But I don't know if it was publicly or privately run."

"Well, you might want to look into that."

"What difference would it make?"

"Oh, there could be all kinds of shenanigans going on in private adoptions. I know, in my time, some young mothers who wanted to keep their babies, but who also wanted to avoid the stigma of illegitimacy for both themselves and the child, would put them up for private adoption. They wouldn't even fill out a birth certificate. Or they would fill out a fraudulent one, with fictitious parents' names, just for the sake of appearances. Then another relative would adopt the child, as part of the arrangement, and the baby would be brought back into the family. This way the mother would have access to her own child without the community suspecting the baby was illegitimate. People can be very critical of babies who were born out of wedlock. Some young mothers did it this way—to protect the child, if nothing else."

"Did that happen often?" I asked eagerly.

"I don't know if it happened very often," she replied. "But I know that it *did* happen. I had a cousin who did just such a thing. She moved out of the area during her pregnancy, had the baby, put it up for private adoption, and an uncle adopted the child. Then she moved back into the area, where she had access to that child during all the years the little girl was growing up. And nobody figured it out until many years later when the girl was much older and living in another part of the country."

IV

As I walked across town, I thought about what the librarian had told me regarding babies being adopted back into families through private adoptions. I didn't know if that applied to me. I doubted it. But it did make my thoughts about Delores's personal background seem a little less like idle speculation.

If such an adoption could have happened in the elderly librarian's family, who was to say it couldn't have happened in ours? That, however, was another issue. At the moment, I was much more concerned about my own birth mother.

The Stevens County Courthouse was located next to the water tower. It was a beautiful old brick building with a steeple on top that made it look more like a church or school than a government building.

The county recorder was standing behind a marble counter when I walked into the office. He was a tall, thin man with large eyeglasses and a folksy manner. "What can I do for you?" he asked in a friendly tone of voice.

"I need some information regarding birth and adoption records," I replied.

"Shoot it to me. What is it you need to know?"

"Well, first of all, could you tell me if all birth records are kept in the county recorder's offices in the county where the baby is born?"

"That's been the practice for many years," he nodded. "That's a pretty uniform policy in the state of Minnesota."

"How about adoption records?" I asked. "Are they also kept in the county where the baby is born?"

"Well, that can get a little more tricky," he replied. "In theory all adoption records are kept by the state. And they are supposed to forward that information to the counties where the babies were born. But I'm afraid it doesn't always happen that way."

"Why?" I asked.

"Oh, all kinds of things could happen. If it was some kind of private adoption, the state might never receive those records. And, years ago, some adoption agencies and orphanages didn't always make it a practice to send out those records as faithfully as they should have. But if an adoption agency or orphanage was run professionally, and they were following the law, they would faithfully send those records out to the state. And the state would forward that information to the county. But did it always happen that way? No, I don't think so."

"How would you know if the state did send the adoption records to the county?"

"The adoption certificate would be attached to the birth certificate. In fact, the adoption certificate seals the birth certificate so that no one has access to either of the documents, except county recorders. They are not available to the public."

I paused to digest what the county recorder was telling me. Then I asked, "If, at the time of an adoption, there was a name change, would that information also be sent out to the county recorder's office where the baby was born?"

"The last name is always changed in an adoption. Do you mean first and middle names?"

"Yes. Would those name changes be forwarded from the state to the county?"

"Yup. Unless the baby is given up for adoption right after the birth. In which case, the baby might only have its adoptive name. But normally new mothers like to name their babies, even when they've planned to put them up for adoption. Still, you have to remember that record keeping wasn't always done as accurately as we do it today. It depends on what period of time you're talking about."

"The early 1920s," I replied.

"That would be about the time the laws regarding record keeping were enforced more vigorously."

"So if someone came into this office and asked for a birth certificate, using either the original name at the time of birth, or the new name at the time of the adoption, you would probably be able to locate it either way?"

"In this office, those names would be cross-referenced. Would that be the case in every county recorder's office in the state of Minnesota? I can't say. Still, like I said, we can't release that information."

"But you would have to tell someone that the information was there, if you had it?" I asked.

"If they gave me the name of someone who had been adopted, I would tell them we had that information. I would also tell them that the records are sealed and unavailable to the public."

I was about to leave, when one more question occurred to me. It would be a question I would ask many times over the next year. "Could you see if you have a birth certificate for Lloyd Augustine Clausen?" I asked.

"Write it out on this piece of paper for me," he replied, pushing a small tablet in my direction.

I wrote the name on the tablet, and he disappeared into a vault in the rear of the room. He walked back out of the vault a few minutes later.

"Nope. Sorry," he said, shaking his head. "I've got nothing back there for Lloyd Augustine Clausen."

That was also something I was to hear many times over the next year.

V

That night, when I returned to the farm, we gathered around the radio with some of our neighbors to listen to President Roosevelt talk about his concerns for world peace. He described the escalating tensions in Europe and called upon our neighbors overseas to do everything in their power to avoid war. He also assured the American people that he would personally do everything in his power to keep this nation out of any foreign war. He said, "I do not want to shed one drop of American blood on foreign soil."

When President Roosevelt was through speaking, an elderly farmer who was sitting in a chair next to the radio leaned back and muttered softly, "Well, there you have it. We'll be fighting in a war in Europe within a year."

"What do you mean?" I asked. "The president just said he was going to do everything in his power to keep us out of a foreign war."

"No president talks like that unless he knows a war is coming," the elderly farmer insisted. "It's the same thing the politicians were saying before they got us into World War I."

VI

After Delores graduated from high school, she took a nurse's training course and then went to work at Morris Hospital, where Raymond Kolden had died. Some weekends she stayed with her parents on the farm, and we would get together occasionally to visit and reminisce. Sometimes we would meet by the rock pile near the oak tree with the split trunk. That was still one of our favorite places to sit and talk.

Even though Buster and Minnie had died many years earlier, I felt at peace when I was near their graves. Nothing could ever take away the memories of those two wonderful dogs. To me, Buster and Minnie had become indistinguishable from the prairie wind song that whispered through the split trunk of the old oak tree near where I had buried them.

On one of our meetings, while we were sitting on the rock pile, I told Delores that I was actively searching for my birth mother.

"Do you think that's a good idea?" she asked.

"It's important to me," I replied. "I can't think of anything in my life that means more to me."

"What if you find her, and she turns out to be different than you wanted her to be? What if she turns out to be a big disappointment?"

For a few seconds, I thought about what Delores had said. I replied, "I can't imagine that anyone would be a bigger disappointment to me than Ma and Pa have been."

"Yes," Delores agreed. "They've been terrible parents to you."

I had never told Delores the whole story about the way Ma and Pa had treated me. And I didn't want to now. I changed the subject. "Buster and Minnie are buried right over there," I said, pointing at a spot near the base of the oak tree. "They were the ones who raised me, not Ma and Pa. I put them there so they could listen to the prairie wind song."

"You really liked that story, didn't you?" Delores mused.

"Yes, I did. It helped me to accept a lot of losses in my life. Buster, Minnie, Tug, Raymond, and many others. I always felt I could come here, sit on this pile of rocks, and be close to them—long after they were gone."

"I liked that story, too," Delores agreed. "I liked it ever since that old hired man told it to me when I was a little girl."

"Who was he?" I asked.

"I don't remember his name. He was just a hired man who stayed with us for a few months, and then he was gone. I don't think there was anyone else in his life. But I think the idea of the prairie wind song made him feel a little bit less alone in the world."

"Do you think it's a true story?" I asked.

"What do you mean?"

"The idea that people who lived and died out here on the prairie still speak to us when the wind whispers through the split trunk of that oak tree."

"Does it really matter?" she replied. "So long as people think it's true, that's all that counts."

"I believe it's true," I said. "I've heard voices as the wind whispers through that tree trunk."

"So have I."

"Do you ever hear your real parents' voices?" I asked.

"I never think about them. Not here, not anywhere."

"Don't you ever want to know who they are?"

"No," Delores replied emphatically. "I don't want to know who they are. They might not be the kind of people I would want in my life. I would rather imagine that they are decent people who had to give me up for a good reason—and let it go at that."

Again, I kept silent about what I suspected. I was not about to play God and tell her something she did not want to know.

"I've always imagined that I could hear my mother's voice here," I said. "But someday I want to hear it in person. That's probably the most important thing in the world to me."

"I hope you're not disappointed," Delores cautioned.

VII

Since the only thing I had to go on was Ma's statement, "He was born not too far from here," I established Alberta at the center of my search. I took a map of Minnesota and circled all of the county seats within a fifty-mile radius.

My idea was to visit the nearest county seats first, and gradually visit those that were farther away. At each county seat, I asked only one question, "Do you have a birth certificate for Lloyd Augustine Clausen?" And each time, after the county recorder walked back out of the vault, I received the same answer, "I'm sorry. But I've got nothing back there for Lloyd Augustine Clausen."

In spite of my best organizational efforts, my search for my birth mother was sporadic. It was impossible to do much searching during our planting and harvesting seasons. In winter, I was greatly limited by the cold weather. So I searched for my birth mother during a few weeks in spring, before the planting season began, and a few weeks in late fall, after the harvest was in.

The farm work had to go on, even as the war drums beat steadily from the eastern horizon.

VIII

Pa hadn't given up on trying to break me and force me to accept my destiny. In August of 1939, during the threshing season, we were short one team of horses. That meant one man was going to have to spike-pitch the cut grain, standing out in a blistering hot sun and loading wagons all day long. It was the most difficult task any hired man could ever be assigned. It was even worse than hand-picking corn nubbins.

Pa asked every hired man, and the members of the threshing crew, if they would spike-pitch all day. He even offered to up that person's wages an extra fifty cents an hour. Since most hired men were earning about five to eight dollars per day, plus room and board, this was a considerable increase. Yet, everyone refused to do the spike-pitching. The extra wages weren't worth the effort. Pa handed me a pitchfork and said, "It's your job."

Spike-pitching was, without question, a man-killer. As I loaded wagon after wagon in the hot August sun, I was aware that the other hired men, as well as the threshing crew, were expecting me to drop from sheer exhaustion at any moment. For me, the task became a battle of wills. Pa was determined to break my spirit. I was equally determined to beat him at his own game.

The sun's heat was relentless. I stopped only to drink an occasional pint of water. On all sides of me, other men were working in the field.

But they rested every time their wagons were full, and they had to drive them over to the thresher to unload. Only I labored non-stop beneath that hot sun.

By late afternoon, I doubted my endurance. I was aware that the other men working in the field were looking at Pa, expecting that he would give me a break. But Pa didn't. He merely supervised the threshing activities. He showed no concern for me.

My back and my arms ached beyond painful exhaustion. Each time I jabbed the pitchfork into the piles of cut grain, I glimpsed the blazing sun. I knew that once it had settled into the western horizon, the threshing activities would cease. So I gritted my teeth and paced myself to the speed of the sun's descent, hoping I would make it.

Then, suddenly, I felt a burst of renewed energy. I don't know why. More than likely it was Pa himself. I watched him drink a pint of water by the threshing machine, and he looked in my direction. I knew that he was waiting for me to collapse. That made me very angry. A burst of fury welled up from all the frustrations I had suffered during the many years that I had been beaten and locked in the cellar and humiliated in every way imaginable.

I remembered the horse Pa had tried to break in our farmyard years earlier. I was not going to let him break me, either. I was going to defeat him.

There was one more wagon to fill. I started spike-pitching at a feverish speed. I was going to fill that last wagon before the sun went down. I saw only the pitchfork, the piles of cut grain on the ground, and the wagon.

As the sun touched the western horizon, I finished loading the wagon. I jabbed my pitchfork into the stubble field. At first, I was panting so hard that I did not notice what was happening around me. Then I heard silence. When I looked up, the other members of the threshing crew were standing on their wagons with their pitchforks raised high in the air. It slowly dawned on me that they were acknowledging my efforts with a spontaneous, soundless gesture of support.

It was a hired man's tribute to another hired man. Many of them knew that Pa had been trying to break me for years, and so they knew they had witnessed more than just an ordeal of spike-pitching. They had witnessed, beneath that hot August sun, my defiance. I had refused to be broken.

As I looked at those pitchforks extended at arm's length toward the sky, I knew I had finally defeated Pa. I had foiled his plans. The sweat poured down my body and rained on that freshly harvested field. The pitchforks remained extended in the air all around me. I felt liberated from a destiny Pa had chosen for me almost two decades earlier.

IX

Pa paid the men in the threshing crew. At their five- to eight-dollar wage, most of them had earned thirty or forty dollars for a week of threshing. When it was my turn to get paid, he handed me fifty cents.

The next day I hitchhiked a ride to Morris. I used the fifty cents to buy a quart of ice cream and take in another movie. All I had left to show for my spike-pitching was the memory that, for one day at least, I was "King of the Hired Men."

I wished Ivar had been there. He would have understood.

X

With the harvest in, I renewed my search for my birth mother. I had already visited the county seats in Stevens, Pope, Becker, Big Stone, Grant, Swift, and Traverse counties. Always the same result: "I'm sorry, but I've got nothing back there for Lloyd Augustine Clausen."

Still, I was determined to visit every county seat within fifty miles in all directions of Alberta. If by that time I had turned up nothing, I would have to devise a new plan.

One autumn day, when Pa was sick and couldn't drive to town to play cards, I decided to search south. I put on my coat and headed the Model-A toward my next county seat: Madison, Minnesota, in Lac Qui Parle County, about forty-five miles south of Alberta.

I knew that this would probably be my last visit to a county seat until spring. So I thought I would take one last shot, and then spend the next few months reassessing my strategies.

The Lac Qui Parle County Courthouse was a two-story brick building in the middle of Madison. When I walked up a flight of stairs to the county recorder's office, a slightly overweight middle-aged woman was standing behind the counter. She was outwardly gracious, but something in her manner was overbearing and intimidating. I asked her if she had a birth certificate for Lloyd Augustine Clausen. I stood by the counter while she disappeared into the vault. For several minutes, I watched the people in the outer hallway walk in and out of their offices. Then the county recorder walked out of the vault.

I was expecting the familiar, "I'm sorry. But we have nothing back there for Lloyd Augustine Clausen." In fact, those words were already in my ears. But this county recorder had a surprise for me. "Was there an adoption involved in that birth?" she asked.

I paused for a moment, not quite knowing what the best response might be. I wanted to solicit more information from her. But she had probably already answered her own question. Asking her another seemed silly. I decided to play it straight with her to see if that would gain me any more information. "Yes," I replied. "I believe there was an adoption."

"I'm sorry," she said. "But those records are sealed."

"Can you tell me the birth date on the birth certificate?" I asked in an attempt to determine if it corresponded to my birthday.

"I'm sorry," she shook her head. "In adoptions, all the records are sealed. I can't tell you what's in that file."

XI

If the county recorder said anything else, I didn't hear her. The next thing I knew I was standing outside the Lac Qui Parle County Courthouse, looking blankly up and down the street. A chorus of questions passed through my mind.

Certainly, there couldn't have been another Lloyd Augustine Clausen who was adopted in west central Minnesota. He had to be me. But how was I going to get the crucial information in that file? How was I going to get my mother's name?

I was struck by the awful irony of my predicament. Only a few feet from where I was standing, in a vault in the Lac Qui Parle County Courthouse, all the information I needed to find my birth mother was stored. And yet, that distance might as well have been the distance between here and Pluto. Those records were sealed, and there was nothing I could do to get into them—even though I was the only person to whom that information could mean anything.

I had never in my life felt so close to something and yet so far away from it. The county recorder knew the name of my birth mother. But I was denied access to that information.

I felt completely frustrated. But I was also elated, because my search had finally paid off. I had been born in Lac Qui Parle County. I looked up and down the street. I had another thought. Somewhere in this town of Madison, Minnesota, maybe even living in one of these houses bordering on Main Street, my birth mother might be looking out her window in my direction right now, without even knowing I was her son.

That thought encouraged me. Sealed documents weren't going to stop me from finding my birth mother. I would comb every square inch of Lac Qui Parle County, if necessary, to find her.

I drove the streets of Madison, thinking about the many possibilities that were available to me now that I had narrowed my search. Every street became an adventure. Every house held the hope that a brother, a sister, or perhaps even my mother lived there. Lac Qui Parle County had other towns. But for the moment, I was content to imagine that Madison was where I was born.

I also pondered my next step. I knew I could not go to the telephone books, or knock on every door in Lac Qui Parle County, asking if anyone knew anything about Lloyd Augustine Clausen, a boy born in their county almost twenty years earlier. My name would do nothing for me, even if my mother had named me Lloyd at birth. I needed the full name my mother had given me. With that information, I could then spread my search across the county and hope that someone still living there would remember my mother, and recall that she had given birth to a child who was given up for adoption in the early 1920s.

I also knew that I could check with some of the local historians and genealogists. From my conversations with the librarian in Morris, I realized that every small town, and every county, had its share of elderly chroniclers who faithfully clung to the past and remembered details about earlier times—even people who were long since buried beneath the prairie soil. But I needed to know the name my mother had given me at birth. Then I could go to the people of Lac Qui Parle County and ask them if they would help me.

In the meantime, every house on every street in Madison, Minnesota, radiated mystery and adventure. Every one of the houses I drove past held potential relatives and family members who could help me escape from my life with Ma and Pa in Alberta, Minnesota.

XII

When I returned home that evening, Ma, Pa, and some of the neighbors were gathered around the radio, listening to the latest news about recent events in Europe. The elderly farmer, who had earlier predicted that America would soon be dragged into a major war, was among them.

"Germany just invaded Poland," someone said to me as I joined the group huddled around the radio.

"France and England are expected to declare war on Germany within the next few days," another exclaimed.

I sat down in a chair and strained to hear over the static as a newscaster announced solemnly, "In the light of recent events in Europe, President Roosevelt will be asking Congress to pass laws to enlist more men and women into the National Guard and the various branches of the Armed Forces."

The elderly farmer leaned back from the radio, stroked his chin and muttered, "Like I said before, it's coming our way. You can count on it."

ECHOES FROM A DISTANT WAR

I

England and France declared war on Germany. America started to mobilize troops in preparation for what most people assumed would be a major role on the European battlefields. Some folks still hoped we could avoid the loss of young American lives. But those people were in the minority. The government and the rest of the country were clearly planning for war.

The Morris Armory became the regular meeting place for National Guardsmen. Most of the young men in Stevens County joined the National Guard. I was one of the first. Even before I was out of high school, I was attending military training sessions on a regular basis.

It wasn't necessarily patriotism that motivated me. Training with the Guard provided my first opportunity to leave Ma and Pa's farm for good. If a circus had come through town, and someone had offered me a job, I would have learned to swing on a trapeze. Pa didn't quite know what to make of my decision to join the Guard. He wasn't the most patriotic fellow in the world, but he didn't kick up too much of a fuss. I suspect he thought the war would be over by the time I finished high school. As long as my National Guard responsibilities didn't get in the way of my chores, he didn't object too much.

I don't think he was too worried that I might someday lose my life. He was more concerned that he might have to go out and plow the fields and milk the cows himself if my National Guard unit was ever called into active duty.

Even before the United States officially declared war on Germany and Japan in December of 1941, America was actively supporting England in a variety of ways. Some young Americans were already dying overseas. The government just didn't publicize those deaths. Some of those young men who died in the undeclared war were from Stevens County. When their bodies were sent back home for burial in local cemeteries, the war overseas became a very personal thing to many of us.

II

I never told Ma and Pa what I learned in Lac Qui Parle County. If they knew what I was up to, they would throw every imaginable obstacle in my way. Nothing threatened them more than the thought that I might somehow manage to locate my birth mother. So as I worked on the farm and attended National Guard training sessions, I quietly bided my time. Whenever Ma and Pa would leave the farm for a few hours, I methodically searched every room and sifted through every drawer in the house. I found nothing that shed the dimmest light on my past. Ma and Pa had hidden those records well.

III

As unlikely as it sounds, I made it to my senior year in the Alberta High School without flunking a grade. I surprised myself as much as I surprised my teachers—and I know they were plenty surprised. They told me they had never known anyone to miss so much school and still get passing grades. My teachers seemed resigned to the fact that someday I would just fade out of school and back to the farm, the way Raymond Kolden had. Still, they were genuinely pleased at the end of every school year, when I passed the final exams in all the subject areas.

Each time the school reported to Ma and Pa that I had passed and could move on to the next grade, they seemed disappointed. I think they were hoping that I would fail. Several times, they even tried to talk me into dropping out. I refused. Nobody realized that I read all the time. Even if I didn't finish chores until nine at night, I would still stay up another couple of hours reading and studying. I was determined to get an education.

Except for my teachers, Ivar was the only one who had ever encouraged me to keep going to school. He even took over some of my chores so I could attend classes. For whatever reason, I sensed that he regretted that he had little in the way of formal education. So he resisted Pa's attempts to turn me into an uneducated hired man. I was not about to let Ivar down. I intended to finish high school, no matter what obstacles Ma and Pa might throw in my way.

IV

My senior year was a series of confrontations with Ma and Pa. At the beginning of the school year, I asked Pa for some money to buy an extra shirt and trousers.

"You already have two shirts and trousers," he insisted. "That's enough for any boy."

"But they're work clothes," I protested.

"They'll do just fine for school."

I took the last of my skunk-trapping money and hitchhiked to Morris to buy a new shirt and trousers. I felt considerably less self-conscious at school.

I told Pa that I didn't intend to miss so many classes during my senior year of high school.

"Chores come first," he said, "then school."

I ignored him. I refused to miss classes unless the weather was so bad the roads were closed.

I told Pa that I had the opportunity to practice my singing one night a week at my music teacher's home. He refused to let me have the car. Every Tuesday night, I ran the three miles to my music teacher's house.

I told Pa I was going out for the football team. He told me football was a complete waste of time. I became a starting halfback.

He did not discourage my playing on the basketball team. But not for the reasons you might expect. One evening, he volunteered to drive me to my game. I was surprised, and somewhat pleased. But after he parked the car, he walked in the opposite direction from the school.

"Pa," I said, "the gym's over here."

"Card room's over here," he replied. "Come get me after your game."

I realized there was only one reason for Pa's sudden interest in my basketball games: he had an excuse to drive to town to be with his friends.

He only watched one of my games. I didn't get to play very much, because I had missed too many practices while I was doing chores. He told me afterwards that he wasn't going to come to another game because I didn't get to play anyway.

"Why are you wasting your time," he said, "when you don't play?"

"I enjoy the games," I replied.

"A bunch of foolishness," he snorted. "You should be home making better use of your time."

I tore a deep gash in my forearm while I was repairing the tractor. Pa examined the wound. "You don't need stitches," he said. "It ain't deep enough. Just wrap it up tight."

Later, when the wound became badly infected, Pa refused to drive me to town to see Dr. Cumming. "Just soak it in hot water," he said. "It'll be fine."

When ugly greenish-brown pus starting seeping out of the wound, he still would not take me to see Dr. Cumming. I finally asked a neighbor to drive me to town.

"You should have gotten this treated a long time ago," Dr. Cumming said after he had examined the wound. "You could have gotten blood poisoning in that arm."

These many disappointments convinced me even more to break free of Ma and Pa's influence. Fortunately, during my trip to Lac Qui Parle County in the fall of 1939, I had learned how I might be able to do just that. Throughout my senior year, I carried in the back of my mind dreams that sustained me. I would graduate with my class in the spring of 1940. I would locate my birth mother, and she would attend my high school graduation.

V

During the winter of 1939, I didn't see much of Delores. Although she had a car, it was a very cold winter, with many blizzards. We didn't have a chance to get together very often. The following spring, we started to meet once again.

One day, I told her about the abandoned windmill. She insisted that we drive over there. Once we had climbed to the top of the windmill, we sat down and gazed out over the prairie.

"Marcus Reece and I used to come up here when I was a boy," I said. "This was a place of high adventure for us. We used to pretend we were on top of a castle, or a guard tower, while our enemies were approaching from all sides."

"Sounds like great fun," Delores mused as she held my hand. "Did any of your enemies ever make it to the top of this windmill and capture you?"

"No." I laughed. "They were never able to shoot their arrows up this high. We dropped imaginary rocks on the ones who tried to climb the ladder to get to us. We were safe. We won every battle."

She gazed at the distant horizon. "It certainly is a beautiful place."

"Yes, it is," I agreed.

"Lloyd," she asked, "what are you going to do after you graduate from high school?"

"I don't know," I replied. "I suppose it depends on whether or not my National Guard unit is called to active duty."

"If the war ends soon, do you plan to stay around here?"

"I don't know where else I could go," I said. "I still plan to locate my birth mother. After that, I'll think about my future."

"Have you had any luck looking for her?"

"I think I was born in Lac Qui Parle County," I replied. "They have adoption records down there for my name, but they're sealed."

"How did you find that out?" she asked quickly.

"I visited just about every county recorder's office in west central Minnesota," I explained. "Last fall, my efforts paid off. Now I need to find out what my name was before I was adopted. Then I'll go back to Lac Qui Parle County and start making some phone calls."

"How can you find out your real name, if those records are sealed?"

"Ma and Pa must have that information in the house somewhere," I replied.

"I found some of our important papers in a chest of drawers," she offered. "There was a concealed compartment in the back. You might want to look in places like that."

"I've already looked in most of the chests of drawers. But I haven't noticed any concealed compartments."

"Lloyd," she asked somewhat wistfully, "have you ever thought about leaving this part of the country for good?"

"Yes," I replied, "I've thought about it."

"I'm thinking about taking a trip to Minneapolis," she said.

"How long will you be gone?"

"A few months. I'll be staying with a friend."

"I'll miss you," I said self-consciously.

"I'll miss you, too, Lloyd."

Below us, the prairie rolled toward the distant western horizon, as though beckoning us to a future far removed from Minnesota's corn and wheat fields. Someday I wanted to walk off into that horizon with Delores.

That was another of my dreams.

VI

Spring came, and I defied Pa by joining the track team. Since I had been jumping barbed-wire fences most of my life, I thought I'd take a shot at the high hurdles. Anyone who could clear a barbed-wire fence could certainly clear a high hurdle. I didn't know that the object of the sport was speed, rather than height. That was the opposite of what I had been doing. Only a fool would jump a barbed-wire fence with anything in mind other than to put as much distance as possible between himself and the sharp metal barbs.

My first two track meets, I didn't do too well. I was still jumping barbed-wire fences. Which is to say, I put a minimum of two feet between myself and the hurdles. I probably looked like some kind of demented jack rabbit running down that track. Eventually, I learned to watch the other hurdlers keep their legs and bodies as close as possible to the hurdles. When I started to imitate what they were doing, my times improved tremendously. Before long, I was able to win some of my races.

I learned to improvise. Whereas my coach taught me to take five steps between each hurdle, that seemed awkward to me. I experimented with three steps. He insisted, however, that I use the traditional five-step approach. That's what I did in practice. But in our next track meet, I used the three-step strategy, and I won my race by a full hurdle. After my victory, my coach agreed that I could use my three-step strategy.

I won the sub-district easily. However, in the district meet I was confronted with the difficult task of running against a hurdler from a northern high school. Everyone expected he would eventually win the state high hurdle event. Of course, I was terribly intimidated by his reputation. I practiced by jumping over just about everything on our farm that was the same height as a high hurdle, including some cows. I did not try to jump our bull. I did not think that was prudent.

In the back of my mind, I was hoping I could make it to the state track meet and get some publicity in the big city newspapers. Perhaps someone in Lac Qui Parle County might read about me, put two and two together, and pass that information on to my birth mother. Perhaps she would then come to my graduation. Needless to say, the district track meet was a very significant event in my life.

I lined up against the hurdler from up north. He was intimidating. He was at least six inches taller than me, and he had the long, slender legs of someone who was born to run the high hurdles. Plus, he had a new pair of track shoes with shiny metal spikes and leather tops. I wore an ancient pair of track shoes, which had been used by several generations of athletes from our small school. There was no money in our school budget for new track shoes. So, I was intimidated by that tall hurdler—and by his new shoes.

In fact, I was looking at his shoes when the starter's pistol went off. I did not get a good start. I was the last one out of the blocks and remained at least five feet behind the pack for the first two hurdles. Then my three-step strategy started to pay off. I gained a few feet on the rest of the pack with each hurdle. I passed one hurdler, then another hurdler, until I was running even with the hurdler from up north. He was running five steps between each hurdle. His form over the hurdles was perfect. But I was gaining on him.

We were dead even clearing the last hurdle. From there, it was a sprint to the finish line. He had longer legs. I was a little faster. I made a lunge at the end. My chest broke the string across the finish line.

That was one of the happiest moments of my life. I was the district champion in the high hurdles. No one, not even Ma and Pa, could ever take that away from me. I thought: maybe my birth mother will read about me in the newspapers when I compete at the state track meet. Maybe she will even decide to come to my graduation.

My victory symbolized that I was breaking free of the destiny Ma and Pa had chosen for me. I was going to be more than just another hired man living from hand to mouth. My life was going to mean something.

VII

A few days later, the principal of our school approached me with the bad news. "Lloyd," he said, "I'm sorry to have to tell you this. But we won't be able to send you to the state track meet."

"Why?" I blurted out.

"We don't have the money." He looked embarrassed. "We're a small school, with limited resources. Room, board, and travel expenses would be more than we could afford. I'm very sorry."

"I want to run in that track meet," I insisted. "It's very important to me."

"You're eligible to run in the state track meet," he said. "You have earned that right. All I'm saying is that we won't be able to pay your expenses."

"But I don't have the money."

"Maybe you should talk to your parents," he suggested. "Maybe they will pay your expenses."

VIII

I pleaded with Pa to loan me the money. I even said I would work extra days for him. But Pa would have none of it.

"Boys jumping fences," he snorted as he turned and walked away from me. "That's a bunch of foolishness."

I knew better than to bring up the issue again.

The day of the state track meet, I did my chores as though it were just any other day. I milked the cows about the time I knew the high hurdle event would start. I paused for a moment, walked out of the barn, and tried to visualize what I would be doing at that very moment if Pa had loaned me the money.

I remembered how I had felt the day the town boys played their practical joke on me, when they invited me to play capture the flag with them. After they drove off, leaving me alone in the grove of trees, I had felt betrayed, defeated. But I had decided to keep right on playing—by myself. I learned that day that the thrill of the game was what you made it out to be in your own mind. Nothing else mattered. Not even if you were the only player left in the game.

I got down into my starting position, right in the middle of the farmyard. Somewhere, deep in my imagination, I heard the starter's pistol. I raced toward a barbed-wire fence. Back and forth, like some insane fool, I jumped that barbed-wire fence. I jumped that fence as many times as I would have jumped the high hurdles at the state meet. I had perfect form. There was no more than an inch of clearance between my legs and that fence.

I almost convinced myself that I had just won the high hurdle event in the state track meet. I waited a few seconds for the reporters to surround and interview me, so my mother in Lac Qui Parle County might see my picture in the newspaper.

Then I realized I was standing alone, in the middle of a stubble field in west central Minnesota. The winner of the high hurdle event was meeting with reporters almost two hundred miles away. Nothing I could do or say was going to change that.

I felt more like a hired man than I had at any other time in my life.

IX

For several months, I thought about the boys from other schools in the district. I felt cheated, bitter. Why didn't I come from a wealthier school district? Why was I always the one left behind?

A few years later, I read in the local papers about the Minnesota boys who were fighting and dying overseas. I recognized the names of several boys I had competed against in the district track meet. Some of those boys had even won at the district level and had competed successfully in the state meet. Now, they were just another war statistic.

Much later, I had an opportunity to drive over to the track where we held the district meet in the spring of 1940. There wasn't another human being in sight, so I walked slowly around the track several times, replaying in my mind the memories from that day long ago. This time, there were no cheers and no loud applause. There was only the sound of the wind blowing through the prairie grass in the fields adjacent to the track.

I remembered the boys I had watched cross the finish line in the spring of 1940. Some were the same ones who were sent home a few years later in wooden boxes. Others had been buried in cemeteries near the battlefields where they fell. They had no inkling when they crossed that finish line in the spring of 1940 that their lives were almost over.

I didn't have to read too many obituaries for these young soldiers before I started to put everything into perspective. That state track meet was a little bump on the rocky road of life. A few years later, I was still alive. Many of the other boys were not. They could only speak to the living in the prairie wind song.

I guess a man can never really judge who are the winners and who are the losers at any point in life. Winners and losers can change places in a heartbeat.

X

Graduation came and went. Ma and Pa came to the graduation ceremony for a few minutes—on their way to visit some friends. They didn't stay long enough to congratulate me.

I stayed afterwards and talked with some of my classmates and their families. I listened as the girls talked about their plans for the future. Some were planning long trips. Others were making plans to start college in the fall. Most of the boys had other plans. Many weren't waiting for the National Guard to become active. They planned to enlist in the Army or the Navy or the Air Force. To so many of my fellow graduates, the war still sounded like high adventure overseas.

When they asked me what I planned to do after graduation, I was evasive. I had no plans for my future. I feared that I was destined to work for the rest of my life on Ma and Pa's farm. I could not see anything in my future that would change that. Unless, of course, my National Guard unit was activated. But I didn't want anyone else to know that was all I could see ahead of me.

After the ceremony, I caught a ride home with a neighbor and his wife. They dropped me off at the farm. I stood in the middle of the yard and looked around at the weathered buildings. I had been very excited about graduating from high school. But now that I was standing alone in the middle of our yard, holding my diploma, I felt empty. The ceremony had meant nothing to Ma and Pa. They probably wouldn't have come at all but for the sake of appearances.

Inside the house, I felt like it was any other day on the farm. I tossed my diploma on the bed, walked outside, and started my chores. Nothing had changed. The fact that I now had a piece of paper that showed I had graduated from high school meant very little. I was still a hired man.

XI

Later that year, Ma and Pa went to Morris to visit a doctor. Pa had been having some chest pains. The doctor was concerned that he might have a heart problem. I stayed on the farm. Around noon, I walked into the house to clean up. I suddenly realized I had the house to myself.

Remembering Delores's suggestion about hidden compartments, I removed every drawer in the house, including those in the kitchen cabinets. But I could find no hidden compartment, no valuable papers.

About to give up, I decided that I would look once again at the piece of paper behind the framed photograph. I took the photograph off the wall and dismantled it. I found the piece of paper behind the matting—right where I had left it almost ten years earlier.

I studied the three words, "For Baby Edward." I noticed that the paper had come from a bound tablet. I could see slight indentations where someone had written something on the preceding page. I could not make out any words from those indentations, but I was able to make out some letters where someone had pressed a pen or pencil more firmly at the bottom of the page.

What I was looking at was some kind of signature. I held the paper up to the light from a nearby window so I could study the individual letters more closely. I was able to decipher five letters from the indentations at the bottom of the page, which appeared to spell Moses. As I held the piece of paper up to the window and studied the letters from every conceivable angle, I realized that what I thought was a letter "s" at the end of the name was probably an "n." There also seemed to be a slight indentation after the final "n," but I could not tell if it was another letter or some kind of punctuation.

Mosen seemed to be part of a signature that had appeared at the bottom of a letter or note someone had written on the previous piece of paper in the tablet. What's more, the carefully scripted name, like the inscription, "For Baby Edward," appeared to be written in the same graceful, elegant handwriting.

Was it possible that my birth mother had sent something to Ma and Pa for me? Or, maybe, she had sent something to the orphanage, and they had forwarded it to Ma and Pa after the adoption. On the other hand, perhaps there was a very innocent and simple explanation for the piece of paper concealed behind the framed photograph—and it had nothing to do with my adoption.

I didn't know what I had found, or if it was of any value whatsoever. But I decided that I would use the information to play a long shot the next time I was able to drive down to Lac Qui Parle County.

XII

My trip to Lac Qui Parle County had to be postponed. A few weeks before Christmas, my unit of the National Guard was called into active duty. Many of the local boys made hasty plans to be shipped out to Camp Haan in Riverside, California. The war overseas was not going to end anytime soon, unless America became involved in a big way. President Roosevelt and Congress activated all National Guard units, and placed the other branches of the armed forces on a state of readiness.

For me, it was a very strange time. I had never been out of the state of Minnesota, and seldom out of Stevens County. Now, I was to be sent all the way across the country to California, a state I had only read about in books. I was excited and fearful of what awaited me at the end of that journey.

Delores drove out to the farm the day before my unit was to leave. She picked me up in her car. We went for a long drive around the countryside.

"How long will you be gone?" she asked.

"We haven't been told anything," I replied. "I don't know if they are planning to train us and then send us back home to await an official declaration of war. Or if they're planning to train us in California and then send us overseas."

"I'm worried," she said somewhat sadly. "What will I do if anything happens to you?"

For the first time in my life, I think I realized that Delores had some deep feelings for me. I had always figured she thought of me as some kind of younger brother. Now, it was clear that her feelings went deeper than that.

As the tears streamed down her cheeks, I helped her guide the car to the side of the road. I turned the key in the ignition and held her while she continued to cry.

"Take care of yourself," she said softly moments later. "I just don't know what I will do if something happens to you."

XIII

We spent the rest of that day together, driving up and down the country roads south of Alberta. A light snow fell sporadically out of a heavy gray sky. When night fell, the cloud cover lifted, and a full moon rose high above the snow-dusted prairie. The night sky reflected in the newly fallen snow, like little stars trying to imitate the much brighter stars in the blackness of space.

As the moon rose higher, it spotlighted the oak tree with the split trunk. The night air was too cold for us to walk out into the field, so we parked the car by the side of the dirt road. We stared silently at the blackened, scorched tree trunk as the moonlight shimmered in the snow all around it.

AT LAST, THE MOUNTAINTOPS

I

The train trip from Minnesota to California in January and February of 1941 is still one of the most memorable experiences of my life. Minnesota National Guardsmen boarded the huge Pullman-style railroad cars, cameras flashed, and newspaper reporters fired questions at us. Every stop along the way, we were treated like celebrities. People couldn't seem to get enough of us.

When the train stopped, there were more cameras flashing and more newspaper reporters asking us questions about the war overseas, and whether or not we were anxious to join in that fight. We responded with patriotic clichés.

"Are you ready to teach Adolph Hitler a lesson, fellas?"

"If there's a war to be fought, we're ready to fight it."

"What did you think of President Roosevelt's decision to activate the National Guard?"

"It was the right decision, sir."

"How do you feel about being so far away from Minnesota?"

"It was hard to leave home. But our country needs us."

I am sure in the back of some of our minds was the question, "Am I really ready to die for my country?" But we were too busy enjoying ourselves to think too much about dying.

It took us a while to figure out why we were treated so well, but eventually we got the drift that the Minnesota National Guard was the first such unit to be deployed to Camp Haan for anti-aircraft training and deployment overseas. Somewhat of a historic first, we were the beneficiaries of all the adulation that came with President Roosevelt's decision to activate the National Guard. The government wanted to milk this event for all it was worth. We were more than willing to be milked. We especially enjoyed it when some of the girls along the way hugged us or posed with us for the benefit of the newspaper cameramen.

Free packages of cigarettes were distributed to all the National Guardsmen. We started smoking—even those of us who had never smoked before. Of course, like everyone else, I had tried a few cigarettes in my youth. But I had never smoked a full pack of cigarettes. At first, I got quite sick to my stomach. I stuck with it, though, because I liked the notion of being a cigarette-smoking National Guardsman heading west to fight for his country.

Little did I know what those cigarettes would eventually do to my health. On my grand heroic adventure out west, however, I needed the cigarette dangling out of my mouth to complete an image. I was a celebrity, by God, and I was going to make the most of it.

I still have vivid memories of the train moving away from the snow-covered prairie, through the Northwestern states, down the coastal states, and into the more arid regions of Southern California. I knew that some parts of the country were never covered with snow in the winter. But actually seeing that miracle right in front of my eyes took a little getting used to. I don't know precisely in which state I saw my first snow-covered mountaintop, but I do remember thinking: "That's where snow belongs, on the top of mountains, not on the prairie where it buries houses and barns and granaries."

II

As we filed off the train at Camp Haan, we were told to line up alongside the railroad tracks, in front of the Pullman cars, so newspaper cameramen could take more pictures of us. Reporters fired more questions our way.

"Can you smile for the girls back home, fellas?"

"What kind of military training have you had so far?"

"If war comes, will the Minnesota National Guard be ready?"

As the cameras flashed, I looked at the beautiful snow-covered mountain peaks in the distance. To the east, the entire horizon was a mountain range. What a breathtaking sight, especially for a Minnesota boy who had never in his entire life seen anything taller than an abandoned windmill.

The camp was a flurry of activity. Men in trucks and jeeps bounced along newly constructed dirt roads, while carpenters and other construction workers lifted walls and poured concrete.

We were all dressed in warm winter jackets that the National Guard had provided for the harsh Minnesota climate. But those jackets were much too warm for Southern California. As soon as the newspaper reporters and cameramen left the area, we shed those coats, pulled out our cigarettes, and started smoking.

I don't know what everyone else was thinking at the time. But I remember what was on my mind. I already knew that I had no desire to go back to the Minnesota prairie. For the first time in my life, in the middle of winter, I was warm.

III

Camp Haan was a hastily erected military community in the middle of a semi-desert region just south of Riverside, California, near March Air Force Base. A dirt road ran about four miles through the middle of the camp. On both sides of the road, various structures had been quickly built out of rough lumber. There was a hospital, many barracks, mess halls, chapels, headquarter buildings, post exchanges and, most importantly to us, a service club.

The service club was the military community's entertainment center. Girls from Riverside and the surrounding areas came to mingle with the National Guardsmen at nights and on Sundays. Bands would play, and, occasionally, Hollywood celebrities entertained us.

Someone in our unit told the Master of Ceremonies that I was a pretty good singer. He invited me to come up on stage and sing with the band. By this time, I knew many songs from the Nelson Eddie and Jeanette MacDonald movies. I sang the theme song from *Rose-Marie*. The audience liked the song so much the M. C. asked me to sing a second one. So I sang the "Song of the Mounties," from the same movie. That song, which celebrates the Mounties' love of freedom and their determination to defend their homeland against all enemies, deeply affected the Guardsmen who were preparing to fight in a war overseas. The song earned me a standing ovation. After that, I sang many times in the service club.

The service club probably ruined me as a farm hand. I quickly grew to love the nightlife. The music. The young women. The laughter. The romance hovering in the smoke-filled air. I had never known anything like it in Alberta, Minnesota. I began to sense in myself some of the same yearnings that had driven Ma to risk so much for love and romance. After hearing loud applause from hundreds of people for singing about love and loss in a smoke-filled dance hall, surrounded by beautiful young women who gaze adoringly in your direction, it is awfully difficult to go back to the Minnesota prairie and slop hogs for a living.

IV

The daily routine at Camp Haan involved performing calisthenics and close-order drills, crawling across the desert terrain, and, mostly, practicing with anti-aircraft equipment and weapons. Then, at night, we would shower, dress in clean clothes, and walk over to the service club to sing and dance.

The newspaper reporters and cameramen showed up periodically to interview and photograph us. We soon learned the proper answers to their questions. Our commanding officers rewarded our good behavior by giving us time off from training activities.

When we weren't training, dancing, or posing for pictures, we often hiked out into the surrounding desert in search of rattlesnakes. For some reason, all of the Minnesota National Guardsmen were fascinated by them. Perhaps because there are no poisonous snakes where we grew up.

We spent many long hours poking around in the dry brush, or searching in the cool shadows of desert rock outcroppings for rattlesnakes.

I didn't find any rattlesnakes. Not when I went looking for them, anyway. But I almost crawled over the top of one during a training session. The rattlesnake was probably six feet away from me when I noticed its beady little eyes staring in my direction. At first, I didn't know what I was seeing. I had expected that a rattlesnake would rattle. But this fellow was more cunning. He was making no noise whatsoever.

When it dawned on me that I was only a few feet away from a rattlesnake, I stood up and ran out of the area screaming. I'm just thankful that no one was firing weapons over our heads. I would have been riddled with bullet holes.

My experiences with that rattlesnake restored some lost loyalty toward my home state. Sure, Minnesota had badgers and skunks and other such wild animals, but at least we didn't have any rattlesnakes. Growing up, I didn't have to worry about sticking my hand into some shadowed area to grab a board or a pitchfork, and pulling it out with a rattlesnake clinging to my forearm. A skunk might spray in my direction, but I could live with that. A rattlesnake bite is a whole different ballgame.

So there was, after all, something to be said for the Midwest.

V

I had written to Delores as soon as I arrived at Camp Haan. Several days later, I received a letter from her. She was working once again at the Morris Hospital. She wrote to me about her daily activities in Stevens County. I shared with her my adventures in Southern California.

In March of 1941, Delores wrote that she and Helen Strubbe, another nurse at the Morris Hospital, were thinking about driving out to Southern California to see some of their friends in the Minnesota National Guard—and maybe they would look for work. Helen had just purchased a new car, and so they both thought that this was as good a time as any to head west.

I didn't know how serious Delores was about coming out to California, but when she stopped writing back to me, I knew something was up. Then, sometime in April, I was informed that I had a visitor waiting for me outside the camp gates. Sure enough, when I walked over to the camp gates, Delores and Helen Strubbe were standing next to a new green Ford coupe. I was delighted to see them. And Delores was obviously delighted to see me.

They were staying with a relative in San Bernardino, while looking for work in the local hospitals. I could tell that Delores was very impressed by my military uniform. That made me very proud.

We hugged and talked for a while. I told Delores I would try to get a one-day pass, and maybe we could do some sightseeing together.

VI

Delores showed up alone in the green Ford coupe. Helen Strubbe had been kind enough to let her have the car so we could have the day to ourselves. I met Delores outside the camp gates. Together, we drove toward the eastern mountain ranges.

"I've been told there's a lake up in the mountains that we might want to visit," Delores said as she placed a map on the seat next to her. "It's supposed to be quite beautiful."

I had never been in the mountains before, except during the train ride from Minnesota, so I was very eager to drive up there and look around. We drove through Riverside and a small town called Redlands, and then we started to drive up a winding road into the San Gorgonio Mountains. The view was extraordinary. I had never experienced anything quite like it. It seemed like you could see a hundred miles to the west.

We entered an area that was dense with beautiful green pine trees. Patches of snow intermingled with green grass beneath the shadows of the forested areas. The sound of rippling mountain streams filled the air. It was truly an enchanted place.

Delores turned off the main road and onto a narrow dirt road. There was a parking area next to a small mountain lake, but not another car or tourist in sight. We had the lake all to ourselves.

When we got out of the car, the air was crisp and clean, like a Midwestern autumn morning. The water in the lake was so blue and calm that it seemed almost part of the sky.

Delores had packed a picnic lunch for us. We sat down on a fallen log near the water's edge and ate. Afterwards, we held hands as we walked around the lake.

The lake was about the size of a large Minnesota slough. But that's where any similarities ended. Most sloughs have muddy bottoms and reed-covered shorelines. The bottom of this mountain lake was sand that extended several feet onto the shoreline.

"Do you remember about five years ago," I asked, "when you took me to the Morris Theater to see Nelson Eddy and Jeanette MacDonald in *Rose-Marie?*"

"I was just thinking about that," she said, giggling.

"This place reminds me of that movie," I said. "The streams, the lakes, the pine trees. After that movie, I always wanted to visit the mountains—"

"And now we're here," she replied softly, finishing my sentence. She held my hand a little tighter.

"I went back to the farm that day and tried to find a mountaintop." I chuckled. "But the only thing tall enough was that old, abandoned windmill. I sang to you on top of that windmill."

"How romantic of you," Delores teased. Then she changed the subject. "Have you heard yet what they plan to do with you once you've finished training at Camp Haan?"

"The scuttlebutt is that we'll be divided into two groups and sent to different war zones overseas. But we haven't heard anything official."

"Let me know as soon as you find out," she said.

"I should know in the next couple of weeks."

We paused next to a huge fallen tree along the water's edge.

"When the war's over, let's come back up here and walk around this lake again." She sat down on the tree and stared across the lake.

"Yes, let's do that," I agreed.

"Do you promise?"

"I promise."

VII

Something happened during my first few months at Camp Haan that seemed insignificant at the time, but several months later it took on a significance beyond anything I could possibly have imagined.

In spite of the camp commander's best efforts to keep us busy and entertained, we all soon grew bored with the daily routine of military life. We started devising all kinds of games and activities just to keep our minds occupied when we were not training, reading military manuals, or drinking beer and dancing and singing at the service club.

We organized lizard races, rattlesnake round-ups, and impromptu touch football games and wrestling matches. During one of those wrestling matches, I competed against a fellow from the southern part of Minnesota. He was strong and lanky, but not terribly quick. I pinned him in less than a minute. He was good-natured about his loss. He smiled and shook my hand as we wiped the dust off ourselves.

Afterwards, we made some small talk for a few minutes. I don't remember his first name, and I don't remember ever running into him again during my stay at Camp Haan. I do remember his last name because it was stitched above the pocket of his shirt: Sandbakken.

VIII

A festive mood prevailed throughout our first few months at Camp Haan. Most of us thought of our experiences in the desert as some kind of a summer camp, a break from our normal lives and responsibilities. We were teenagers who had been released from our Midwestern schools and farms. We gave little serious thought to the war. We were much more concerned about news from back home, which we shared with everyone who would listen. We constantly sought new ways to entertain ourselves. And we spent hours taking photographs of ourselves sitting on sun-bleached desert rocks. We were just pretending to be soldiers. None of us had any idea what it meant to be a real one. In spite of the long hours we spent training to become anti-aircraft gunners, fighting in a war was the farthest thing from our minds.

The mood changed as we approached our last months of training. Word trickled in to us about German and Italian victories overseas. The names of European and North African cities became as familiar to us as the names of the small Minnesota towns—and as important. We could be assigned to any one of those war zones in a few short weeks. We began to listen attentively to any news from abroad.

We also spent much of our time telling our life's stories to each other. No one said as much, but everyone was probably thinking the same thing: in combat, some of us would survive, and some of us would be killed. We wanted at least one other person to know our life's story, someone to go back to our home towns and tell the people we loved how we had died.

I talked a lot about Delores. I also told some of my buddies that I was adopted, and that my dream had always been to locate my birth mother. Each man listened sympathetically. One of them even said that he would find her for me if I didn't make it through the war.

IX

I received word that I was to meet with one of my commanding officers. I thought maybe it had something to do with dividing our unit into two groups and sending each to a different location overseas. I thought perhaps my c. o. would tell me where I was going.

I walked over to one of the headquarters buildings and waited on a bench in a hallway for a few minutes before I was ushered into the officer's quarters. The officer gestured for me to sit down in a wooden chair in front of his desk. "Private Clausen," he began solemnly, "I'm sorry to be the one to have to tell you this, but we received word this morning that your father had a heart attack a few days ago."

"Is he okay?" I asked.

"Yes, his doctor expects him to recover. But he can no longer farm by himself. So this does change our plans for you."

"How?"

"Son," the officer slowly explained, "this war will be fought and won on two fronts—on the battlefield and at home. Since you are the only son of a farmer who can no longer farm his land by himself, we will be sending you back home to help your father grow the crops that we will need to feed our troops. You will, of course, receive an honorable discharge."

I was too stunned to know what to say at first. A part of me understood that this quirk of fate may very well have saved my life. But I would be leaving behind other men in the Minnesota National Guard unit to whom I had grown incredibly close over the previous months. I would also leave behind my grand adventure in California—and return to my life as Ma and Pa's hired man.

I had a vision of Pa standing in the open doorway of my classroom in the Alberta High School, telling my teacher that he needed to pull me out of school so I could do chores. Now, he had managed to pull me out of World War II. I half expected him to show up at the open doorway of the officer's quarters and escort me back home. Of all the ways my experiences at Camp Haan might have ended, this was the one I would never have predicted.

"When do I leave?" I asked the officer.

"Tomorrow morning," he replied. "We'll process your discharge papers immediately. Stop by this office and pick them up before you board the train."

X

I tried to reach Delores by telephone and tell her what had happened. I was unable to get ahold of her. The next morning, I said good-bye to my friends and buddies and boarded the train that would take me back to the Minnesota prairie.

The train ride back home was in contrast to the trip out west. I was all alone. There were no other National Guardsmen traveling with me. There were no cameras flashing, no newspaper reporters asking questions about the war, no running jokes to be shared with my buddies.

As the train sped north and then east, I watched the landscapes pass steadily by the window. When we entered the Midwestern states, I could see the darker brown and gray colors of late autumn spreading across the trees and sloughs and open fields. The landscape was the color of the cloud-covered sky. Everything was dead or dying.

I felt bewildered by the hand fate had dealt me. Many of my buddies had expressed envy for my good luck. I was going back to my life as a hired man on Ma and Pa's farm. They were going overseas to fight, and possibly die, in a war. Some of them would have readily changed places with me. Given the chance, I would have done so in an instant.

XI

The train pulled into the Morris depot late at night. I knew there would be no one to greet me, because no one even knew I was coming home. The depot agent seemed to sense my dilemma because he asked if I needed a ride. I said, "Yes, I do—to Alberta."

"Let me see what I can do for you." He picked up a telephone and spoke into the receiver. A few seconds later he set the receiver down. "A friend of mine will drive you to Alberta," he said. "He likes to help out the servicemen."

Minutes later, an elderly man pulled up in a battered pick-up truck. I learned during the drive to Alberta that he was a veteran of World War I. He remembered all too vividly being stranded in railroad depots during his days in the service. He made himself available to the Morris Depot for other servicemen who were in a similar predicament.

As we turned off Highway 28 and onto the dirt road that ran by Pa's farm, I began to think that maybe my experiences in Southern California had been a dream. Maybe I had imagined everything, including my trip with Delores up into the San Gorgonio Mountains.

When the elderly driver dropped me off in the middle of the farmyard, I was again alone. I stood for a few moments and listened to the sounds around me. The breezes whispered across the farmyard, carrying just a hint of the much colder winter winds that were soon to come. An owl hooted somewhere over by the barn.

As I stood under a star-filled sky, I was convinced that no matter what I did with my life, I would always end up back on the farm with Ma and Pa. Apparently, nothing could change that. Not even a war.

I dropped my duffel bag on the ground and lit up a cigarette. Then I stared at the stars twinkling in the vast darkness of space. About all I had left to show for my experiences in Southern California were a couple of free cartons of cigarettes.

I was still a farm hand.

XII

The National Guardsmen who journeyed with me from the Minnesota prairie to the semi-desert regions of Southern California in the early months of 1941 were divided into two different anti-aircraft groups. One of those groups fared quite well, and most of the men returned safely home after the war. The other group suffered heavy causalities.

I knew many of the men who were killed. They were the men I had trained with at Camp Haan. Most likely, I would have served with them overseas.

THE SEARCH CONTINUES

I

The morning after I had returned from Camp Haan, I rose at 4 a.m. and did chores I had been doing for most of my life. The cows still had to be milked. The livestock still had to be fed. The cream still had to be separated.

Pa had neglected much of the farm work in the months before his heart attack. As a result, almost every piece of equipment was in need of repair, and some of the farm animals were terribly undernourished.

In the days and weeks that followed, I was too busy to think about Delores out in California. She didn't write and that worried me somewhat. But I figured when I talked to her again, there would be some simple explanation. The most logical explanation was that she was probably making plans to return to the Morris, or she was already on her way back home.

Ma and Pa seemed to have aged considerably during my absence. Pa, especially, seemed older. The heart attack had drained him of strength. He was no longer the man who used to strike terror in my heart. When Ma and Pa looked up at me from the kitchen table, the morning after I returned, they reminded me of two people who were lost and looking for someone to save them.

For better or worse, I was the only one who *could* save them.

II

A few weeks later, when I walked into the house after doing my afternoon chores, Ma was reading a letter by the kitchen table. As I washed my hands in the sink, she looked up at me. "This is from Delores," she said, holding up the letter.

I tried not to appear too interested in the letter.

"How's she doing?" I asked.

"She seems to be doing fine," Ma replied. Then she read from the letter. "She writes, 'I won't be coming home for another month or two. I've met someone out here in California, and he's been taking me to the beaches and all the other places of interest. So I'll be staying a while longer.'"

I didn't bother to look at Ma's face, or to ask her to read the rest of the letter. I knew from what she had already read that Delores had more than a passing interest in the man she had met. I knew she was probably going to stay in California. I couldn't deal with that possibility.

I had just lost another of my dreams. Somehow, in the back of my mind, I had been convinced that Delores and I would someday live by that mountain lake together. But now she had met someone else.

I hurried outside and drove the Model-A over to the abandoned windmill. I climbed to the top and sat down on the same spot where Delores and I had held hands and talked about our future.

I remembered how Nelson Eddy had felt when his Rose-Marie left the Canadian Rocky Mountains—and he was convinced that he had lost her for good. I wanted to stand and sing one of the songs from that movie in the hope that Delores could still hear me. But I couldn't utter a word. I sat silently, watching the sun vanish into the grayish-brown Minnesota prairie.

III

Pa's health improved enough that he could do some of the lighter farm work. However, after an hour or two of pretending he was working, he generally made some excuse to hop in the car and drive to Alberta.

I normally wouldn't see him for the rest of the day. I knew he was playing cards, but I didn't say anything to him. He wasn't much help on the farm anyway. The only thing that annoyed me was that he always had the car, so I was stuck on the farm without any transportation.

As soon as Pa started playing cards again, Ma went back to her kitchen-window reveries. One day, while she was gazing forlornly out the kitchen window, I decided it might be a good time to see if she had mellowed enough to help me with my search for my birth mother. I was a little apprehensive, because I had never been allowed to discuss my adoption. Still, I was hoping to catch her at a weak moment.

"Ma," I said, sitting down by the kitchen table, "I need to talk to you for a minute."

"About what?" she replied absentmindedly, not bothering to look at me.

"My birth mother."

Ma slowly turned. She looked directly at me. "What about her?"

"I've been searching for her the past two years," I explained.

"Is that what you were doing when you were gone all those times?" she asked with an accusing stare.

"Yes. I drove to all the county seats in a fifty-mile radius to see if I could find any information on her."

"How do you even know she's from Minnesota?" she asked. "She could be from another state."

"Because Delores once heard you say to someone that I was born not too far from here," I said.

"I don't remember saying anything like that," Ma replied.

"I've also been searching through this house to see if I can find my birth or adoption records," I explained firmly.

"They're not here."

"Where are they?" I insisted.

"Pa kept all of our family records in a hidden compartment in one of the walls of the barn on our old farm," she explained matter-of-factly. "All of those papers disappeared when the tornado struck."

I eyed Ma carefully to try to determine if she was lying to me or telling the truth. But I could not get a reading on her. "Even if they disappeared in the tornado," I reminded her, "you still must have known what was on my adoption papers and birth certificate."

"We didn't have a birth certificate for you," she replied. "And your adoption papers said nothing about your birth mother."

"Did they say anything about my name before I was adopted?" I asked.

Ma slowly shook her head. "You didn't have a name before we adopted you," she said. "Your mother didn't give you a name. At least that's what the orphanage told us."

"So what did they call me before I was adopted?" I insisted.

"They had some kind of nickname for you. And you had a number. It was on your crib in the orphanage."

I studied Ma again to see if she was lying or telling the truth. It was still impossible to tell.

"Did my birth mother ever try to get in touch with you after the adoption?" I asked.

"No," Ma shrugged. "We heard nothing from her."

Ma had deflected my questions so deftly, so brusquely, that I decided I had no choice but to play my trump card. "Does the name Edward Mosen mean anything to you?" I asked.

Ma slowly shook her head. "No. I've never heard that name before. Why do you ask?"

"Because I think that was my name before I was adopted."

"I've never heard that name before," Ma insisted.

IV

Shortly before the first winter snow, Pa started to have chest pains again. His doctor in Morris recommended bed rest for three days. If the symptoms continued after that time, the doctor wanted to hospitalize Pa and run more extensive tests to determine the extent of the damage to his heart.

At long last I had an opportunity to drive the car down to Lac Qui Parle County to continue my search. I didn't even ask for permission to take the car. I simply slipped behind the driver's wheel and drove out of the yard.

During the trip to Madison, I thought about what I had learned in Lac Qui Parle County before I was shipped out to Camp Haan. I needed to test my adoptive name against the name I had found on the piece of paper hidden behind the picture frame.

With so many dead ends in my search for my birth mother, I was afraid to get my hopes up too high. At times, I felt like someone was teasing me along, letting me find little enticing tidbits of information, but with no intention of allowing me to find my mother. Still, I was determined to continue my search.

When I arrived in Madison, I walked up to the second floor of the Lac Qui Parle County Courthouse. The middle-aged woman who had helped me earlier was standing behind the counter of the county recorder's office.

"What can I do for you?" she asked.

"I'm looking for a birth certificate," I explained.

"What's the name?"

"Edward Mosen."

"Please write it on this tablet," she said, sliding a pen and tablet across the counter in my direction.

I wrote the name "Edward Mosen" on the tablet, and then I waited patiently while she walked back into the vault. I nervously ran my fingers along the lines and veins in the marble counter top.

"I'm sorry," she said as she walked back out of the vault. "I've got nothing back there for Edward Mosen."

I was greatly disappointed. I'm sure it showed. I had allowed my hopes to get too high. I suffered an immediate, overwhelming sense of despair.

"Are you sure there's nothing back there under that name?" I pleaded.

"Yes, I'm sure. I'm sorry."

"Okay," I said. "Thank you for your help."

I started walking toward the hallway. Then I heard her say, "Are you sure you spelled that last name correctly?"

"What do you mean?" I asked, turning and looking back at her.

"I've never heard of anyone around these parts with the last name Mosen," she explained. "But there are many people in this county with the last name of Mo-seng. With a 'g' at the end. Are you sure you're not looking for Edward Moseng?"

"I don't know," I stammered, not knowing quite what to say. "I suppose it could be."

"Do you want me to see if I have a birth certificate for Edward Moseng?" she asked.

"Yes, please, I would appreciate that."

Once again she disappeared into the vault in the rear of the room. Moments later, she walked back to the counter. "Was there an adoption involved in that birth?" she asked.

"Yes," I said nervously. "I believe there may have been an adoption."

"Then I'm sorry," she said. "But those records are sealed."

"Is there any way—"

"What are you trying to find out about Edward Moseng?" she asked, interrupting me.

"I'm ... I'm doing a genealogy," I lied. "He's one of the people I'm trying to locate."

She smiled slightly and then she started to write something down on the tablet lying on the counter. When she looked up at me, there was a twinkle in her eye. I had the distinct impression that she knew I was lying. I also sensed that she was trying to help me.

"If you're trying to locate someone who once lived in this county," she explained gently, handing me the piece of paper, "this is the person you need to talk to. Her name is Elma Harbaugh. She's an amateur historian, and she knows everything there is to know about Lac Qui Parle County. I'll call and tell her you're on your way over to see her."

V

Excitement and anxiety nearly overwhelmed me. I drove from the Lac Qui Parle County Courthouse to the address written on the piece of paper. When the county recorder had converted the name to "Edward Moseng," and then when she told me that he was also involved in an adoption, I knew that Edward Moseng and Lloyd Augustine Clausen were the same person. It had to be me. It could not be a coincidence.

An elderly white-haired woman in her early seventies was waiting for me on the porch of a small Victorian home when I pulled up in front of the address.

She greeted me as I got out of the car and walked over to where she was standing. "The county recorder's office just called and said you were on your way over," she said warmly. "I understand you're trying to find a resident of our county."

I could sense her lively spirit and inquisitive intelligence behind her otherwise humble manner and appearance. I decided I would trust her and tell her the truth about my real reasons for being in Lac Qui Parle County.

"Yes, I'm looking for someone," I admitted. "But it's not exactly the way I described it to the county recorder."

"Well, come inside and we'll talk about it," she said, opening the screen door wide and gesturing for me to step inside. She led me over to a small living room. I sat down on a couch, and she settled into a rocking chair. "Now," she said, "who is it you're looking for in Lac Qui Parle County?"

"To tell you the truth, I'm not doing a genealogy," I admitted. "I was adopted. My adoptive name is Lloyd Augustine Clausen. But I believe my name before I was adopted was Edward Moseng. I'm trying to locate my birth mother. I believe she once lived in Lac Qui Parle County."

"There are a lot of Mosengs in this county," she replied.

"Can you help me?" I asked softly.

"What if you're disappointed by what you find?" she cautioned me.

"I'm prepared for that," I replied. "I just want to find my birth mother. That's the most important thing in my life right now."

She stared at me for what seemed like an eternity. Then she reached for the telephone on a stand next to the rocking chair. "I'll make a few telephone calls and see what I can come up with," she said. "You just make yourself at home."

I listened to her talk with the operator. She asked for two numbers in quick succession. In each case, she said pretty much the same thing to the parties at the other end of the line. She said she had a young man in her home who was adopted, and who was trying to find his birth mother. She also explained that I thought my name prior to the adoption was Edward Moseng, and that I had been born in Lac Qui Parle County. In both cases, she hung up the telephone when the parties at the other end of the line were unable to be of any assistance to her.

"You know," she mused softly to herself, "I just remembered something. I believe there is an Edward or Edwin Moseng who lives on a farm outside of Dawson, about twenty-five miles southeast of here. I wonder—"

I felt my spirits drop as I realized that this might be the person whose birth certificate I had just discussed with the county recorder. If so, it had nothing to do with me—and I had just hit another dead end in my search for my birth mother.

"Do you know if he was adopted?" I asked apprehensively.

"I don't know anything about him," she replied. "I just remember the name from some of the work I've been doing on local history. Let's see if he's home."

She picked up the telephone and said to the operator, "Phyllis, could you connect me to Edward Moseng in Dawson. He lives on a farm as I remember."

There was a long pause as the operator made the connection.

Elma spoke again, "Is this Edward Moseng?... This is Elma Harbaugh in Madison.... No, I don't think we've ever met.... I do a lot of work with local history.... You're interested in those kind of things, too?... Listen, I've got a young man down here who may be related to you.... No, he says he was adopted.... Oh, I'd say he's about nineteen or twenty years old.... Wait a second and I'll ask him." Then she turned to me, cupped the telephone in her palm, and said, "He wants to know what year you were born."

"I was told I was born in 1922," I replied. My heart was thumping so loud I was sure she could hear it. "That's what my adoptive parents told me."

"He says he was born in 1922," she said into the telephone. "He believes his name before he was adopted was the same as yours.... Does that mean anything to you?... You don't say.... You're sure about that? ... Well, I'm sure he'll be interested.... What time?... I'll tell him.... Yes.... Thank you, too."

"What did he say?" I asked eagerly as she hung up the telephone. "Did he remember me?"

"Yes," she smiled gently. "He remembers you. From what I described to him, he said he is probably your uncle. He said his sister had a baby boy she gave up for adoption in 1922. She named that child Edward Moseng, after her brother, the person I just spoke to. The child who was given up for adoption must be you."

"Are you sure?" I blurted out.

"That's what he said," she replied. "He asked me to bring you out to the farm tomorrow so you can meet your mother and some of your relatives."

VI

I do not remember much about my drive back to Alberta. After all those years, at last I was going to meet my birth mother and my real family. Nothing else in the universe meant a thing to me. Someone could have offered me ten million dollars, and it would not have meant as much to me as what I had just learned in Lac Qui Parle County.

I remembered all those times I had thought about her when Ma and Pa had locked me up in the dark cellar, or after they had beaten me. Now, I was actually going to meet her. It would be impossible to describe in words how that made me feel.

I decided right then and there that I would not tell her too much about my life with Ma and Pa. I did not want to cause her any more pain. I would just tell her that my life with Ma and Pa had been a hard life, but it had been a good life—and let it go at that. There was no reason to make her feel guilty for giving me up for adoption—whatever her reasons might have been.

Besides, I was too happy to think very much about what my life had been like with Ma and Pa. I could only think about the people I would meet the next day. It was a day I thought would never come.

VII

I did not sleep at all that night. I was too excited to do anything except stare at the ceiling and think about what it was going to be like to meet my mother for the first time. In the morning, I rushed through my chores and walked back upstairs to get dressed. I put on the shirt and trousers I had purchased with my skunk-trapping money. They were both a little worn and faded, but they were still the best clothes I owned. I wanted to look good for my mother. I did not want her to be ashamed of me.

Ma and Pa were sitting by the table when I walked downstairs and into the kitchen. They were both still in their robes. Pa looked pale and tired. Ma just looked old and worn out.

"I'll be taking the car again today," I said.

Ma looked up at me and asked, "Where are you going?"

"Lac Qui Parle County," I answered.

"What's down there?"

"I think you know what's in Lac Qui Parle County," I replied as I walked out the door.

I thought about going into more detail, but I didn't.

As I drove to Madison, I thought about how Ma and Pa had looked that morning. They seemed so old, so weary. We had gone through so much together, survived so many tragedies and crises, and yet in my heart I felt nothing for them. They had denied me every opportunity to be their son. And now I was on my way to meet the people who should have been my family.

As I thought about the family I had never met, I was suddenly filled with fear. I had waited so long for this moment that I was alarmed that something terrible might happen, and my dream would all be taken away from me.

Disappointment after disaster pulsed through my mind. Perhaps, my Uncle Edward had second thoughts about having me come out to the farm. Would I find that my relatives did not want to meet me? Perhaps, I was someone they preferred to forget, a blight on the family tree that should remain permanently in the past. Perhaps, I would be told never to come back. Perhaps, I was not worthy to be anyone's son. Perhaps, my true calling in life was to be Ma and Pa's hired man.

I had experienced so much rejection from Ma and Pa that I had to consider whether or not I was worthy of being accepted into anyone's family. Still, I was determined to complete my search for my birth mother. I would live with whatever truth awaited me at the Moseng farm.

I also thought about Ivar. I respected him more than anyone else I had ever met. Yet, I did not want his life. Nor would I wish his life on anyone else. Ivar seemed content to be disconnected from everything he had once known, whatever that might have been. He wandered through life without worrying too much about his parents or brothers or sisters—if he had any. In truth, he seemed to have no past. That sad possibility did not appear to disturb him in the least. He accepted whatever came his way and did the best with it. He lived on the edge of other families, but he was never part of one. When it was time to move on, he moved on—and never looked back.

I was not like that. I had lived in isolation for so long that the one thing that mattered the most to me was to be connected to the people who brought me into this world. For better or worse, that's what I was going to do—in less than an hour. No wonder I was scared.

VIII

I arrived at Elma Harbaugh's house about eleven o'clock in the morning. She was waiting for me on the front porch. She gestured for me to get in her car. We drove south.

"I spoke to Edward Moseng again last night," she explained. "He's putting together an impromptu family reunion for you."

"Will my mother be there, too?" I asked.

"She'll be there," Elma said, nodding reassuringly. "Some of the other people in the area who are related to you will also be there."

"Then ... they remember me?"

"Some of them do. Your Uncle Edward has told the others who you are. He'll explain everything to you when we get there."

As I watched the tall prairie grass flow past the car window, I thought about the many people who had stood by me and helped get me to this point in my life. Mr. Jensen, who had lectured Pa for beating me and offered to take me into his home when I was a little boy. Clyde Roberts, our mailman, who somehow knew that a boy who had very little going for him in life, would take great pride in a mailman's cap. Dr. Cumming, who saved my life when the whooping cough epidemic swept through our area. Buster and Minnie, those two wonderful dogs who were my real adoptive parents. Ivar, who was more of a father to me than Pa. The farmers on the school board who defended me and refused to allow a powerful member of our community to expel me from our country school. Tug, who went blind pulling me safely through a raging blizzard. Raymond Kolden, who stood up for me against the town bullies, and then, later, threw a wrestling match to me to end the teasing I had to endure at school. Hans Anderson, who confronted Pa when he refused to pay me the money he owed me. Jack Schultz, the kindly grocer who had shared his food so I, and many others like me, would not starve during the drought years and the Depression.

From them, and so many others, I had learned that for every person who is ready to knock you down, there's another person somewhere who's ready to pick you up again. These were the people, and the creatures, who had raised me up. I was forever grateful to them for their kindness and decency. My long journey back home would have been impossible without their assistance every step of the way. They had all helped get me to the threshold, but now I had to take the step through the doorway by myself. I had to take that last step into my personal past alone. And yet, I felt them alongside of me, and we were together as I completed my personal odyssey back home to my birth mother and her family.

IX

The local historian parked her car in front of an unpretentious two-story farmhouse. We both got out and walked up to the front door.

A kindly middle-aged man opened the door even before we could knock. He smiled broadly as he shook my hand and introduced himself. "I'm your Uncle Edward," he said warmly.

He led us into the living room, where about fifteen people were seated on couches and chairs. My first thought was, which one of these women is my mother?

They must have read my mind because one of them immediately explained that my mother, Clara, was driving down from Cottonwood, Minnesota. She would arrive shortly. Another woman told me that I had my mother's eyes. Others agreed.

"You'll see for yourself when your mother arrives," Uncle Edward said.

That comment, more than any of the others, made me feel welcome in the Moseng home.

They each shook my hand and warmly introduced themselves. They also explained who they were in relation to the rest of the family. They showed me around the house, which I learned had been in the Moseng family for several generations. They showed me the bedroom where I was born. They showed me where my mother would sit with me in a rocking chair as the sunlight streamed through a nearby window.

"Right here," my Uncle Edward said, tears filling his eyes. "It was right here that she handed you over to the representative from the orphanage. I still remember how you cried. You clung to your mother with all the strength you had in your two little arms. It was heartbreaking. Your mother didn't get over that for many years. I don't think she ever got over it."

"I remember holding onto her," I replied.

"You were very young," he said gently as he wiped his eyes with the back of his hand.

"I know," I replied. "But I remember."

We all went back to the living room and sat down. They told me more about the family history, including the fact that all of my mother's brothers and sisters had wanted her to keep me when I was born out of wedlock. It was a grandmother who insisted that I should be given up for adoption, because she did not want to bring shame onto the family. No one in that room seemed to have a very high opinion of that grandmother, and how she forced her will on the rest of the family.

They told me my mother kept me for almost five months, hidden away on the farm. No one in the community knew she had given birth to a child. She defied her grandmother, as did her brothers and sisters, until she was finally shamed into giving me up for adoption. They said she never fully accepted the decision to give me up. In later years, she lamented that she had let her grandmother talk her into doing something she did not really want to do. But they also acknowledged that times were different then, and not too many single mothers had the means, or the courage, to raise a child alone.

What they told me reaffirmed the decision I had made earlier not to tell my mother what life had really been like with Ma and Pa. I knew she did not need to bear that burden, along with the other burdens she had carried through life. I could only imagine what it must have been like for her to have to give up a child she loved. To learn later that the child had been beaten repeatedly, and turned into a common field hand, would have been too much for her to bear. That knowledge was best kept to myself.

They said I was born on February 23, 1922, whereas Ma and Pa had told me I was born on August 18, 1922. I speculated that August 18, 1922, was the day Ma and Pa took me home with them from the orphanage. They had not only changed my name. They had also changed my birthday.

Ma and Pa had apparently decided very early to wipe out my identity, and my personal past, so they could build a completely new identity for me. Perhaps the name change from Edward to Lloyd was understandable. But there seemed to be no valid reason to change my birthday, unless they preferred to think that my life began the day they took me out of the orphanage.

One of my relatives, an elderly aunt, remembered that my mother had sent some toys and clothing to the orphanage in the weeks and months after she had given me up for adoption. The aunt remembered that my mother kept sending toys and clothing to the orphanage for almost a year, until someone convinced her that it was time to let go of those memories and get on with her life. She did so reluctantly.

I surmised that the orphanage had forwarded some of those items to Ma and Pa, and that was how the piece of paper was placed behind the picture frame. If Ma or Pa hadn't placed the paper behind the picture frame, or if another piece of paper had been available and placed there instead, I might never have been able to locate my family. As much as I had often felt like I had been cruelly betrayed by the forces that control human destinies, those same forces had seemingly been kind enough to provide me with the one clue I needed to find my way back home.

We talked for a while longer, and then I heard another car drive up to the house. Moments later, there was a knock on the door, and two women stepped into the living room. One of the women was a few years younger than me. I was told later that she was my half-sister. The other woman, who was tall with slightly graying hair, was about twenty years older than me. She radiated a quiet, gentle presence, and her eyes, which were the same color as mine, misted up as I stood to greet her.

"Edward?" she asked warmly as she walked slowly over to me. Tears quickly filled her eyes and flowed down her cheeks.

With that one word, I knew that I was no longer a hired man. I was Edward Moseng. I was someone's son.

She held her arms out and slowly drew me to her. No one had to tell me that she was my mother. I had felt those arms around me before. I had waited all my life to feel them around me again.

New Voices in the Prairie Wind

I

Well, son, I'm sure by now you know more about your old man than you ever wanted to know. I hope you are not too disappointed. I did not talk about some of these things when you were a young boy because I did not want to burden you with my problems. I hope you will not be burdened with them now. As I am sure you know by now, there were some things in my life that I could not control. On the other hand, I have made more than my share of mistakes, and I accept full responsibility for them.

I will try to answer some of the questions you might still have about my life's story. I'm sure you are wondering who my real father was. Well, his name was Judd Thompson, and he lived most of his life in Dawson, Minnesota. He was about twelve years older than my mother, and he was married when he met her. They had a brief romantic relationship. My mother became pregnant. I am told that Judd Thompson expressed a desire to divorce his wife and marry my mother. But perhaps that is just a rumor. Maybe it is even wishful thinking on my part. I suspect every child wants to think that the two people who brought them into the world really wanted to be together, no matter what the consequences might be for everyone else involved.

I never met my real father. He was killed in a construction accident in 1947. He was working near the top of a silo when the scaffold collapsed. He fell to the ground and was seriously injured. I am told he lingered on in the hospital for several days before finally succumbing to his injuries. The interesting thing about Judd Thompson—my father, your grandfather—is that he was somewhat of a legend as an amateur wrestler in that part of the state. Apparently, they had wrestling competitions in National Guard armories and at county fairs, and I am told that he was never defeated.

So I guess wrestling came naturally to me when I had to defend myself at school. I would have liked to meet my father, and maybe even wrestle him—but that was not to be.

II

By the time I found my mother, she was married to a farmer by the name of Oscar Sandbakken. They lived in Cottonwood, Minnesota, and had two children together. The Private Sandbakken I had wrestled at Camp Haan was one of my cousins. So, I guess it is a small world, after all.

The day I met my mother and my half-sister was, without question, the high point of my life. I continued to keep in touch with my mother until she died of cancer in the late 1950s. I also kept in touch with other members of the family, including my half-brother and half-sister. However, I never did tell any of them what my life had been like with Ma and Pa on the farm. I did not want to risk the possibility that any of that information might get back to my mother.

On one of my visits, my mother grasped my hand and asked, "Were your adoptive parents good to you?"

I could tell this was a question that had been on her mind for years. I knew if I told her the truth, she would be filled with guilt for the rest of her life. I knew it was better to lie than to tell her what my life had really been like with Ma and Pa.

"Yes," I reassured her, "they were very good parents."

She seemed happy and greatly relieved to hear that. We never discussed the subject again.

My half-brother and half-sister went to college and did very well. Apparently, learning came very easy for them. If there is anything to be said for heredity, I suppose that my Moseng blood helped me to make passing grades in school without attending very many classes. The Mosengs and Sandbakkens (my mother's married name) were also people who enjoyed drama and music. Some of them were talented singers and musicians. We had much in common. Perhaps this also explains why I was temperamentally unsuited to be a hired man. Perhaps some people are genetically prepared for a life of mindless, daily toil. I was not.

As much as I might have wanted to, I never did become a part of the Moseng or Sandbakken families. They had their own personal histories and experiences, most of which did not include me. And I had my own personal history and experiences with Ma and Pa, none of which included them. Although the Mosengs and the Sandbakkens were always very warm and gracious to me, I did not fit comfortably into their world.

Don't get me wrong. My reunion with my mother and her family was the biggest thrill of my life. But it would have been expecting too much to think we could enter into a family relationship. Too much water had gone under too many bridges. It was enough for me to know that they were there, and that I could go to them whenever I needed to feel that I belonged someplace. Just knowing there was a place where I was considered a son or a brother meant the world to me.

III

I eventually returned to the only life I knew, and that was the life I had shared with Ma and Pa. After I had met my birth mother, however, I was no longer willing to accept life on Ma and Pa's terms—and they knew it. In one very important respect, my reunion with my birth mother enabled me to step away from the destiny Ma and Pa had chosen for me. I worked a few more years on their farm, with better pay I might add, and then I set out on my own. One day, I simply announced that I was quitting as their hired man—and that was the end of it.

Without me to work for them, Ma and Pa had to leave the farm and move to Morris, where they both went to work: Pa as a custodian; Ma as a cook and dishwasher. Pa died of heart disease in 1951 after several years of failing health. Ma outlived him by nine years before she died of cancer in the spring of 1960.

Ma outlived many of the people who were our neighbors in Alberta. During the last years of her life, she became lonely, isolated, and despondent. She turned to her Bible for some comfort, and, I believe, for the first time she really began to understand what that book was trying to tell her. She never apologized for the way she had treated me when I was a boy growing up on the farm, but I could tell she had some regrets. Also, in spite of her many differences with Pa throughout their lives, I could tell that she missed him.

Ma was a terrible mother; yet, she became a good grandmother. The children, fathered by the adopted son she had rejected, became the sole source of love and companionship in her old age. The fact that she turned to her grandchildren for comfort and solace speaks volumes. She had mellowed. Having made more than my share of mistakes, I want to be careful that I do not condemn others, including Ma, too quickly. I sincerely believe that everyone, even the most hardened criminal among us, can be redeemed. Ma was not a hardened criminal, but she was a very frustrated, lonely woman who took her misery out on me. Later, she tried to atone through her grandchildren. That is all we need to know. God can judge the rest.

I learned that Ma and Pa were unhappily married from the start. Pa made it very clear to Ma that he regarded their relationship primarily as a marriage of convenience. He needed someone to cook, clean, and care for his house. So in a way, Ma, as Pa's wife, and I, as his hired man, merely provided services for him. We freed Pa up to do the things he loved best in life—and that was to fish and sit in smoke-filled bars and card rooms.

Ma's situation was made much worse by the fact that she was alone in the middle of the barren Minnesota prairie. When the man I came to know as Ma's company entered her life, he must have brought hope into a world where there was only despair. Perhaps out of desperation, Ma eventually yielded to those temptations. Her company became the only thing that made her life tolerable.

Pa probably knew what was going on when he was away from the farm, but he just looked in the other direction. As long as Ma—or someone else—didn't throw it in his face, he ignored it.

Ma and Pa are buried next to each other in the Morris Summit Cemetery. Ma's company and his wife are buried together in a different cemetery. And Judd Thompson and his wife are buried together in a cemetery near Dawson, Minnesota. Three husbands and three wives, who caused so much pain and suffering for each other during their married lives, would nonetheless spend eternity lying next to each other a few feet below the prairie soil.

Maybe there is a lesson for all of us in there someplace. Maybe we all need to remember that we do not live forever. If married people would remember that simple truth about life, perhaps they would treat each other better, and there would be less sorrow and misery in the world.

But again, I am the last person who should be lecturing anyone about marriage. I have made more than my share of mistakes in that area of my life. I married your mother when I was on the rebound. Your mother deserved better. One of my biggest regrets is that I did not work with her to make our marriage a success. Our marriage failed because of me. I take full responsibility. I had it all, and I didn't even know it.

IV

Delores eventually married the fellow she met in California. They became world travelers. He worked for an oil company as a driller, and so they toured the world many times over. I saw her only a handful of times after she drove out to California in the early 1940s. Once, long after she was married, she told me she still missed me, and I could tell she meant it.

Every time I saw her, she looked more and more the way Ma had looked as she got older—although Delores had a very different spirit and personality. I will go to my grave with my suspicions regarding Delores's past. And if my suspicions are not on target, I will go to my grave convinced that the fates are even more inscrutable for conspiring to bring an adopted daughter into our family who grew up to look so much like Ma. In either case, the supreme irony of my life is that I fell in love with a young woman who strongly resembled the woman who adopted me and treated me so terribly in my youth.

One of the last times I saw Delores was in the mid-1950s. We both happened to be in Stevens County to attend a funeral and burial in Reque Cemetery. Delores's husband was working overseas and couldn't make it to the funeral. After the graveside service, we wandered off to talk and reminisce. Nothing had changed. I could tell she still cared about me deeply. I know she could tell I cared about her. But she never tried to explain why she had gotten married so quickly after she drove out to California. I never asked.

We enjoyed a long walk across the prairie that day. I felt like I had never been away from her. It was perhaps that day, more than any other, that made me realize how Ma could carry a romantic dream from decade to decade throughout much of her life. In some ways, I realized that I had done the same thing with Delores that Ma had done with her company. I refused to let go even after Delores was married. Perhaps Ma became a bit more human to me that day.

When Delores and I parted, she didn't tell me she loved me. I didn't tell her, either. We didn't have to say it. Ever since we were kids, growing up together as adopted children on the Minnesota prairie, that love was always there. It was and always will be a deeper love than most married people share. It was something no one could ever take away from us. As the car Delores was driving disappeared in the distance, I knew my love for her would be as much a part of my life as the air I breathed every day.

V

I did not return to Alberta for many years after my last meeting with Delores. Then, in the early 1970s, I started going back again. My final trip was in the fall of 1979, shortly after the doctors told me I had lung cancer. The cigarettes I had started smoking on my trip out to Camp Haan finally caught up with me. I was told that I had less than a year to live. In the time that I had left, I decided to revisit some old memories.

I caught a plane from Houston, Texas, to Minneapolis, where I rented a car. Then I drove across the Minnesota prairie for what I knew would be the last time.

I visited the country cemetery outside of Cottonwood, Minnesota, where my mother, Clara Moseng Sandbakken, is buried. The cemetery reminds me of Reque Cemetery, south of Alberta. It is quiet and peaceful, surrounded on all sides by corn and wheat fields. Before leaving, I picked some wildflowers from a nearby field and placed them on my mother's grave.

I also visited the Dawson cemetery, where my real father, Albert Judson Thompson, is buried. I paused briefly to pay silent homage to a man I had never met.

I even stopped by Madison to visit the grave of the woman who worked in the county recorder's office. She was the one who had helped me make the initial contact with the elderly historian, who, in turn, had helped me locate my birth mother through my Uncle Edward Moseng.

I thought I understood everything that had happened the day I located my birth mother. Years later, I realized that once again I was probably only seeing a small part of what was really going on. I began to suspect that there was probably something else at work just below the surface.

I eventually heard rumors that the woman behind the desk in the Lac Qui Parle County Recorder's Office had quietly helped some other adopted children locate their birth parents. I don't know if that is true. But when I added that bit of information to the fact that the elderly historian had located my Uncle Edward after only three telephone calls, I started to suspect something.

I believe the woman in the county recorder's office remembered me from my first visit. Subsequently, I suspect she may have cross-referenced the adoption and birth records, and realized that my real name was Edward Moseng, and that my birth mother's name was Clara Moseng. She just didn't know how to pass that information on to me without violating state laws regarding sealed adoption records.

When she called the elderly historian, I believe she told her who my birth mother was and how to get ahold of her—through my Uncle Edward. So the historian's first two telephone calls, which produced no leads, were probably a ploy to make everything look legitimate—and to keep the woman in the county recorder's office from getting into trouble for revealing confidential information regarding my adoption. In her line of work, she probably understood the pain all adopted children feel when they come up against the obstacles the government puts in their way. And I believe she saw my pain, and she decided to help me by making that telephone call to the elderly historian.

So on my last trip back to Minnesota in the fall of 1979, I found her grave and placed some wildflowers on it, too.

VI

My next stop was the Summit Cemetery in Morris, where Ma and Pa are buried. The cemetery is located on the eastern edge of town. I drove through the gates and parked the car on a dirt path in the middle of the cemetery.

As I stepped out of the car, I felt winter in the air. High overhead, a flock of Canada geese winged its way south. Pheasants clucked contentedly in some underbrush on the edge of the cemetery. In the distance, chimney smoke lingered lazily in the still air above two homes. My shoes crunched through the crisp autumn leaves as I searched for Ma and Pa's graves.

Even though I had been back to Stevens County several times, I had not been out to the cemetery since Ma had died in the spring of 1960. I had thought about visiting the graves. But something always held me back. I probably did not want to revisit those memories, and feel the rush of anger and bitterness. I wanted to put all of that behind me. But since I knew this would be my last trip back home, I decided I needed to say good-bye to Ma and Pa, as well as to all the other people I had known as a boy.

I found the two gravestones, set level with the ground. I knelt to brush away the autumn leaves and other debris that covered the inscriptions. As I stared at the gravestones, it seemed strange to me that the names "Claus Clausen" and "Marie Clausen" were carved there. The names "Ma" and "Pa" seemed more appropriate. It was how I remembered them.

As I stood by the graves, a rush of cold wind blew in from the prairie. Dead autumn leaves were torn from trees and scattered across the cemetery. Two squirrels nibbled tenderly on fallen acorns beneath one of the trees. They paused to sniff the air, then darted up a tree trunk to store the acorns.

I remembered how Ma, Pa, and I had survived blizzards, epidemics, drought, the Great Depression, and other calamities that had destroyed so many people in Stevens County. We were spared, not because we were stronger or better prepared. We were just luckier than those who had perished.

We were certainly never much of a family. We had stayed together because none of us had anywhere else to go. Still, we had survived so very much together. It made no sense to hold onto the anger and the bitterness. It was time to let go of those feelings.

While the autumn leaves scattered across the cemetery, I prayed that Ma and Pa had found some peace with God, and with each other—and I forgave them.

VII

Finally, I drove out to Alberta for what I knew would be my last visit to the area where I had been raised. I visited all of the farms where I had lived as a boy. The farm we lived on ten miles south and three miles west of Alberta is now abandoned. Weeds and prairie grass grow right up to the front door of the house. The cellar door has rotted away, so I was able to walk down into the darkness where Ma had imprisoned me so many times. The cellar did not seem to be so frightening anymore. I had learned that there are things in this world that are far more frightening than darkness. Things that we carry deep inside of ourselves, and that we don't even know are there.

The farm we lived on three miles south and almost three miles west of Alberta, the one that was torn apart by the tornado, is, ironically, the only farm we lived on that is still functioning. The drainage ditch still meanders across the property and empties into Lake Hattie farther north. The trees that were splintered and decimated by the tornado have been replaced by new growth. The barn, where Ivar came to my rescue, still stands on the edge of the farmyard.

The buildings on our last farm, the one located two miles south and one mile east of Alberta, have either burned or been dismantled. The lumber has been hauled away. There is nothing left except a dirt road and a driveway leading into a tangle of brush and trees. There are rocks, tin cans, and other junk scattered across the area where the house once stood. But everything else, even the basement foundation, is buried beneath dirt, weeds, and debris. Each year the tangle of trees and brush grows thicker, as the prairie gradually reclaims what little there is left of the farm.

Many of our neighbors' houses south of Alberta are also abandoned, and the buildings look like gray mirages shimmering among groves of dead trees. Everywhere I looked, the prairie was slowly erasing the memories of everything and everyone I had known as a boy. But I understood now why all things fade back into the soil, and I did not object.

During my last visit, I drove over to the old abandoned windmill I had climbed so many times as a young boy. The ladder was worn and rusted, and it was impossible to climb to the top to view the immense, rolling prairie—even though I was desperate to do so. The rust had frozen the metal blades so they no longer groaned in the breeze. Still, that lofty perch reawakened some distant memories of an enchanted world that had once existed for me on top of the windmill.

I also walked through Reque Cemetery to say hello and good-bye to old friends like Raymond Kolden. As I stood by those graves and pondered the dreams that had vanished in that obscure, insignificant place, I realized that the people buried there were more than neighbors to me. Ma and Pa were poor substitutes as a family, and Judd Thompson and Clara Moseng were never married and could never be my family. So the neighbors buried in that country cemetery had protected me in ways that most families protect their own children.

I was filled with gratitude.

VIII

Before I left Alberta for the last time, I drove down the dirt roads and over to the oak tree with the split trunk. The tree is still there. It will probably always be there. I believe that oak is the only thing on the prairie that is eternal. Everything else fades back into the soil—but not that oak tree. It just keeps producing leaves and acorns season after season, as it has done for well over a hundred years.

I sat on the rock pile where Delores and I had sat and talked so very often, and I stared at the ground where Buster and Minnie are buried. Whenever I looked at that spot of soil, I always felt like I was looking at the graves of my real parents. In my entire life, no one had ever meant quite so much to me as Buster and Minnie. Without them, I had always felt very much alone. I still miss them terribly.

I remembered how, years earlier, I left the dirt trails and gravel roads on the Minnesota prairie to follow the paved roads that eventually led me to just about every major city in America. I worked on more construction crews than I can count. And I pursued my own Rose-Marie through too many city streets and into too many piano bars.

Singing to my enchanted vision from the smoke-filled darkness, I became the very thing I resented in other people. I lost all meaningful contact with the people I never should have left behind. I pursued the adventure and excitement of romance, even if it meant I had to sacrifice those who might otherwise have loved me. I became more like Ma than I cared to admit. We both pursued a distant, unreachable dream—and thought it was love.

I lived for that kind of love, while real love was the one emotion I least understood. City streets led me into relationships that dead-ended before I got my bearings. I became the most forlorn and lonely of all the lost children wandering in that darkness, searching for any dream that had a song attached to it.

In time, I learned that life is a puzzle beyond all human comprehension. That the winds flickering through the autumn leaves are like the fingers of destiny nudging individual human lives onward and sending them scurrying across the world in directionless patterns. In the end, I could not escape from my destiny, the one Ma and Pa had chosen for me when they picked me out of the orphanage. Like Ivar, I became a wanderer, moving from city to city, living on the edge of other people's families, but never forming any real attachments to anyone. I made the mistake of thinking romance was love—and, in the process, I found neither.

As I sat next to the oak tree and gazed out over the empty fields near the area where I grew up, I realized something else: I was the one person who wanted most desperately to escape from this flat, uninspiring prairie, and yet I was also the one person who returned to it each fall with an even more desperate need to be touched once again by its desolate beauty. So the game goes on, as when I was a boy playing capture the flag in a nearby grove of trees. The other players have all gone home, and I am the only player left in the game.

As I listened to the sound of the wind blowing through the split trunk of the old oak tree, I again heard the voices of all those people who lived and died on the prairie.

I know I will soon be one of those voices.

And I no longer feel alone.

Love,
Dad

POSTSCRIPT

On Father's Day, June 15, 1997, a florist placed a vase filled with wild-flowers on Section 409, Lot 1356, Space 5 of the Forest Park Cemetery in Houston, Texas. It was the first time in seventeen years that there were flowers on the grave of Lloyd A. Clausen.

ABOUT THE AUTHOR

Dennis Clausen was born and raised in Morris, Minnesota. His first book was *Ghost Lover*, a bestselling gothic mystery set on the prairie. He has also authored two textbooks, a chapbook of poetry, numerous articles on higher education, and opinion pieces and essays for various newspapers, magazines, and journals. He lives in Escondido, California, with his wife, Alexa, and son, Derl, and is a professor of English at the University of San Diego, where he teaches American literature and writing.

CPSIA information can be obtained
at www.ICGtesting.com
Printed in the USA
LVHW081545080522
718201LV00010B/1336

9 781541 357761